D0864529

THE SECOND VATICAN COUNCIL

The Four Constitutions

THE SECOND VATICAN COUNCIL

The Four Constitutions

Sacrosanctum Concilium

Lumen Gentium

Dei Verbum

Gaudium et Spes

IGNATIUS PRESS   SAN FRANCISCO

CATHOLIC TRUTH SOCIETY   LONDON

Original Latin editions of the four constitutions and
Benedict XVI's address to the Roman Curia in English
© Libreria Editrice Vaticana
Vatican City

English translations of the four constitutions
© 1964, 1965 and 1966 by Catholic Truth Society, London

Cover image: Second Vatican Council, September 1, 1962
© David Lees/CORBIS

Cover design by Alison Faulkner

General introduction © 2013 by Ignatius Press, San Francisco
All right reserved
ISBN 978-1-58617-839-0
Library of Congress Control Number 2013935551
Printed in the United States of America ∞

CONTENTS

- General Introduction by Archbishop Salvatore
  Cordileone   vii
- The Second Vatican Council: Excerpt from
  Pope Benedict XVI's address to the Roman
  Curia, December 22, 2005   xi

Sacrosanctum Concilium
(Constitution on the Sacred Liturgy)

- Introduction by Francis Cardinal Arinze   3
- Constitution   13

Lumen Gentium
(Dogmatic Constitution on the Church)

- Introduction by Paul Cardinal Poupard   61
- Constitution   69

Dei Verbum
(Dogmatic Constitution on Divine Revelation)

- Introduction by Archbishop Charles Chaput   161
- Constitution   167

Gaudium et Spes
(Pastoral Constitution on the Church in the Modern World)

- Introduction by Angelo Cardinal Scola   189
- Constitution   195

GENERAL INTRODUCTION
by Archbishop Salvatore Cordileone
Archbishop of San Francisco

At the writing of this General Introduction, the Church is living in historic, indeed in some ways unprecedented, times. In a move of profound humility and true concern for the good of the Church, Pope Benedict XVI freely resigned the Papacy; the ensuing Conclave then elected the first Roman Pontiff to come from outside that part of the world where Christianity has been established from ancient times: Cardinal Jorge Mario Bergoglio of Buenos Aires, now Pope Francis.

It is within this historic backdrop that Ignatius Press has published this translation of the four Constitutions to have emanated from the Second Vatican Council: the Constitution on the Sacred Liturgy, *Sancrosanctum Concilium*; the Constitution on Divine Revelation, *Dei Verbum*; the Constitution on the Church, *Lumen Gentium*; and the Constitution on the Church in the Modern World, *Gaudium et Spes*.

The publication of this work is made all the more timely in that it occurs during the Year of Faith called by Pope Benedict as a time of renewal on the occasion of the fiftieth anniversary of the opening of the Second Vatican Council and the twentieth anniversary of the publication of the *Catechism of the Catholic Church*. Appropriately, then, this book begins with Pope Benedict's speech to the Roman Curia for Christmas of 2005. It is here where he lays out most clearly the experience that has marked—dare I say plagued?—the Church since even before the Council was concluded: the "hermeneutic of discontinuity and rupture" versus the "hermeneutic of reform". One of the great legacies that Pope Benedict has bequeathed to the Church is indeed his call for a re-reading, re-interpretation and authentic appropriation of the Council within the vision of continuity and reform.

The treatise on the Sacred Liturgy logically follows, at the beginning, immediately after this speech by Pope Benedict, for nowhere has this divergence of understanding of what the Council really meant been more felt than in the Church's life of worship. Given the fundamental importance of worship for the entire faith life of the Church—another principle frequently emphasized by Pope Benedict XVI—the Council's teaching in this area can serve as a paradigm for a correct and pastorally beneficial interpretation of the Council. If one places *Sancrosanctum Concilium* within the context of the 150 years of history of liturgical renewal that preceded it, one can readily see that the Council Fathers seized the moment of opportunity to advance the active ("*actuosa*") participation of the faithful in the liturgy that had been growing in the years prior to the Council, going all the way back to 1903 when Pope Pius X first coined this phrase in his instruction on the Sacred Liturgy, *Tra le sollecitudini*. The liturgical renewal movement was coming to maturity at the time of the Council, and the letter of the Council's teaching was clearly championing its vision. What actually took place in the vast majority of parishes and even religious communities, however, was something quite different: a stark displacement, and sometimes even outright rejection, of the Church's two-thousand-year continuous development of sacred art, architecture and—especially—music, and replacing it with something quite different, even completely new. What was really new, though, was a form of iconoclasm that placed emphasis on people's experience of the liturgy in the sense of seeking to create an emotional intensity resulting from a sense of bonding with the community at worship, rather than a truly sacramental understanding of the liturgy in which every detail— every gesture made, every word spoken, every note sung, every liturgical appointment used, every vestment worn—has a meaning far beyond the object itself, a physical or audible object that reveals the invisible truth that God communicates to us in the Church's liturgy.

However, before going further here, perhaps we should back up and consider what these four documents have in common: they are all constitutions. After all, the documents of the Council are themselves multiple in kind: constitutions, decrees, declarations and instructions. Herein the constitutions have the highest authority among all the documents that were promulgated.

This is not the case because the other documents—decrees and declarations—are not considered objectively true, or are not considered as containing any definitive teachings of the Church. On the contrary, decrees such as *Nostra Aetate* and *Dignitatis Humanae* form part of the Extraordinary Magisterium of the Catholic Church. However, they are not the central points of reference of the Council. The pillars, so to speak, of the edifice of the Council are the constitutions. They are the reference points for understanding all the rest, the center in which or from which all other teachings at the Council have their bearings and upon which they build.

Two are entitled "Dogmatic Constitutions"—*Dei Verbum* and *Lumen Gentium*—and these treat the subjects of divine revelation and of the Church, respectively. In calling these writings "dogmatic", the Council Fathers seemed to be underscoring the fact that they contain the core theoretical teachings of the Council. One way to think about this is to say that at the heart of Vatican II is an attentiveness to the uniqueness of the divine revelation given to us in Jesus Christ, and an awareness of the Church as the mystical body of Christ, the bride of Christ, the universal sacrament of salvation, and a communion of life, charity and truth. If we are properly to understand everything else—the Sacred Liturgy, the mission of evangelization, the dignity of the human person, the dialogue with other religions—all of this has to be seen in relation to the revelation of Jesus Christ as the God-man, and all of this has to be understood in relation to the mystery of the Church and her sacraments. Without these two truths at the center of our evangelization and our preaching, the mission of the Church is made meaningless. With them at the center of our preaching, the Church's message is forever what is most vital and most valuable in human civilization.

Sacrosanctum Concilium is the "Constitution on the Sacred Liturgy" while *Gaudium et Spes* is envisaged as a "Pastoral Constitution". The latter seems to be written particularly with a view toward the Church's situation in an epoch marked by political democracy and modern humanism. Here we see the pastoral applications of the Dogmatic Constitutions. If the Church in Christ is a "sign and instrument" of man's unity with God, as *Lumen Gentium* states (no. 1), then the Sacred Liturgy should really present human beings with a sense that they are encountering the holiness and beauty of God. If modern governments truly seek to give their citizens a life of well-being and the pursuit of happiness, then the message of the Gospel needs to be at the center of any true humanism, and it should inform the workings of modern democratic societies. The experience of the twentieth century, after as well as before the Council, certainly demonstrated the horrendous destruction and dehumanization that results from a purely materialistic understanding of the human person. The Gospel, as preserved intact by the Church and developed especially in her social teaching, keeps the focus on an authentic anthropology, understanding the human person as primarily a spiritual and social being.

Only with this proper understanding can democratic societies promote a humanism that is actually capable of attaining the goal of human flourishing for their citizens.

Already, then, in the four Constitutions of Vatican II we find a complex but unified message that informs the whole of the Council. If we want rightly to understand its teaching, we have no better place to begin than with these four core documents. That is why it is so fitting that Ignatius Press has provided us with this translation of these documents.

They have done this in great part so as to respond to the call of Pope Emeritus Benedict XVI: that the Council be interpreted within a hermeneutic of continuity with the longstanding previous tradition of the Church. That is to say, we should read the language and the theology of the Second Vatican Council in harmony with previous statements of sacred Tradition and of the Magisterium. This insistence for an interpretation of the Council in keeping with Tradition is nothing novel or recent. We should recall that Pope Paul VI himself asked that an explanatory note be issued as an addendum to *Lumen Gentium*. This note made it clear that the ecclesiology of the hierarchy presented in that document had to be understood in light of the perennial teaching of the Catholic Church with regard to the authority of the Pope, the nature of the episcopacy and the unity of the visible Catholic Church. This is why the teaching in that Constitution, which is properly dogmatic, has such a traditional character, and yet the Constitution seeks to present the Church in an evangelical light, as is proper to the pastoral aims of the Council.

Catholic Christians today have great need to understand rightly the Second Vatican Council and to assimilate its fundamental teachings in depth. Pope Emeritus Benedict XVI's address to the Roman Curia of December 22, 2005, will no doubt serve as a guidepost for years, and quite likely generations, to come in providing much needed direction and inspiration to the Church in the much needed project of re-reading the Council through the hermeneutic of reform and continuity.

Indeed, it is in this sense that the Council continues to present today a beautiful and vital expression of the traditional teaching of the Catholic Church. That teaching needs to be readily available to all in an accessible language that is also theologically precise. This book from Ignatius Press undoubtedly will be of great service to many, in view of that very end.

May 30, 2013

THE SECOND VATICAN COUNCIL

An excerpt from Pope Benedict XVI's Address to the Roman Curia,
December 22, 2005

What has been the result of the Council? Was it well received? What, in the acceptance of the Council, was good and what was inadequate or mistaken? What still remains to be done? No one can deny that in vast areas of the Church the implementation of the Council has been somewhat difficult, even without wishing to apply to what occurred in these years the description that St Basil, the great Doctor of the Church, made of the Church's situation after the Council of Nicea: he compares her situation to a naval battle in the darkness of the storm, saying among other things: "The raucous shouting of those who through disagreement rise up against one another, the incomprehensible chatter, the confused din of uninterrupted clamouring, has now filled almost the whole of the Church, falsifying through excess or failure the right doctrine of the faith ..." (*De Spiritu Sancto*, XXX, 77; PG 32, 213 A; SCh 17 ff., p. 524).

We do not want to apply precisely this dramatic description to the situation of the post-conciliar period, yet something from all that occurred is nevertheless reflected in it. The question arises: Why has the implementation of the Council, in large parts of the Church, thus far been so difficult?

Well, it all depends on the correct interpretation of the Council or—as we would say today—on its proper hermeneutics, the correct key to its interpretation and application. The problems in its implementation arose from the fact that two contrary hermeneutics came face to face and quarreled with each other. One caused confusion, the other, silently but more and more visibly, bore and is bearing fruit.

On the one hand, there is an interpretation that I would call "a hermeneutic of discontinuity and rupture"; it has frequently availed itself of the sympathies of the mass media, and also one trend of modern theology. On the other, there is the "hermeneutic of reform", of renewal in the continuity of the one subject-Church which the Lord has given to us. She is a subject which increases in time and develops, yet always remaining the same, the one subject of the journeying People of God.

The hermeneutic of discontinuity risks ending in a split between the pre-conciliar Church and the post-conciliar Church. It asserts that the texts of the Council as such do not yet express the true spirit of the Council. It claims that they are the result of compromises in which, to reach unanimity, it was found necessary to keep and reconfirm many old things that are now pointless. However, the true spirit of the Council is not to be found in these compromises but instead in the impulses toward the new that are contained in the texts.

These innovations alone were supposed to represent the true spirit of the Council, and starting from and in conformity with them, it would be possible to move ahead. Precisely because the texts would only imperfectly reflect the true spirit of the Council and its newness, it would be necessary to go courageously beyond the texts and make room for the newness in which the Council's deepest intention would be expressed, even if it were still vague.

In a word: it would be necessary not to follow the texts of the Council but its spirit. In this way, obviously, a vast margin was left open for the question on how this spirit should subsequently be defined and room was consequently made for every whim.

The nature of a Council as such is therefore basically misunderstood. In this way, it is considered as a sort of constituent that eliminates an old constitution and creates a new one. However, the Constituent Assembly needs a mandator and then confirmation by the mandator, in other words, the people the constitution must serve. The Fathers had no such mandate and no one had ever given them one; nor could anyone have given them one because the essential constitution of the Church comes from the Lord and was given to us so that we might attain eternal life and, starting from this perspective, be able to illuminate life in time and time itself.

Through the Sacrament they have received, Bishops are stewards of the Lord's gift. They are "stewards of the mysteries of God" (1 *Cor* 4:1); as such, they must be found to be "faithful" and "wise" (cf. *Lk* 12:41-48). This requires them to administer the Lord's gift in the right way, so that it is not left concealed in some hiding place but bears fruit, and the Lord may end by saying to the administrator: "Since you were dependable in a small matter I will put you in charge of larger affairs" (cf. *Mt* 25:14–30; *Lk* 19:11–27).

These Gospel parables express the dynamic of fidelity required in the Lord's service; and through them it becomes clear that, as in a Council, the dynamic and fidelity must converge.

The hermeneutic of discontinuity is countered by the hermeneutic of reform, as it was presented first by Pope John XXIII in his Speech inaugurating the Council on 11 October 1962 and later by Pope Paul VI in his Discourse for the Council's conclusion on 7 December 1965.

Here I shall cite only John XXIII's well-known words, which unequivocally express this hermeneutic when he says that the Council wishes "to transmit the doctrine, pure and integral, without any attenuation or distortion". And he continues: "Our duty is not only to guard this precious treasure, as if we were concerned only with antiquity, but to dedicate ourselves with an earnest will and without fear to that work which our era demands of us ...." It is necessary that "adherence to all the teaching of the Church in its entirety and preciseness ..." be presented in "faithful and perfect conformity to the authentic doctrine, which, however, should be studied and expounded through the methods of research and through the literary forms of modern thought. The substance of the ancient doctrine of the deposit of faith is one thing, and the way in which it is presented is another ...", retaining the same meaning and message (*The Documents of Vatican II*, Walter M. Abbott, S.J., p. 715).

It is clear that this commitment to expressing a specific truth in a new way demands new thinking on this truth and a new and vital relationship with it; it is also clear that new words can only develop if they come from an informed understanding of the truth expressed, and on the other hand, that a reflection on faith also requires that this faith be lived. In this regard, the programme that Pope John XXIII proposed was extremely demanding, indeed, just as the synthesis of fidelity and dynamic is demanding.

However, wherever this interpretation guided the implementation of the Council, new life developed and new fruit ripened. Forty years after the Council, we can show that the positive is far greater and livelier than it appeared to be in the turbulent years around 1968. Today, we see that although the good seed developed slowly, it is nonetheless growing; and our deep gratitude for the work done by the Council is likewise growing.

In his Discourse closing the Council, Paul VI pointed out a further specific reason why a hermeneutic of discontinuity can seem convincing.

In the great dispute about man which marks the modern epoch, the Council had to focus in particular on the theme of anthropology. It had to question the relationship between the Church and her faith on the one hand, and man and the contemporary world on the other (cf. Abbott, 715). The question becomes even clearer if, instead of the generic term "contemporary world", we opt for another that is more precise: the Council had to determine in a new way the relationship between the Church and the modern era.

This relationship had a somewhat stormy beginning with the Galileo case. It was then totally interrupted when Kant described "religion within pure reason" and when, in the radical phase of the French Revolution, an image of the State and the human being that practically no longer wanted to allow the Church any room was disseminated.

In the 19th century under Pius IX, the clash between the Church's faith and a radical liberalism and the natural sciences, which also claimed to embrace with their knowledge the whole of reality to its limit, stubbornly proposing to make the "hypothesis of God" superfluous, had elicited from the Church a bitter and radical condemnation of this spirit of the modern age. Thus, it seemed that there was no longer any milieu open to a positive and fruitful understanding, and the rejection by those who felt they were the representatives of the modern era was also drastic.

In the meantime, however, the modern age had also experienced developments. People came to realize that the American Revolution was offering a model of a modern State that differed from the theoretical model with radical tendencies that had emerged during the second phase of the French Revolution.

The natural sciences were beginning to reflect more and more clearly their own limitations imposed by their own method, which, despite achieving great things, was nevertheless unable to grasp the global nature of reality.

So it was that both parties were gradually beginning to open up to each other. In the period between the two World Wars and especially after the Second World War, Catholic statesmen demonstrated that a modern secular State could exist that was not neutral regarding values but alive, drawing from the great ethical sources opened by Christianity.

Catholic social doctrine, as it gradually developed, became an important model between radical liberalism and the Marxist theory of the State. The natural sciences, which without reservation professed a method of their own to which God was barred access, realized ever more clearly that this method did not include the whole of reality. Hence, they once again opened their doors to God, knowing that reality is greater than the naturalistic method and all that it can encompass.

It might be said that three circles of questions had formed which then, at the time of the Second Vatican Council, were expecting an answer. First of all, the relationship between faith and modern science had to be redefined. Furthermore, this did not only concern the natural sciences but also historical science for, in a certain school, the historical-critical method claimed to have the last word on the interpretation of the Bible and, demanding total exclusivity for its interpretation of Sacred Scripture, was opposed to important points in the interpretation elaborated by the faith of the Church.

Secondly, it was necessary to give a new definition to the relationship between the Church and the modern State that would make room impartially for citizens of various religions and ideologies, merely assuming responsibility for an orderly and tolerant coexistence among them and for the freedom to practice their own religion.

Thirdly, linked more generally to this was the problem of religious tolerance—a question that required a new definition of the relationship between the Christian faith and the world religions. In particular, before the recent crimes of the Nazi regime and, in general, with a retrospective look at a long and difficult history, it was necessary to evaluate and define in a new way the relationship between the Church and the faith of Israel.

These are all subjects of great importance—they were the great themes of the second part of the Council—on which it is impossible to reflect more broadly in this context. It is clear that in all these sectors, which all together form a single problem, some kind of discontinuity might emerge. Indeed, a discontinuity had been revealed but in which, after the various distinctions between concrete historical situations and their requirements had been made, the continuity of principles proved not to have been abandoned. It is easy to miss this fact at a first glance.

It is precisely in this combination of continuity and discontinuity at different levels that the very nature of true reform consists. In this process of innovation in continuity we must learn to understand more practically than before that the Church's decisions on contingent matters—for example, certain practical forms of liberalism or a free interpretation of the Bible—should necessarily be contingent themselves, precisely because they refer to a specific reality that is changeable in itself. It was necessary to learn to recognize that in these decisions it is only the principles that express the permanent aspect, since they remain as an undercurrent, motivating decisions from within.

On the other hand, not so permanent are the practical forms that depend on the historical situation and are therefore subject to change.

Basic decisions, therefore, continue to be well-grounded, whereas the way they are applied to new contexts can change. Thus, for example, if religious freedom were to be considered an expression of the human inability to discover the truth and thus become a canonization of relativism, then this social and historical necessity is raised inappropriately to the metaphysical level and thus stripped of its true meaning. Consequently, it cannot be accepted by those who believe that the human person is capable of knowing the truth about God and, on the basis of the inner dignity of the truth, is bound to this knowledge.

It is quite different, on the other hand, to perceive religious freedom as a need that derives from human coexistence, or indeed, as an intrinsic consequence of the truth that cannot be externally imposed but that the person must adopt only through the process of conviction.

The Second Vatican Council, recognizing and making its own an essential principle of the modern State with the Decree on Religious Freedom, has recovered the deepest patrimony of the Church. By so doing she can be conscious of being in full harmony with the teaching of Jesus himself (cf. *Mt* 22:21), as well as with the Church of the martyrs of all time. The ancient Church naturally prayed for the emperors and political leaders out of duty (cf. 1 *Tm* 2:2); but while she prayed for the emperors, she refused to worship them and thereby clearly rejected the religion of the State.

The martyrs of the early Church died for their faith in that God who was revealed in Jesus Christ, and for this very reason they also died for freedom of conscience and the freedom to profess one's own faith—a profession that no State can impose but which, instead, can only be claimed with God's grace in freedom of conscience. A missionary Church known for proclaiming her message to all peoples must necessarily work for the freedom of the faith. She desires to transmit the gift of the truth that exists for one and all.

At the same time, she assures peoples and their Governments that she does not wish to destroy their identity and culture by doing so, but to give them, on the contrary, a response which, in their innermost depths, they are waiting for—a response with which the multiplicity of cultures is not lost but instead unity between men and women increases and thus also peace between peoples.

The Second Vatican Council, with its new definition of the relationship between the faith of the Church and certain essential elements of modern thought, has reviewed or even corrected certain historical decisions, but in this apparent discontinuity it has actually preserved and deepened her inmost nature and true identity.

The Church, both before and after the Council, was and is the same Church, one, holy, catholic and apostolic, journeying on through time; she continues "her pilgrimage amid the persecutions of the world and the consolations of God", proclaiming the death of the Lord until he comes (cf. *Lumen Gentium*, no. 8).

Those who expected that with this fundamental "yes" to the modern era all tensions would be dispelled and that the "openness towards the world" accordingly achieved would transform everything into pure harmony, had underestimated the inner tensions as well as the contradictions inherent in the modern epoch.

They had underestimated the perilous frailty of human nature which has been a threat to human progress in all the periods of history and in every historical constellation. These dangers, with the new possibilities and new power of man over matter and over himself, did not disappear but instead acquired new dimensions: a look at the history of the present day shows this clearly.

In our time too, the Church remains a "sign that will be opposed" (*Lk* 2:34)—not without reason did Pope John Paul II, then still a Cardinal, give this title to the theme for the Spiritual Exercises he preached in 1976 to Pope Paul VI and the Roman Curia. The Council could not have intended to abolish the Gospel's opposition to human dangers and errors.

On the contrary, it was certainly the Council's intention to overcome erroneous or superfluous contradictions in order to present to our world the requirement of the Gospel in its full greatness and purity.

The steps the Council took towards the modern era which had rather vaguely been presented as "openness to the world", belong in short to the perennial problem of the relationship between faith and reason that is re-emerging in ever new forms. The situation that the Council had to face can certainly be compared to events of previous epochs.

In his First Letter, St Peter urged Christians always to be ready to give an answer (*apo-logia*) to anyone who asked them for the *logos*, the reason for their faith (cf. 3:15).

This meant that biblical faith had to be discussed and come into contact with Greek culture and learn to recognize through interpretation the separating line but also the convergence and the affinity between them in the one reason, given by God.

When, in the 13th century through the Jewish and Arab philosophers, Aristotelian thought came into contact with Medieval Christianity formed in the Platonic tradition and faith and reason risked entering an irreconcilable contradiction, it was above all St Thomas Aquinas who mediated the new encounter between faith and Aristotelian philosophy, thereby setting faith in a positive relationship with the form of reason prevalent in his time. There is no doubt that the wearing dispute between modern reason and the Christian faith, which had begun negatively with the Galileo case, went through many phases, but with the Second Vatican Council the time came when broad new thinking was required.

Its content was certainly only roughly traced in the conciliar texts, but this determined its essential direction, so that the dialogue between reason and faith, particularly important today, found its bearings on the basis of the Second Vatican Council.

This dialogue must now be developed with great openmindedness but also with that clear discernment that the world rightly expects of us in this very moment. Thus, today we can look with gratitude at the Second Vatican Council: if we interpret and implement it guided by a right hermeneutic, it can be and can become increasingly powerful for the ever necessary renewal of the Church.

CONSTITUTION ON THE LITURGY

Sacrosanctum Concilium

INTRODUCTION
by Francis Cardinal Arinze

The celebration of the mysteries of our redemption, especially of the paschal mystery of the suffering, death, and resurrection of Our Lord and Saviour Jesus Christ in the Sacred Liturgy, is central in and to the life of the Church. Participation in liturgical celebrations is seen by the Second Vatican Council as the primary and indispensable source "from which the faithful may be expected to draw the true Christian spirit" (SC, no. 14).

It was, therefore, very fitting that the first of the sixteen documents to be issued by the Second Vatican Council was on the Sacred Liturgy. As *Sacrosanctum Concilium* was promulgated on December 4, 1963, "the first fruit of the Council" (VQA, no. 1) was offered to the entire Church. Through the rich doctrine and wise directives offered by this Constitution, the road to liturgical renewal was marked out for the Church "in accordance with the conciliar principles of fidelity to tradition and openness to legitimate development" (VQA, no. 4; cf. also SC, no. 23).

The crucial role of *Sacrosanctum Concilium* becomes clearer when we consider that a very close and organic bond does exist between sound liturgical renewal and the renewal of the whole life of the Church. After all, "the Liturgy is the peak towards which the Church's activity tends, just as it is also the fountain–head from which all its vitality flows" (SC, no. 10). "The Church not only acts but also expresses herself in the liturgy and draws from the liturgy the strength for her life" (DC, no. 13). In particular, "the Church draws her life from the Eucharist" (EE, no. 1), "the source and culmination of all Christian life" (LG, no. 11).

In the liturgical life of the Church, some very good developments have taken place since *Sacrosanctum Concilium* was promulgated. Pope John Paul II, in commemoration of twenty–five years of the document, lists five of these positive results (VQA, no. 12).

The first is the place given to the Bible in the liturgy. *Sacrosanctum Concilium* insisted that the table of God's word is to be made more abundantly available to the people of God in the liturgy. If we reflect back over the past forty years, we see how the renewed liturgical rites have been made much richer with biblical texts. In the Mass, the lectionary is so arranged as to cover most of the Bible in a three–year Sunday reading and a two–year weekday lessons programme. The responsorial psalms help to elucidate the readings. The sacramental rites and the celebrations of the sacramentals are suitably fitted with rich biblical texts. So is the Liturgy of the Hours. In this way not only are the faithful exposed, as it were, to a greater part of Holy Scripture so as to become more familiar with it, but each community has the opportunity, in the specific setting of the liturgical celebration, to enter ever more deeply at all the levels of the human person into the great mystery of God's transforming love which the Scripture proclaims. In country after country, immense effort is undertaken to provide the Christian people with translations of the Bible.

A second happy development is the sustained effort to translate the various liturgical texts into the current language of the people, and also to face the challenges of adapting liturgical celebration to the culture of each people.

A third reason for gratitude is "the increased participation of the faithful by prayer and song, gesture and silence, in the Eucharist and the other sacraments".

We are also encouraged because of "the ministries exercised by lay people and the responsibilities that they have assumed in virtue of the common priesthood into which they have been initiated through Baptism and Confirmation".

Lastly, and as a summary of the above four areas, we must thank God "for the radiant vitality of so many Christian communities, a vitality drawn from the wellspring of the liturgy".

Each of these five positive results offers us reasons for joy and encouragement. But each also assigns us a further task, poses us a challenge and enjoins on us to see that the developments remain truly positive, according to the desire and directives of the Council expressed in *Sacrosanctum Concilium*, and of the Pope and the Bishops who guide us today and tomorrow in the Church that Christ founded.

Bible and Liturgy

In his commentary on Isaiah, St Jerome tells us that, "Ignorance of the Scriptures is ignorance of Christ". Ignorance of the Bible is a great handicap to an understanding of the liturgy and the hoped for fruit of participation in its celebration. A great part of the liturgy is based on Holy Scripture, not only in the readings but also in the inspiration of the prayers, in the symbols and in the images dear to the public worship of the Church. Without a biblical understanding of exodus, covenant, chosen people, Isaac, paschal lamb, Passover, manna and promised land, how can the liturgy be understood? The Psalms, in particular, are an indispensable source of liturgical language, signs and prayers.

"The Church is nourished on the word of God as written down in the books of the Old and New Testaments. When the Church proclaims the word in the liturgy, she welcomes it as a way in which Christ is present" (VL, no. 23). It is Christ "himself who speaks when the Holy Scriptures are read in the Church" (SC, no. 7).

Everyone in the Church needs to make progress in contact with the Bible: clerics, consecrated people and the lay faithful. The growing desire of many lay people to receive better and deeper biblical formation should be met with adequate programmes. The translation of the Bible into the people's language is the first and indispensable step. People also need guidance individually and in groups in how to read, understand and pray the Bible. This is essential for a Catholic approach to the Bible, in which it is clearly understood that it is the Church which presents the Bible to the faithful, explaining its significance in the light of the Tradition that goes back to the Lord's Apostles. Liturgical experts and pastors should help people to see how selected biblical texts fit into specific liturgical celebrations. Homilies should also be rich in biblical foundations.

Translation—Adaptation—Inculturation

The Second Vatican Council introduced the vernacular into the liturgy and also allowed for properly considered adaptations and inculturation in the rites. This poses a considerable challenge and requires careful consideration.

While retaining Latin as the language in the Latin rite, the Council appreciated the usefulness of the use of the mother tongue among the various peoples of the world (cf. SC, no. 36). However, Vatican II did not abolish Latin. It would be good that occasionally a parish sings the more popular parts of the Mass in Latin: think of what this means in terms of preserving and respecting our patrimony, showing the Church as a community that has a memory, and facilitating international Eucharistic celebrations.

Liturgical translations into the mother tongue pose the demanding challenge of producing translations which are faithful to the Latin original, which are excellent literary productions, which can be set to music, which will stand the test of time and which will nourish the piety and spiritual sensitivity of the people. Dangers and abuses arise from *ex tempore* translations, hurried works and illegitimate translations not approved by the Conference of Bishops and ratified by the Apostolic See.

When we go into the area of adaptation and inculturation of rites, we are faced with still more demanding challenges. *Sacrosanctum Concilium* is very clear in its principles and directives (SC, no. 37). The carrying out of these directives will engage the Church for generations, especially in the countries of recent evangelization. Writing on the Holy Eucharist, Pope John Paul II says that "the 'treasure' is too important and precious to risk impoverishment or compromise through forms of experimentation or practices introduced without a careful review on the part of the competent ecclesiastical authorities ... 'because the Sacred Liturgy expresses and celebrates the faith professed by all, and being the heritage of the whole Church, cannot be determined by local Churches in isolation from the universal Church'" (EE, no. 51).

It is therefore reasonable and indeed obvious that there must be liturgical regulations and norms. With reference to the Holy Eucharist, for example, Pope John Paul II says that "These norms are a concrete expression of the authentically ecclesial nature of the Eucharist; this is their deepest meaning. Liturgy is never anyone's private property, be it of the celebrant or of the community" (EE, no. 52). That is why *Sacrosanctum Concilium* already declared that the regulation of the sacred liturgy depends solely on the authority of the Church, that is, on the Apostolic See and, as laws may determine, on the Bishops and the Bishops' Conference. "Wherefore, no one else at all, not even a priest, may, of his own authority, add to, take from, or modify anything in the Liturgy" (SC, no. 22).

The danger is that some people seem to think that inculturation in the liturgy encourages free and uncontrolled creativity. Pope John Paul writes that "it must be lamented that, especially in the years following the postconciliar liturgical reform, as a result of a misguided sense of creativity and adaptation, there have been a number of *abuses* which have been a source of suffering for many" (EE, no. 52).

True and lasting inculturation demands long study, discussions among experts in interdisciplinary platforms, examination and decision by Bishops, recognition from the Apostolic See and prudent presentation to the people of God. Moreover, it should be noted that in religious matters, people's sensitivity and piety can easily be hurt by ill–considered and hasty novelties. In religious practices, most people are understandably conservative in the good sense, and unwilling to endure frequent changes.

Active Participation

The Fathers of the Second Vatican Council stress the importance of the active participation of all the faithful in liturgical celebrations. "Mother Church greatly desires that all the faithful may be brought to take that full, intelligent, active part in liturgical celebrations which the nature of the Liturgy itself requires, and which, in virtue of their baptism, is the right and duty of the Christian people, 'a chosen race, a royal priesthood, a holy nation, God's own people' (1 *Pet* 2:9; cf. 2:45)" (SC, no. 14).

It is important to realize that the internal aspect of participation is indispensable as a basis, a requirement and the aim of all external participation. That is why personal prayer, Scriptural meditation and moments of silence are necessary. "The sacred Liturgy is not the whole of the Church's activity. Before men can come to the Liturgy, they must be called to faith and to conversion" (SC, no. 9). It is highly advisable to promote moments of silence for individual reflection and prayer during the Eucharistic celebration, at such times as after each reading, and after the homily and Holy Communion. Choirs should resist the temptation to fill every available quiet time with singing.

A sense of reverence and devotion is conducive to interiorized active participation. Prominent among those who influence the congregation in this matter is the priest celebrant. But the altar servers, the readers, the choir, and the extraordinary ministers of Holy Communion where they are really needed, do also influence the people by every move of theirs. Reverence is the exterior manifestation of faith. It should show our sense of adoration of God most holy and most high. And our belief in the Real Presence of Jesus Christ in the Holy Eucharist should come across in how the ministers handle the Blessed Sacrament, how they genuflect and how they recite the prescribed prayers.

Liturgical music promotes worship. The Gregorian chant has an honoured place in the history of the Latin rite. It is to be noted that even young people today do appreciate it. Most liturgical singing will understandably be in the mother tongue. The diocesan or national music commission should see that such texts are suitable from the theological and musical points of view before they are approved for Church use.

The *General Instruction on the Roman Missal* wisely notes the importance of common gestures by the worshipping congregation (nos. 4244). Examples are times for the congregation to stand, kneel or sit. Bishops' Conferences can and do make some specifications. Care should be taken not to regiment the congregation, as if it were an army. Some flexibility should be allowed, more so as it is easy to hurt people's eucharistic sensitivity with reference, for example, to kneeling or standing.

Church architecture also influences active participation. If a church is built and the seats are arranged as in an amphitheatre or as in a banquet, the undeclared emphasis may be horizontal attention to one another, rather than vertical attention to God. In this sense the celebration of Mass facing the people demands from the priest and altar servers a high level of discipline, so that as from the offertory of the Mass it be seen clearly that both priest and people are turned towards God, not towards one another. We come to Mass primarily to adore God, not to affirm one another, although this is not excluded.

Some people think that liturgical renewal means the removal of kneelers from Church pews, the knocking down of altar rails or the positioning of the altar in the middle of the sitting area of the people. The Church has never said any such thing. Nor does liturgical restoration mean iconoclasm or the removal of all statues and sacred images. These should be displayed, albeit with good judgment. And the altar of the Blessed Sacrament should be outstanding for its beauty and honored prominence, otherwise in some so-called restored churches one could rightly lament: "They have taken my Lord away, and I don't know where they have put him" (*Jn* 20:13).

Lay Liturgical Roles

For proper celebration of the sacred liturgy and fruitful participation in it by all Christ's faithful, it is important to understand the roles proper to the ministerial or ordained priest and those proper to the lay faithful. Christ is the priest, the high priest. He gives all baptized people a share in this role of offering gifts to God. The common priesthood of all the baptized gives people the capacity to offer Christian worship, to offer Christ to the Eternal Father through the hands of the ordained priest at the Eucharistic celebration, to receive the sacraments and to live holy lives and by self–denial and active charity make of their entire lives a sacrifice.

The ministerial priest, on the other hand, is a man chosen from among the baptized and ordained by the Bishop to the Sacrament of Holy Orders. He alone can consecrate bread into the Body of Christ and wine into the Blood of Christ and offer to the Eternal Father in the name of Christ and the whole Christian people. It is clear that, though they differ from one another in essence and not only in degree, the common priesthood of all the baptized and the ministerial or hierarchical priesthood are closely related (cf. LG, no. 10).

The major challenge is to help the lay faithful appreciate their dignity as baptized persons. From this follows their role at the Eucharistic sacrifice and other liturgical acts. They are the people of God. They are insiders. Their share as readers of lessons, as leaders of song, and as the people offering with and through the priest is based on Baptism. The high point is when they communicate at the Eucharistic table. This crowns their participation at the Eucharistic sacrifice.

There should be no attempt to clericalize the laity. This could happen when, for example, lay people chosen as extraordinary ministers of Holy Communion no longer see this role as being called on to help when the ordinary ministers (bishop, priest, and deacon) are not available in sufficient numbers to cope with the high number of communicants.

We have also the opposite mistake of trying to laicize the clergy. When the priest no longer wishes to bless the people with the formula "May Almighty God bless you", but prefers the seemingly democratic wording, "May Almighty God bless us", then we have a confusion of roles. The same thing happens when some priests think that they should not concelebrate a Mass but should just participate as lay people in order to show more solidarity with the lay faithful. "In liturgical celebrations, each participant, whether minister or simple member of the faithful, in the performance of his office, is to do all that and only that which belongs to him from the nature of things and the rules of liturgy" (SC, no. 28).

Conclusion: Revitalization of Church Life

There is no doubt that *Sacrosanctum Concilium* has continued to sustain the Church along the paths of holiness by fostering genuine liturgical life. It remains important to see that the Council's genuine directives are actually followed.

It is a fact that as the Pope says, "some have received the new books with a certain indifference, or without trying to understand the reasons for the changes; others, unfortunately, have turned back in a one-sided and exclusive way to the previous liturgical forms which some of them consider to be the sole guarantee of certainty in the faith" (VQA, no. 11). Ongoing formation continues to be necessary.

Moreover we have to note that the liturgy of the Church goes beyond the liturgical reform. Many young priests, consecrated brothers and sisters, and lay faithful are not conversant with the liturgical books of fifty years ago, either because they were born after Vatican II, or because they were infants when it was celebrated. What is above all needed is "an ever deeper grasp of the liturgy of the Church, celebrated according to the current books and lived above all as a reality in the spiritual order" (VQA, no. 14). There should be a widespread formation of the lay faithful in the theology and spirituality of the liturgy.

+ Francis Cardinal Arinze
Emeritus Prefect, Congregation for Divine Worship
and the Discipline of the Sacraments

Abbreviations

DC	Dominicae Cenae
EE	Ecclesia de Eucharistia
LG	Lumen Gentium
SC	Sacrosanctum Concilium
VQA	Vicesimus Quintus Annus
VL	Varietates Legitimae

PAUL, BISHOP
SERVANT OF THE SERVANTS OF GOD
TOGETHER WITH THE FATHERS
OF THE SACRED COUNCIL PUTS ON
PERMANENT RECORD THE

CONSTITUTION
ON THE SACRED LITURGY

1. THE SACRED COUNCIL has set itself the following aims: to increase daily among the faithful the vigour of their Christian life; to
adapt in the best way possible to the needs of our time those institutions that admit of change; to foster anything at all that may contribute
to the union of all those who believe in Christ; to give added support to anything that may help to call all men into the bosom of the
Church. For the better achievement of these aims, it considers that it
should give particular attention to the restoration and encouragement
of the Liturgy.

2. The reason for this is that the Liturgy, by which is put into effect,
especially in the divine sacrifice of the Eucharist, 'the work of our redemption',[1] contributes in the highest measure to enabling the faithful
to express in their lives and show forth to others the mystery of Christ
and the real nature of the true Church. It is, of course, characteristic
of the Church to be at once human and divine, visible and yet endowed with invisible values, pulsating with activity and yet given over
to contemplation, present in the world and withal a stranger there.
In all this there is order: the human in the Church is ordered to and,
indeed, subordinate to the divine, the visible to the invisible, action to
contemplation, the present to the city which is to come, that we seek.[2]

---

[1] *Roman Missal*, Ninth Sunday after Pentecost, Prayer over the Offerings.
[2] Cf. *Heb* 13:14.

With the result that, whereas the Liturgy daily builds up those who are in the Church into a holy temple in the Lord, into a dwelling place of God in the Spirit,[3] until they attain to the measure of the stature of the fullness of Christ,[4] it gives them, at the same time, a remarkably increased vitality for the publishing abroad of Christ, and, by so doing, to those who are outside her confines, displays the Church as an ensign raised up for the nations,[5] an ensign under which may be gathered into one the children of God who are scattered abroad,[6] until there be but one flock and one shepherd.[7]

3. Therefore, the Sacred Council thinks it advisable, firstly, to restate the following principles which apply in the matter of encouraging and restoring the Liturgy, and, secondly, to fix certain practical guiding lines.

Among these principles and guiding lines, there are some that can and ought to be applied both to the Roman rite and to all the other rites, but it must be clearly understood that the practical directions that follow concern the Roman rite only, except when they treat of matters which, from the very nature of things, affect the other rites also.

4. Finally, remaining in this matter faithful to tradition, the Sacred Council declares that Holy Mother Church holds all legitimately recognized rites in equal right and honour, and that she wishes them to be kept and fostered unreservedly for the future. The Council desires that, where there may be need, they should be carefully and thoroughly revised in accordance with sound tradition and endowed with a new vigour to suit the needs and circumstances of the present day.

---

[3] Cf. *Eph* 2:21-2.
[4] Cf. *Eph* 4:13.
[5] Cf. *Js* 11:12.
[6] Cf. *Jn* 11:52.
[7] Cf. *Jn* 10:16.

Chapter I

GENERAL PRINCIPLES GOVERNING THE
RESTORATION AND ENCOURAGEMENT
OF THE SACRED LITURGY

I. THE NATURE OF THE SACRED LITURGY
AND ITS IMPORTANCE
IN THE LIFE OF THE CHURCH

5. God, 'who desires all men to be saved and to come to the knowledge of the truth' (1 *Tim* 2:4), 'in many and various ways spoke of old to our fathers by the prophets' (*Heb* 1:1) and, when the fullness of time had come, sent his Son, the Word made flesh, anointed by the Holy Spirit, to preach good news to the poor, to bind up the broken-hearted,[8] 'the one physician at once both flesh and spirit',[9] the mediator between God and man.[10] His humanity, in the Word's oneness of Person, was the instrument by which our salvation was effected, and that is why we can say that in Christ 'the perfect satisfaction required for our reconciliation has been already made, and on us has been bestowed the whole fullness of divine worship'.[11]

This work—the redemption of mankind and the perfect glorification of God—was foretold by the mighty works of God wrought on behalf of the people of the Old Testament and effectively accomplished by the Lord Christ, above all in the paschal mystery of his

---

[8] Cf. *Is* 61:1; *Lk* 4:18.
[9] St Ignatius of Antioch, *Ad Ephesios*, 7,2.
[10] Cf. 1 *Tim* 2:5.
[11] *Sacramentarium Veronese (Leonianum)*; Ed. C. Mohlberg, Rome, 1956, No. 1265, p. 162.

blessed Passion, his Resurrection from the netherworld and his glorious Ascension. In this paschal mystery 'he destroyed death by his dying and remade life by his rising',[12] for, from the side of Christ sleeping on the cross the wondrous sacrament of the whole Church came forth.[13]

6. So then, as Christ was sent by the Father, even so did he send the apostles, filled with the Holy Spirit, to preach the gospel to the whole creation[14] and to proclaim that the Son of God, by his death and resurrection, had rescued us from the power of Satan[15] and from death, and transferred us to the Father's kingdom. At the same time, the work of salvation they were making known, this same work they were to put into effect, through the sacrifice and the sacraments round which, of course, all liturgical life revolves. For, in baptism men are grafted into Christ's paschal mystery—they die with him, they are buried with him, they are raised with him.[16] They receive the Spirit of adoption into sonship 'in which we cry, "Abba! Father!"' (*Rom* 8:15) and so become true worshippers, such as the Father seeks to worship him.[17] Likewise, each time they eat the Lord's Supper, they proclaim his death until he comes.[18] For this reason, on the day of Pentecost, the very day on which the Church appeared before the world, 'those who received [Peter's] word were baptized'. 'And they devoted themselves to the apostles' teaching and fellowship, to the breaking of bread and the prayers ... praising God and having favour with all the people' (*Acts* 2:41-7). From that day on, the Church has never failed to assemble together for the celebration of the paschal mystery, reading 'in all the scriptures the things concerning [Christ]' (*Lk* 24:27), celebrating the Eucharist in which 'are set forth the victory and triumph of his

---

[12] *Roman Missal*, Preface for Easter.
[13] Cf. St Augustine, Enarr. in Ps., 138, 2 (*Corpus Christianorum*, 40, Turnhout, 1956, p. 1991); *Roman Missal*, Collect after the second prophecy on Holy Saturday (before the 1956 reform).
[14] Cf. *Mk* 16:15.
[15] Cf. *Acts* 26:18.
[16] Cf. *Rom* 6:4; *Eph* 2:6; *Col* 3:1, 2 *Tim* 2:11.
[17] Cf. *Jn* 4:23.
[18] Cf. 1 *Cor* 11:26.

death',[19] and also giving thanks 'to God for his inexpressible gift' (2 *Cor* 9:15) in Christ Jesus, in 'praise of his glory' (*Eph* 1:12) through the power of the Holy Spirit.

7. For the perfect and complete accomplishment of this great work Christ is ever present in his Church, more particularly in her liturgical acts. He is present in the sacrifice of the Mass, first of all in the person of the minister—'he now offers himself by the ministry of priests, who then offered himself on the cross',[20]—but chiefly under the eucharistic species [of bread and wine]. His presence is realized, by his active power, in the sacraments, for whenever anyone baptizes, it is Christ himself who baptizes.[21] His presence is realized, by his spoken word, since it is he himself who speaks when the Holy Scriptures are read in the Church. Finally, his presence is realized when the Church makes supplication and sings, his presence who promised that 'where two or three are gathered in my name, there am I in the midst of them' (*Mt* 18:20).

It is true to say that Christ always joins with himself in this great work, in which God is perfectly glorified and men sanctified, the Church his most dearly loved Bride: she calls upon her Lord and through him presents her worship to the Eternal Father.

It is, therefore, only right to see in the Liturgy the exercise of Jesus Christ's priestly office. For, in the Liturgy, first, by means of sensible signs the sanctification of man is both signified and, in a manner proper to each sign, brought about; second, by the Mystical Body of Jesus Christ, of the Head, that is to say, and its members, there is carried out a complete public worship.

From this it follows that every liturgical celebration, inasmuch as it is a work of Christ the Priest and of his Body the Church, is pre-eminently a sacred action, the efficacy of which no other act of the Church can equal on the same basis and to the same degree.

---

[19] Council of Trent, Sess. XIII, Decree *De Ss. Eucharistia*, 5 (Denz, 878; *Concilium Tridentium*, Ed. Gorres-Gesellschaft, 7, 4, Freiburg, 1961, p. 202).
[20] Council of Trent, Sess. XXII, Doctrine De Ss. *Missae Sacrificio*, 2 (Denz. 940; Ed. Cit., 8,5, p. 960).
[21] St Augustine, *In Ioann. Ev.* Tr., 6, 1, 7; PL 35, 1428.

8. In our liturgy here on earth, we receive a foretaste of and a share in the heavenly liturgy that is celebrated in the holy city Jerusalem towards which we are wending our pilgrim way and in which Christ is, seated at the right hand of God, a minister in the sanctuary and the true tabernacle.[22] With all the host of the army of heaven we join in singing to the Lord the hymn of glory. Reverencing the memory of the saints, we hope for some part and fellowship with them. We await the Saviour our Lord Jesus Christ until the day when he who is our life appears, and we appear with him in glory.[23]

9. The sacred Liturgy is not the whole of the Church's activity. Before men can come to the Liturgy, they must be called to faith and conversion. 'How are men to call upon him in whom they have not believed? And how are they to believe in him of whom they have not heard? And how are they to hear without a preacher? And how can men preach unless they are sent?' (*Rom* 10:14-15).

The Church, therefore, proclaims to unbelievers the message of salvation to the end that all men may come to know the only true God and Jesus Christ whom he has sent, and may repent and turn from their own ways.[24] As for the believers, she must ever preach to them faith and repentance; she must also fit them for the sacraments, teach them to observe all that Christ has commanded,[25] and encourage them in all those works of charity, devotion and apostolate that make it obvious that Christians, though they are not of this world, are yet the light of the world, glorifying the Father in the sight of men.

10. Nevertheless, the Liturgy is the peak towards which the Church's activity tends, just as it is also the fountain-head from which all its vitality flows. For the labours of the apostolate have but one end, namely, that all men made God's sons by faith and baptism should be

---

[22] Cf. *Rev* 21:2; *Col* 3:1; *Heb* 8:2.
[23] Cf. *Phil* 3:20; *Col* 3:4.
[24] Cf. *Lk* 24:27; *Jn* 17:3; *Acts* 2:38.
[25] Cf. *Mt* 28:20.

drawn together, praise God in the midst of the Church, share in the sacrifice and eat the Lord's Supper.

In return, the Liturgy moves the faithful whom it has heaped with the delights of 'the paschal sacraments' to be 'of one mind in the service of God',[26] and prays that 'they may hold fast in their everyday life what they have received in faith'.[27] Furthermore, the renewal of the Lord's covenant with men in the Eucharist attracts the faithful to and fires them with the compelling love of Christ. And so, from the Liturgy, and especially from the Eucharist, grace flows out into us as from a fountain, procuring with the greatest possible effect that sanctification of men in Christ and that glorification of God which are the end of all the other works of the Church.

11. In order that this full effect may be realized, it is, however, essential that the faithful should come to the Liturgy in the right frame of mind, suiting their thoughts to their voices and cooperating with the grace from on high, lest they receive it in vain.[28] Therefore, pastors must see to it, on the one hand, that in the performance of the liturgy the laws of valid and licit celebration are observed, and, on the other hand, that the faithful take part in its performance intelligently, actively and fruitfully.

12. However, the spiritual life is not limited to participation in the sacred Liturgy and nothing but that. For the Christian, called to take part in common prayer, must also go into his private room and pray to the Father in secret,[29] or rather, as the apostle teaches, pray without ceasing.[30] We are further taught by the same apostle always to carry in

---

[26] *Roman Missal*, Easter Sunday, Postcommunion.
[27] *Ibid.* Tuesday in Easter Week, Collect.
[28] Cf. 2 *Cor* 6:1.
[29] Cf. *Mt* 6:6.
[30] 1 *Thess* 5:17.

our body the death of Jesus, so that the life of Jesus, also, may be manifested in our mortal flesh.[31] For this reason, we pray the Lord in the sacrifice of the Mass that he would accept the offering of our spiritual victim and make for himself of our selves 'an everlasting offering'.[32]

13. The devotional practices of the Christian people, provided they are in agreement with the Church's laws and directives, are warmly recommended, especially when it is the Apostolic See that has ordered them.

A special dignity is also enjoyed by such pious practices of particular Churches as are performed by order of the bishops in accordance with properly approved customs or books.

However, taking account of the liturgical seasons, these exercises are to be so arranged as to conform with the sacred Liturgy, flow from it, as it were, and lead the people to it, for the Liturgy is, of its nature, far superior to them.

II. TEACHING THE LITURGY
AND ACTIVE PARTICIPATION
IN THE LITURGY

14. Mother Church greatly desires that all the faithful may be brought to take that full, intelligent, active part in liturgical celebrations which the nature of the Liturgy itself requires, and which, in virtue of their baptism, is the right and duty of the Christian people, 'a chosen race, a royal priesthood, a holy nation, God's own people' (1 *Pet* 2:9; cf. 2:4-5).

This full, active participation on the part of the whole people is something that deserves the utmost attention when the reformation and fostering of the sacred Liturgy are under consideration, because this active taking part is the first, indeed it is the necessary, source from

---

[31] Cf. 2 *Cor* 4:10-11.

[32] *Roman Missal*, Whit Monday, Prayer over the Offerings.

which the faithful may be expected to draw the true Christian spirit. Therefore, by proper education it is to be zealously sought after by the shepherds of souls in all their pastoral work.

Moreover, since it cannot be hoped that this will occur unless the pastors themselves are, first, so thoroughly imbued with the spirit and power of the Liturgy as to become past masters in it, there is an even greater need to make the best possible provision for the liturgical education of the clergy. To this end, the Sacred Council has decided on the following measures.

15. Professors who are charged with teaching the subject Sacred Liturgy in seminaries, the houses of studies of religious, and theological faculties, are to receive a thorough training for their task in institutes specially appointed for this purpose.

16. Sacred Liturgy as a subject in seminaries and the houses of studies of religious is to be considered one of the necessary, key subjects; in theological faculties it will rank as a major subject *(disciplina principalis)*; it will be taught not only under its theological and historical aspects, but also under its spiritual, pastoral and juridical aspects. Professors of other disciplines, more particularly Dogmatic Theology, Holy Scripture, Spiritual and Pastoral Theology, will take good care, each according to the intrinsic requirements of his particular subject, to explore the riches of the mystery of Christ and of redemptive history in such a way as to make abundantly obvious both their connexion with the Liturgy and the whole unity of the clerical education given.

17. Clerical students in seminaries and religious houses are to receive a liturgical education to the spiritual life. This will comprise suitable guidance to enable them to understand the sacred rites and join in them wholeheartedly; it will also include the actual celebration of the holy mysteries, as well as other devotional exercises steeped in the spirit of the sacred Liturgy. In addition, they will learn to observe the

liturgical laws, so that life in the seminaries and religious institutes may be wholly penetrated by the liturgical spirit.

18. Priests, both secular and religious, already at work in the Lord's vineyard, are to be helped by all opportune means to gain an ever increasing understanding of what they are doing when they celebrate the functions of the Church; they are to be helped to lead a liturgical life and to share this with the faithful entrusted to them.

19. As for the faithful, their liturgical education and active participation—both internal and external—according to their age, status, mode of life and degree of religious culture, are to be pursued by their pastors with zeal and patience. These latter will know that in this they are performing one of the greatest tasks of the faithful dispenser of God's mysteries. Let them lead their flock in this domain by example as well as by word.

20. Any radio or television broadcasts of church services, especially if they concern the Holy Sacrifice, must be produced with dignity and taste, under the direction and responsibility of some fit person appointed by the bishops.

III. THE REFORM OF THE SACRED LITURGY

21. In order that the Christian people may the more surely gain an abundance of graces in the sacred Liturgy, the Church, their loving Mother, desires to apply herself with due care to a general reform of the Liturgy, for the Liturgy consists of a part that is unchangeable because it is divinely instituted and of parts that can be changed. These latter can, and indeed must, vary with the passage of time, if ever they come to contain things not altogether consonant with the real nature of the Liturgy as such, or things that are no longer appropriate.

In this restoration, it is important to give to texts and rites a form that will express clearly the sacred content they are meant to signify, a form such that the Christian people will be able to grasp this content as easily as possible and share in it in a full, active, congregational celebration.

Wherefore, the Sacred Council has drawn up these general directives.

A. General Directives

22. § 1. The supervision and general ordering of the sacred Liturgy are vested solely in the authority of the Church. This authority resides in the Apostolic See and, according to the terms of the law, in the bishop.

§ 2. In virtue of a power granted by law, the supervision and general ordering of liturgical matters within certain fixed limits also belong to the various sorts of competent territorial assemblies of bishops legitimately constituted.

§ 3. Wherefore, no one else at all, not even a priest, may, of his own authority, add to, take from, or modify anything in the Liturgy.

23. In order that sound tradition may be maintained and, at the same time, that the way may be opened to legitimate progress, the revision of the different parts of the Liturgy is always to be prepared by a thorough theological, historical and pastoral investigation. Moreover, the general laws of the structure and spirit of the Liturgy, and the experience deriving from recent liturgical reform and from a large number of grants of indults, are to be taken into consideration. To conclude, innovations should not be made unless when a real and definite advantage will accrue to the Church and when due care has been taken to ensure that the new forms shall, as it were, grow out organically from those already existing.

In addition, steps should be taken to see that, as far as possible, no notable differences in rites arise between neighbouring regions.

24. The importance of Holy Scripture in the celebration of the Liturgy is very great. From it come the passages that are read and expounded in the homily, and the psalms that are sung. Inspired and suggested by

it, prayers, collects and liturgical hymns pour forth. From it liturgical actions and signs receive their meaning. Therefore, in order to provide for the restoration, progress and adaptation of the Liturgy, it is important to spread that keen and loving affection for Holy Scripture that is attested by the venerable tradition of the rites of both East and West.

25. The liturgical books are to be revised as soon as possible. For this work experts must be employed and the bishops of different parts of the world consulted.

B. Directives drawn from the Nature of the Liturgy as a Hierarchical and Congregational Action

26. Liturgical services are not private activities but celebrations of the Church, the 'sacrament of unity', that is, a holy people gathered together and drawn up in order under the bishops.[33]

That is why the liturgical services belong to the whole body of the Church, why they manifest it and affect it, and why they also affect its individual members, but in different ways varying with the diversification of their orders, tasks and effective participation.

27. Whenever any rite, of its very nature, implies a congregational celebration with the attendance and active participation of the faithful, let it be emphatically taught that this congregational celebration is to be preferred, as far as possible, to any individual and more or less private celebration.

This is particularly true of the celebration of Mass—without prejudice to the unalterably public and social nature of each and every Mass—and the administration of the sacraments.

28. In liturgical celebrations, each participant, whether minister or simple member of the faithful, in the performance of his office, is to do all that and only that which belongs to him from the nature of things and the rules of liturgy.

---

[33] St Cyprian, *De Catholicae Ecclesiae Unitate*, 7 (CSEL 3, 1, Vienna, 1868, pp. 215-6); cf. Ep.,66, 8, 3 (Ed.cit., 3, 2, pp. 732-3).

29. Servers, readers, commentators and members of choirs exercise a true liturgical ministry. Therefore, they are to perform their office with all the sincere devotion and discipline that befit so great a ministry and that the people of God has every right to require of them.

They must, therefore, be zealously instructed in the spirit of the Liturgy, each according to his capacity, and taught how to do in a correct and dignified manner what they have to do.

30. To encourage the people to take an active part, their acclamations, answers, singing of psalms, antiphons and hymns, even their actions, for example gestures and attitudes of body, are to be gone into, and a holy silence should be observed at the appropriate times.

31. In the revision of the liturgical books, let care be taken to see that the rubrics provide for the people's part.

32. In the Liturgy, except for the distinction based on liturgical function and Sacred Order, and except for the honours prescribed by the liturgical laws as due to secular authorities, no differences are to be made between private persons or classes of persons either in the ceremonies or in any outward display.

C. Directives deriving from the Educative and Pastoral Character of the Liturgy

33. Though the Liturgy is above all else the worship of the Divine Majesty, it nevertheless contains a great deal of teaching for the faithful.[34] In the Liturgy God speaks to his people, Christ still proclaims the good news. In their turn the people answer God by their hymns and prayer.

The prayers addressed to God by the priest who presides over the assembly in the person of Christ are proffered in the name of the

---

[34] Cf. COUNCIL OF TRENT, Sess. XXII, *Doctrine De Ss. Missae Sacrificio*, 8 (DENZ. 946; Ed. cit., 8, p. 961).

25

whole holy people and of all those present. The visible signs employed by the sacred Liturgy for the signifying of invisible divine realities have been chosen by Christ or the Church. It follows, therefore, that it is not only when the words are read that were 'written for our instruction' (*Rom* 15:4), but also when the Church prays, sings or does something, that the faith of the participants is nourished, their minds are stirred up to offer their reasonable service and duty to God, and they receive in more abundant measure his grace.

That being so, the following general directives must be observed in carrying out the reform.

34. The rites should shine with a noble simplicity, be concise and clear, and avoid useless repetitions. They should be intelligible to the faithful and should not, as a rule, require any considerable explanation.

35. In the Liturgy, the intimate union of rite and word should appear clearly, therefore:

(1) In the services a richer, more varied and more appropriate reading of Holy Scripture should be introduced.

(2) The best place for the sermon, since it is a part of the liturgical action, is to be noted in the rubrics, taking into account the structure of the rite. The ministry of preaching is to be performed properly and with great fidelity. Let it draw, in the first place, on the source of Holy Scripture and the Liturgy, and it will be like a proclamation of God's mighty deeds in redemptive history, i.e. in the mystery of Christ ever present and at work in us, especially in liturgical services.

(3) Instruction of a more directly liturgical nature should also be given in every way possible; and, if necessary, during the rites themselves, but only at the more suitable moments, provision should be made for short addresses by the priest or competent minister, in prescribed terms or words similar to those suggested.

(4) The sacred celebration of the Word of God is to be encouraged

on the eves of the greater feasts, on certain weekdays in Advent and Lent and on Sundays and feast days, particularly in places where there is no priest. In this case, a deacon or other person appointed by the bishop should conduct the service.

36. § 1. The use of the Latin tongue is to be maintained in the Latin rites, except where some special law obtains.

§ 2. However, in the Mass, the administration of the sacraments and other parts of the Liturgy, the use of the vernacular can not infrequently be very useful to the people. Therefore, it would be well to grant it some considerable place, above all in the readings and addresses to the congregation, in some prayers and chants, along the lines laid down for this in detail in the chapters that follow.

§ 3. Provided these lines are followed, the decision about the use and extent of the vernacular rests with the competent territorial authority of the Church mentioned in Art. 22, § 2. If the case should arise, this authority is to discuss the question with the bishops of neighbouring regions using the same language and its acts must be approved, i.e. confirmed by the Apostolic See.

§ 4. Any translation of the Latin text into the vernacular destined for use in the Liturgy must be approved by the competent territorial authority of the Church, as above.

D. Directives for the Adapting of the Liturgy to the particular genius and traditions of various peoples

37. In matters that do not affect the faith or good of the whole community, the Church has no desire to impose a rigid uniformity, not even in the Liturgy. On the contrary, she cultivates and develops the mental and spiritual graces and gifts of the different nations and peoples. Anything at all in peoples' customs that is not inescapably identified with superstition and error she examines favourably and, if possible, maintains whole and entire. Sometimes, indeed, she gives it a place in the Liturgy itself, provided it conforms with the principles of the true, genuine liturgical spirit.

38. On condition that the substantial unity of the Roman rite is pre-served, room should be found in the revision of the liturgical books for legitimate variations and adaptations to different groups, regions and peoples, especially in the Missions. This necessity should, on occasion, be kept in mind in the ordering of the rites and the drawing up of the rubrics.

39. Within the limits laid down in the typical editions of the liturgical books, it will depend on the competent territorial authority of the Church mentioned in Art. 22, § 2, to determine any adaptations, particularly in the administration of the sacraments and in sacramentals, processions, the liturgical language, church music and the arts; always, of course, according to the basic lines contained in this Constitution.

40. However, in various places and in differing circumstances, a more fargoing and, consequently, more difficult adaptation may be required. Therefore:

(1) The competent territorial authority of the Church mentioned in Art. 22, § 2, is to consider carefully and wisely, what contributions to divine worship it would be right to accept, in this matter, from the traditions and nature of each people. Any adaptations deemed useful or necessary are to be submitted to the Apostolic See for introduction if its consent is obtained.

(2) In order that any adaptation may be effected with all due care and consideration, the Apostolic See will, if advisable, grant the aforesaid territorial authority of the Church a faculty to allow and conduct the necessary preliminary experiments in certain suitable groups over a fixed period.

(3) Seeing that liturgical laws often entail special difficulties where adaptation is concerned, particularly in the Missions, specialists in the matter dealt with should be present when the laws are being framed.

IV. FOSTERING THE LITURGICAL LIFE
IN DIOCESE AND PARISH

41. The bishop is to be reckoned the great high priest of his flock. From him is derived and on him depends, in some sense, the life in Christ of his faithful.

For this reason, all must hold in the greatest respect the liturgical life of the diocese centred on the bishop, especially in the cathedral. Let them be quite certain that the chief manifestation of the Church is to be found in the full, active participation of the whole holy people of God in the same liturgical services, particularly in the same Eucharist—in one prayer at one altar—presided over by the bishop surrounded by his whole body of priests and subordinate ministers.[35]

42. Since the bishop in his Church cannot himself always and everywhere preside over his whole flock, he needs must set up groups of the faithful, and among these the chief are the parishes established on a local basis having each its pastor who takes the bishop's place. These, in some sort, represent the worldwide visible Church.

For this reason, the liturgical life of the parish and its relation to the bishop should be fostered in the theory and practice of clergy and faithful alike. Efforts should be made to encourage a real parish community sense, above all in the common celebration of the Sunday Mass.

V. THE PROMOTING OF
PASTORAL LITURGICAL ACTIVITY

43. The interest shown in the encouragement and restoration of the Liturgy is rightly held to be a sign of God's providential dispositions in favour of our time, as a visiting of his Church by the Holy Spirit. Indeed, it gives a characteristic distinguishing mark to the Church's life and to the whole religious thought and practice of our time.

---

[35] Cf. St Ignatius of Antioch, *Ad Magn.*, 7; *Ad Phil*, 4; *Ad Smyrn.*, 8.

To give still greater encouragement to this pastoral liturgical activity in the Church, the Sacred Council decrees:

44. It will be useful if the competent territorial authority of the Church mentioned in Art. 22, § 2, will appoint a Liturgical Commission with the aid of experts in liturgical matters, music, sacred art and the pastoral ministry. Of assistance to this commission would be, if it could be managed, an Institute of Pastoral Liturgy consisting of members of special competence in this domain, among whom might well be, in certain circumstances, lay people. The commission's duty will be, under the guidance of the aforementioned territorial authority of the Church, to direct pastoral liturgical activity in its area, and to further studies and necessary experiments in the case of adaptations to be submitted to the Apostolic See.

45. In the same way, each diocese should have its Liturgical Commission for a furthering of the Liturgy under the bishop's general direction.

Sometimes it might be wise for several dioceses to appoint a single commission for the promotion of the Liturgy on a common basis.

46. In addition to the Liturgical Commission each diocese should appoint, if possible, further Commissions for Church Music and Sacred Art.

These three commissions must work closely together; indeed, quite often it will be best for them to coalesce into one single commission.

CHAPTER II

THE HOLY MYSTERY OF THE EUCHARIST

47. Our Saviour, at the Last Supper on the night on which he was betrayed, instituted the eucharistic Sacrifice of his Body and Blood whereby he might perpetuate the sacrifice of the cross throughout the ages until he should come, and, moreover, entrust to the Church, his beloved Bride, a memorial of his death and resurrection: the sacrament of love, the sign of unity, the bond of charity,[36] the paschal banquet, in which Christ is received, our mind and soul are filled with grace and a pledge is given us of glory to come.[37]

48. Therefore, the Church takes very special care to see that the faithful do not assist at this mystery of faith like strangers or dumb spectators. On the contrary, she wants them to have a good understanding of the mystery through the rites and prayers, and thus to take an intelligent, devout and active part in the sacred action. They should find instruction in the word of God and refreshment at the table of the Lord's Body; they should give thanks to God. Offering the spotless victim not only at the priest's hands, but also, themselves, offering it together with him, they should learn to make the oblation of themselves. Day by day through Christ the Mediator,[38] they should grow into an ever more perfect unity with God and one another, until at last God becomes all things in all of them.

49. Therefore, in order that the sacrifice of the Mass, even in the form of its rites, may obtain its full pastoral effect, the Sacred Council, having in mind those Masses that are celebrated with a congregation, particularly on Sundays and holy days of obligation, makes the following decrees.

[36] Cf. St Augustine, *In Ioann. Ev.* Tr, 26, 6, 13; PL 35, 1613.
[37] Roman Breviary, *Corpus Christi*, II Vespers, Antiphon for Magnificat.
[38] Cf. St Cyril of Alexandria, comment. *In Ioann. Ev.*, 11, 11-12; PG 74, 557-64.

50. The Ordinary of the Mass (*Ordo Missae*) is to be revised in a way that will reveal more clearly the real function of each of the parts and the connexions of the various parts with one another. This revision is also to facilitate the devout, active participation of the faithful.

To this end, while the substance of the rites is to be preserved, they themselves should be simplified. Doublets and any additions of little value that have accrued in the course of the centuries are to be omitted. Certain things that have fallen out through the wearing processes of time are to be reinstated after the ancient model of the holy Fathers, according as they may seem advisable or necessary.

51. In order to lay a more richly furnished table of God's Word for the faithful, the larder of the Bible is to be opened up more generously, so that in the space of a fixed number of years, the more important part of Holy Scripture may be read to the people.

52. The homily which, in the course of the liturgical year, uses the sacred text to set forth the mysteries of the faith and the rules of Christian living, is to be strongly recommended, for it is a real part of the liturgy. At Masses celebrated with a congregation on Sundays and holy days of obligation it must not be omitted, unless for a grave reason.

53. 'The common prayer', i.e. 'the prayer of the faithful' ['the bidding prayer'] after the Gospel and the homily, is to be reintroduced, especially on Sundays and holy days of obligation, so that the people may join in and pray for the Holy Church, those in authority over us, those in various troubles and afflictions, as well as for all men and the situation of the whole world.[39]

54. It should be possible to give a fitting place to the vernacular in Masses celebrated with a congregation, especially in the readings and

---

[39] Cf. 1 *Tim* 2:1-2.

the bidding prayer, and also, depending on local conditions, in those parts that concern the people, as laid down in Art. 36 of this Constitution.

Provision should be made, however, to see that the faithful can say or sing together in Latin those parts of the Ordinary of the Mass that concern them.

If in any place a wider use of the vernacular in the Mass should seem called for, the measures prescribed in Art.40 of this Constitution are to be followed.

55. The more perfect sharing in the Mass whereby, after the communion of the priest, the faithful receive the Lord's Body from the same sacrifice is greatly recommended.

Communion under both kinds, without prejudice to the dogmatic principles laid down by the Council of Trent,[40] can, if the bishops so rule, be granted to clerics and religious and also to lay people, in cases to be determined by the Apostolic See. Examples would be the giving of communion in an ordination Mass to those just ordained, in a profession Mass to the newly professed, and in a Mass following baptism to the neophytes.

56. The two parts which, in one sense, make up the Mass, that is the Liturgy of the Word and the Eucharistic Liturgy, are so intimately linked that they make up one single act of worship. The Holy Synod, therefore, earnestly exhorts pastors that in their instructions they should zealously teach the faithful to take their part in the whole Mass, especially on Sundays and holy days of obligation.

57. § 1. Concelebration, which is an excellent illustration of the oneness of the priesthood, has remained in use in the Church until the present in both East and West. Therefore, the Council has been pleased to extend the permission to concelebrate to the following cases:

---

[40] Sess. XXI, *Doctrine De Common, sub utraque specie et parvulorum*, 1-3 (Denz. 930-2; Ed. cit., 8, pp. 698-9).

(1) (a) Maundy Thursday [Holy Thursday] in both the Chrism Mass and the evening Mass;

(b) Masses at Councils, Bishops' Meetings and Synods;

(c) Mass at the Blessing of an Abbot.

(2) In addition, with the permission of the Ordinary, whose right it is to judge of the advisability of concelebration:

(a) Conventual Mass and the principal Mass in churches when the needs of the faithful do not require that each of the priests present should say a separate Mass;

(b) Masses at any kind of meeting of priests whether secular or religious.

§ 2. (1) It is the bishop's right to regulate the discipline of concelebration in his diocese.

(2) Any priest, however, is always to have the possibility of celebrating a separate Mass, except that it must not be at the same time in the same church, or on Maundy Thursday.

58. A new rite of concelebration is to be composed for insertion in the Roman Pontifical and Missal.

Chapter III

THE OTHER SACRAMENTS
AND THE SACRAMENTALS

59. The end of the sacraments is the sanctification of men, the building of the Body of Christ, and the worship of God, and since they are signs they also have an educative function. They not only suppose faith; they also, by words and objects, nourish, strengthen and express it. This is why they are called 'the sacraments of faith'. To be sure, they confer grace, but their celebration is the best possible means of disposing the faithful for a fruitful reception of this grace, for the fitting worship of God and for the practice of charity.

Hence it follows that it is of the greatest importance that the faithful should be able to understand easily the signs conveyed in the sacraments and that they should be most zealous in their frequentation of those sacraments that were instituted to nourish the Christian life.

60. In addition, Holy Mother Church has instituted sacramentals. These are sacred signs by which, somewhat after the pattern of the sacraments, certain effects—chiefly spiritual ones—are both indicated and, as a result of the Church's advocacy, obtained. The sacramentals have a twofold function: they dispose men for the reception of the chief effect of the sacraments; they hallow a number of circumstances in the lives of men.

61. As a consequence, those of the faithful who are well disposed find that, in the liturgy of the sacraments and sacramentals, practically every happening of their lives is sanctified by the divine grace that flows from the paschal mystery of the Passion, Death and Resurrection of Christ, the source from which all the sacraments and sacramentals derive their power. Indeed, there is scarcely any right use of material things that cannot be directed to the sanctification of man and the praise of God.

62. However, with the passage of time, certain things have found a place in the rites of both sacraments and sacramentals, that rather obscure to men of our day their real nature and end. In so far as this is so, some adaptations must be made to the needs of our time. The Sacred Council sets out the following rules to govern this revision.

63. As in many cases it may be found extremely useful for the people if the vernacular is adopted in the administration of the sacraments and sacramentals, it is only right that some considerable place should be given to this, as follows:

(a) In the administration of the sacraments and sacramentals the vernacular may be used as laid down in Art. 36.

(b) In accordance with the new edition of the Roman Ritual, proper Rituals, adapted—in language also—to meet the special needs of each region, are to be prepared as quickly as possible by the competent territorial authority of the Church (see Art. 22, § 2 of this Constitution). After inspection by the Apostolic See, they will be used in their respective regions. When these Rituals or proper Smaller Rituals (*Collectiones Rituum*) are being prepared, the instructions—pastoral, rubrical, or of special social importance—that precede the various rites in the Roman Ritual are not to be omitted.

64. An adult catechumenate divided into several stages is to be restored, the introduction of which will depend on the judgement of the local Ordinary. In this way, it should prove possible to sanctify the time of the catechumenate, which is meant to be given over to the fitting instruction of the catechumen, with a succession of sacred rites to be performed each in its right time.

65. In missionary countries, over and above the elements already found in Christian tradition, there should be no difficulty in admitting further initiation ceremonies that may be in use among different

peoples, in so far as they can be adapted to the Christian rite, as laid down in Art. 37-40 of this Constitution.

66. Both rites of adult baptism, the simple one and the more solemn that takes account of the restored catechumenate, are to be revised. A proper Mass 'For the Conferring of Baptism' will be inserted in the Roman Missal.

67. The rite of infant baptism is to be revised and made to suit the real state of infants. The roles of both parents and godparents, and their duties also, are to be made more obvious in the rite itself.

68. In the rite of baptism there should be modifications, to be used if the local Ordinary approves, when there is a large number of candidates. A shorter service will also be drawn up to be used, particularly in the Missions, by catechists, and generally, in danger of death, when no priest or deacon may be had, by the faithful.

69. Instead of the rite called *The Supplying of the Ceremonies when Baptism has been Administered without them*, a new and more suitable one is to be devised making it clear that the child, though baptized with the shorter rite, has already been received into the Church.

Another new rite is to be composed for converts to Catholicism who have already been validly baptized. This should indicate that they are being admitted to the communion of the Church.

70. Outside Paschaltide, baptismal water may be blessed in the service of baptism, using the approved shorter form.

71. The rite of confirmation is to be revised in such a way that the intimate connexion of this sacrament with the whole scheme of Christian initiation may become more obvious. Therefore, a renewal of the baptismal promises will fittingly precede the actual reception of the sacrament.

Confirmation may, if convenient, be conferred during Mass. When given outside Mass, a text is to be prepared that can be used as an introduction [to the whole ceremony].

72. The ceremonies and texts of [the sacrament of] penance are to be revised in order that they may express more clearly the nature and effect of the sacrament.

73. 'Extreme Unction', which may also, and indeed preferably, be called 'The Anointing of the Sick', is not a sacrament reserved to those who are at life's last gasp. It follows, therefore, that the time for receiving it has certainly come when a Christian begins to be in danger of death either from sickness or old age.

74. In addition to the separate services of *Anointing of the Sick and Viaticum* a single rite is to be drawn up providing for the anointing of the sick person after he has made his confession and before he receives Viaticum.

75. The number of the anointings will be varied according to circumstances, and the prayers in the *Anointing of the Sick* revised so as to suit the various states of the sick people who receive the sacrament.

76. Both the ceremonies and the texts of the ordination services will be revised. The addresses read by the bishop at the beginning of each ordination or consecration may be made in the vernacular.

In the consecration of a bishop, it is allowed that the laying on of hands should be performed by all the bishops present.

77. The marriage service contained in the Roman Ritual is to be revised and enriched; it should indicate more clearly the grace of the sacrament and emphasize the duties of the partners in marriage.

The Other Sacraments and Sacramentals

'If any countries have other laudable customs and use other ceremonies in celebrating the sacrament of matrimony, the Holy Synod much desires that these should by all means be retained.'[41]

Furthermore, complete liberty is left to the competent territorial authority of the Church (see Art. 22, § 2 of this Constitution) to devise, on the lines of Art. 63, a proper rite in conformity with the customs of the local population, provided the law is observed that a priest is present to ask for and receive the consent of the contracting parties.

78. Marriage is normally to be celebrated during Mass after the Gospel and homily, before the bidding prayer. The prayer over the bride is to be amended to convey that the duty of mutual fidelity obliges bride and bridegroom equally. It may be said in the vernacular.

If, however, the sacrament of matrimony is celebrated without Mass, the Epistle and Gospel from the Wedding Mass are to be read at the beginning of the service and a blessing is always to be given to the bride and bridegroom.

79. The sacramentals will be revised taking into account the overriding principle of an intelligent, active and easy participation on the part of the faithful and considering also the needs of our day. In the revision of Rituals as laid down in Art. 63, new sacramentals may be added, if called for.

'Reserved blessings' are to be very few in number, and even these shall be reserved only to bishops or Ordinaries.

Provision will be made that certain sacramentals, at least in special circumstances and with the Ordinary's approval, may be administered by lay people possessing the requisite qualifications.

80. The rite of the consecration of virgins contained in the Roman Pontifical is to undergo a revision.

---

[41] COUNCIL OF TRENT, Sess. XXIV, *De Reformatione*, 1 (Ed. cit., 9, 6, p. 969); cf. Roman Ritual, VIII, 2, 6.

In addition, a rite for religious professions and renovations of vows will be drawn up with a view to obtaining more unity, sobriety and dignity. Provided that particular laws are respected, this rite can then be adopted by those who make their profession or renew their vows during Mass.

It will be a praiseworthy thing if religious professions are made during Mass.

81. The funeral rite will give more obvious expression to the paschal character of Christian death and correspond more closely with the conditions and traditions of each country, e.g. in such things as the liturgical colour used.

82. The rite of the burial of infants will be revised and provided with a special Mass.

Chapter IV

THE DIVINE OFFICE

83. The High Priest of the New and eternal Covenant, Jesus Christ, when he took human nature, brought with him into this earthly exile that hymn which to all eternity is sung in the courts on high. He draws about him the whole community of men and makes them his companions in singing with him this song of praise.

He continues this priestly task through his Church, which unceasingly praises the Lord and intercedes for the salvation of the whole world, not only by the celebration of the Eucharist, but in other ways too, and chief among these, by the performance of the Divine Office.

84. The Divine Office, as it has come down from ancient Christian tradition, is so composed that the whole course of day and night is consecrated by praise offered to God. Now, when this wonderful song of praise is duly performed by priests and others set aside for this purpose by the Church's ordinance, or by the Christian faithful praying according to the approved form with their priest, then this is truly the voice of the Bride speaking to the Bridegroom, or rather, the prayer of Christ with his Body to the Father.

85. Therefore, all those who offer this service are at that time accomplishing the Church's duty, are at that time sharing in the supreme honour of Christ's Bride, for, as they pay their praises to God, they stand before God's throne in the name of Mother Church.

86. Priests occupied in the sacred pastoral ministry will find an added incentive to the offering of the praise of their Hours with special fervour in their awareness of their need to observe St Paul's precept: 'Pray constantly' (1 *Thess* 5:17). God alone can give efficacy to and produce results from the task at which they labour, he who said: 'Apart from me you can do nothing' (*Jn* 15:5) With this in mind the apostles, when appointing [the first] deacons, said: 'We will devote ourselves to prayer and to the ministry of the word' (*Acts* 6:4).

87. To achieve a better and more perfect performance of the Divine Office in the present circumstances, whether by priests or by other members of the Church, the Sacred Council, following in this the movement of reform so happily undertaken by the Apostolic See, has been pleased to lay down the following points concerning the Office in the Roman rite.

88. Since the end of the Office is the sanctification of the day, the traditional cycle of the Hours will be restored in such a way that, as far as possible, its true correspondence in time shall once more be given to each Hour. This will be done taking into account the conditions of present-day life as these affect those, above all, who are occupied in apostolic labours.

89. Therefore, in revising the Office, these principles will be followed:

(a)   Lauds, the morning prayer, and Vespers, the evening prayer, which the venerable tradition of the universal Church recognizes as the double hinge of the daily Office, are to be considered and celebrated as the chief Hours.

(b)   Compline will be drawn up so as to make of it a fitting end to the day.

(c)   The Hour called Matins, though retaining in choir its nature as a nocturnal [offering of] praise, will be adapted so that it can be recited at any hour of the day, and will be composed of fewer psalms and longer readings.

(d)   Prime will be deleted.

(e)   In choir, the Lesser Hours of Terce, Sext and None will be maintained. When the Office is not recited in choir, it is allowed to choose one of the three corresponding most nearly to the time of day.

90. Furthermore, since the Divine Office, the Church's public prayer, is the fountain of devotion and food of personal prayer, priests and all others who take part in the Divine Office are begged in the Lord [to see to it] that, when they perform it, their minds should accord with their voices. That they may the better achieve this, they should set about acquiring a rich liturgical and biblical culture, particularly as concerns the psalms.

In the work of revision, the venerable, age-old treasure of the Roman Office should be adapted in such a way that all those to whom it is committed may more easily find in it still more abundant fruit.

91. In order that it may be practically possible to keep to the cycle of Hours set out in Art. 89, the psalms will no longer be distributed over one week but over some longer period.

The work of revising the Psalter, already happily begun, will be concluded as quickly as possible, giving due consideration to [the following points:] Christian Latinity, liturgical use including [the requirements of] singing, the whole tradition of the Latin Church.

92. In the matter of the readings, these are the points to be noted:

(a)   The reading of Holy Scripture will be arranged so that the treasures of God's Word may be made readily accessible in yet greater fullness.

(b)   The lessons to be taken from the Fathers, Doctors and ecclesiastical writers will be better chosen.

(c)   The 'Passions' or lives of the saints will be given in versions that are historically true.

93. The hymns, in so far as it may seem desirable, will be re-established in their original text, with the removal or modification of any mythological elements or things that have little place in Christian piety. Other texts contained in the Church's treasury of hymns may also be adopted in suitable cases.

94. It is better, both for the real sanctification of the day and for the

spiritually fruitful recitation of the Hours themselves, if the time chosen for their performance corresponds closely to the real time of each canonical Hour.

95. Communities with the obligation of Office in choir, must, in addition to the conventual Mass, perform the Divine Office in choir each day, as follows:

(a) Orders of canons, monks and nuns, as well as of other regulars bound to choir either by law or by their constitutions, must say the whole Office.

(b) Cathedral or collegiate chapters must say those parts of the Office with which they are charged by the common or a particular law.

(c) All members of the above communities who are either in Major Orders or solemnly professed—lay brothers and sisters excepted—must recite alone those canonical Hours they do not perform in choir.

96. Clerics who are not bound to choir, if they are in Major Orders, have the obligation of performing the whole Office every day as laid down in Art. 89. This they can do either in common or alone.

97. Occasional substitution for the Divine Office of some liturgical function will be laid down by the rubrics.

In particular cases and for a just cause, Ordinaries can dispense their subjects from the obligation of reciting either the whole Office or a part thereof, or can replace it with something else.

98. The members of any Institute dedicated to the pursuit of perfection who, in accordance with their constitutions, perform certain parts of the Divine Office, engage in the public prayer of the Church.

Similarly, they engage in the public prayer of the Church, if, in accordance with their constitutions, they recite some kind of Little Office, provided this reproduces the pattern of the Divine Office and is duly approved.

99. Since the Divine Office is the voice of the Church, that is, of the whole Mystical Body engaged in the public praise of God, it is suggested that some part at least of the Divine Office might well be recited in common by clerics who are not obliged to choir, and more especially by priests, where these live in the same house or when they meet together.

All those who perform the Office in choir or in common should accomplish the task entrusted to them as perfectly as they can, with real internal devotion and external decorum.

It is better, moreover, that, when possible, the Office in choir and in common should be sung.

100. Pastors should see to it that the chief Hours, Vespers particularly, are celebrated in common in church on Sundays and great feasts. The recitation of the Divine Office by lay folk either with priests or in their own gatherings or, indeed, by themselves each one alone, is commended.

101. § 1. In accordance with the age-old tradition of the Latin rite, Latin is to be maintained by clerics in the Divine Office. However, the Ordinary is given authority to concede the use of a vernacular version compiled in conformity with the rules of Art. 36. He may use this faculty in particular cases in favour of those clerics who find in the use of Latin a grave impediment to the due performance of the Office.

§ 2. Nuns, and members of Institutes dedicated to the pursuit of perfection whether men not in orders or women, can receive from their competent superior permission to use the vernacular in the Divine Office even when celebrated in choir, provided the version has been approved.

§ 3. Any cleric bound to the Divine Office who celebrates the Divine Office in the vernacular with a group of the faithful or with the persons mentioned in § 2, satisfies his obligation, provided the text of the translation is an approved one.

Chapter V

THE LITURGICAL YEAR

102. A devoted Mother Church has thought it only right that she should, on certain appointed days in the course of the year, hold a sacred celebration recalling the saving work of her divine Bridegroom. Each week, on Sunday, the Lord's day, she remembers the Lord's Resurrection, and again, once a year, at Easter, the greatest solemnity of all, she repeats her experience of the Lord's Resurrection and blessed Passion.

Indeed, as the year passes, she unfolds the whole mystery of Christ from his incarnation and birth to his ascension, to the day of Pentecost and to the awaiting of the blessed hope and appearing of the Lord.

The Church recalls in this fashion the mysteries of redemption, the rich treasures of her Lord's virtues and merits, and opens them up to the faithful in such a way that they may, as it were, be made at all times present. The faithful can thus be brought into contact with them and be filled with the grace of salvation.

103. Celebrating this yearly cycle of the mysteries of Christ, Holy Church venerates with an especial love Blessed Mary the Mother of God who is joined by an unbreakable bond with the saving work of her Son. In her the Church admires and exalts the fruit *par excellence* of the Redemption, joyfully contemplating this unsullied image of what she, in her entirety, desires and hopes to be.

104. In the yearly cycle the Church has also inserted commemorative days in honour of the martyrs and other saints. These holy men and women, brought to perfection through God's manifold gifts of grace and having now laid hold on everlasting salvation, sing to God a perfect praise in heaven and intercede for us. In these birthdays of the saints [to eternal life, the Church] proclaims the paschal mystery in the saints who have suffered and been glorified with Christ, sets before

the faithful their examples drawing all men through Christ to the Father, and by their merits obtains the blessings of God's good favour.

105. Finally, throughout the year at various times fixed by tradition, the Church undertakes the further education of the faithful by means of pious exercises for both mind and body, through instruction, prayer and works of penance and mercy.

For these reasons the Sacred Council has been pleased to make the following orders.

106. Following the apostolic tradition that originated on the very day of Christ's resurrection, the Church celebrates the paschal mystery every seventh day, which day is, therefore, rightly called the Lord's day, or Sunday. On this day, Christians must gather together to hear the word of God, to partake of the Eucharist, and, in this way, to call to mind the passion, resurrection and glory of the Lord Jesus, giving thanks to God by whom they 'have been born again to a living hope through the resurrection of Jesus Christ from the dead' (1 Pet 1:3). Therefore, Sunday is the first of all feastdays, to be presented to and urged upon the faithful as such, so that it may also become a day of gladness and rest from work. Other celebrations, unless they are really of the very greatest importance, should not take its place, since it is the foundation and nucleus of the whole liturgical year.

107. The liturgical year will be revised. While safeguarding the traditional customs and disciplines connected with sacred seasons, or restoring them to suit the conditions of our day, their proper nature will be retained so that the piety of the faithful may find its due nourishment in the celebration of the mysteries of our redemption in Christ, especially of the paschal mystery. Local adaptations where necessary will be made in accordance with Art. 39 and 40.

108. The attention of the faithful is to be focused, in the first place, on the feasts of the Lord that celebrate throughout the year the mysteries of salvation. This means that the Proper of the Season must be given

its rightful place above the feasts of saints, so that the complete cycle of the mysteries of salvation may be duly observed.

109. The Lenten season bears a twofold character: it creates in the faithful the right dispositions for the celebration of the paschal mystery, chiefly by baptism, on the one hand, calling it to mind and preparing for it, and, on the other hand, by repentance, as it recommends a more zealous listening to the word of God and a more ardent devotion to prayer. This twofold character will be made more plainly apparent in the Liturgy itself and in liturgical instruction. Therefore:

(a) The baptismal elements proper to the Lenten liturgy will be used more liberally; certain features from an older tradition will, where advisable, be restored.

(b) The same will be done with the penitential elements. As far as instruction is concerned, the faithful will be carefully taught to understand, together with the social consequences of sin, the specific nature of repentance which is a detestation of sin precisely because and in so far as it is an offence against God. In addition, the place of the Church in the whole work of repentance will be taught and prayer for sinners urgently commended.

110. Lenten penance should be not only an inward, individual thing; it should also be an outward, social concern. Penitential practices are to be encouraged and recommended by the authorities mentioned in Art. 22 according to the possibilities of our time and of the various countries concerned, and, also, according to the conditions in which the faithful live.

Let it, however, be a sacred rule that the paschal fast be celebrated everywhere on Good Friday, the day of the Lord's Passion and Death. Where possible, this fast should be continued on Holy Saturday, so that, with hearts and minds free and uplifted, all may come to the joys of the resurrection on Easter Sunday.

111. Traditionally, the saints are honoured in the Church and their genuine relics and images are held in veneration. The feasts of the saints show forth the mighty works of Christ in his servants and provide the faithful with excellent examples they can imitate.

The feasts of the saints should not take the place of the feasts that celebrate the mysteries of salvation. To prevent this from happening, many of these feasts of saints will be left to the celebration of particular Churches, nations or religious families; to the universal Church will be extended only those that commemorate saints who really did have some universal importance.

Chapter VI

CHURCH MUSIC

112. In the musical tradition of the universal Church is contained a treasure of inestimable value. It occupies a place higher than that of other art forms chiefly because it is a sacred chant wedded to words and, as such, constitutes a necessary and integral part of solemn liturgy.

Sacred song has, of course, been praised by Holy Scripture,[42] and also by the Fathers and the Roman Pontiffs who, in modern times, following in this the example of St Pius X, have insisted at some length on the role of music in the Lord's service.

So then, the more intimately church music is linked with the liturgical action the holier it will be. This close connexion is achieved in various ways: the music can express prayer more persuasively; it can help in producing unanimity; it can add increased solemnity to the sacred rites. But it is the Church that approves all the forms of true art that possess the necessary qualities; it is the Church that gives them their place in divine worship.

Therefore, the Sacred Council, adhering to the norms and precepts of ecclesiastical discipline and tradition, and keeping in view the end of church music, which is the glory of God and the sanctification of the faithful, makes the following provisions.

113. The work of the Liturgy takes on a nobler form when the divine offices are celebrated solemnly with singing, with the assistance of sacred ministers and with the active participation of the people.

For the language to be used, follow the rules of Art. 36; for Mass, Art. 54; for the sacraments, Art. 63; for the Divine Office, Art. 101.

114. The treasury of church music will be maintained and cherished with the greatest care. Choirs will be diligently fostered in their efforts, more particularly in cathedral churches. Bishops and other pastors will

---

[42] Cf. *Eph* 5:19; *Col* 3:16.

take good care to see that in all sung services the whole congregation may be able to take therein the active part that is theirs, as laid down in Art. 28 and 30.

115. Great importance is to be attached to the teaching and practice of music in seminaries, in the novitiates and houses of studies of religious of both sexes, and also in other Catholic institutions and schools. To this end, every care is to be taken to ensure that persons who will be able to assume responsibility for the teaching of church music receive a thorough training.

Any higher institutions for church music that may be founded as opportunity occurs, are recommended.

The musicians themselves, the singers and above all the boys, are to be given a thorough liturgical education.

116. The Church recognizes Gregorian chant as the chant proper to the Roman liturgy. Therefore, other things being equal, it should have the chief place in liturgical functions.

Other kinds of church music, especially polyphony, are by no means excluded from the celebration of divine worship, provided they accord with the spirit of liturgical action, as laid down in Art. 30.

117. The typical edition of the books of Gregorian chant will be completed. Indeed, a more truly critical edition will be prepared of the books already published since St Pius X's restoration.

It will likewise be of advantage if an edition can be prepared containing simpler melodies for use in smaller churches.

118. Popular religious music should be carefully fostered, so that the faithful may be able to raise their voices in their devotions and pious exercises and, indeed, in the liturgical functions themselves, according to the rules and prescriptions of the rubrics.

119. In some countries, particularly in the missionfield, peoples can be found with a musical tradition of their own that plays an important part in their religious and social life. Due esteem should be had for this music and a fitting place found for it both in the moulding of these peoples' religious sense and in the adapting of the pattern of worship to their particular genius, as suggested in Art. 39 and 40.

Therefore, in the musical training of missionaries, great care must be taken to see that, in as far as possible, they may be made capable of furthering the traditional music of these peoples both in the schools and in liturgical worship.

120. The pipe organ is to be held in high honour in the Latin Church as the traditional musical instrument, the sound of which has the power not only to add a wonderful splendour to the Church's ceremonies, but also to lift up men's minds in a remarkable way to God and the things on high.

Other instruments, too, as approved and agreed by the competent territorial authority (see Art. 22, § 2; 37 and 40), can be permitted in divine worship provided they are—or can be made to be—suited to a sacred use, and provided they accord with the dignity of a church building and really contribute to the edification of the faithful.

121. Musicians, filled with the Christian spirit, should feel that they have a vocation to cultivate church music and to enrich its treasure.

They should see that their compositions display the notes of truly sacred music. These compositions should not be of a kind that can be sung only by the larger choirs; they should also be suitable for smaller choirs and encourage an active participation on the part of the whole congregation.

The texts to be set to music should agree with Catholic teaching; indeed, they could best be taken from Holy Scripture and liturgical sources.

Chapter VII

SACRED ART AND CHURCH FURNISHINGS

122. Among the noblest occupations of the human mind we are certainly right in numbering the fine arts and especially religious art and the supreme expression of this latter—sacred art. Of their nature, these are concerned with the infinite divine beauty and with the attempt at expressing it through human endeavour. Their consecration to God and to the furtherance of his praise and glory is manifested by the singleness of their aim, which is to make in their works the greatest possible contribution to the turning of men's thoughts to God.

For this reason, the Church, like a loving mother, has always been a friend of the fine arts. She has trained artists and unfailingly sought out the noble ministry of the arts, chiefly so that the things needed in divine worship should be worthy, comely and beautiful, signs and symbols of the things on high. Furthermore, the Church has, rightly, always looked upon herself as an arbiter of the arts, choosing among artists' works those that are in conformity with the faith, true religion and faithfully preserved traditional laws, and are, moreover, adapted to a sacred use.

The Church has taken particular care to ensure that sacred furnishings should serve as worthy and beautiful instruments to enhance the comeliness of worship, admitting such changes in materials, design or ornament as technical progress has introduced in the course of time.

That being so, the Fathers have been pleased to make the following orders in these matters.

123. The Church has never had its own peculiar artistic style. It has accepted the idiom of each age according to the genius and circumstances of peoples and the requirements of the various rites. In this way, it has, down the centuries, amassed an artistic treasure that must be preserved with every care. The art of our day and of all peoples and countries is to have free exercise in the Church, provided it can be used in the service of sacred buildings and sacred rites with due

reverence and honour. Then it will be able to join its voice in that admirable chorus of glory which the greatest talents have in the past sung to the Catholic faith.

124. Let Ordinaries in their furtherance and encouragement of a truly sacred art take care that their aim is noble beauty rather than mere display. This holds good for sacred vestments and ornaments.

Bishops will take care diligently to keep out of the churches of God and other holy places, works of art opposed to faith and morals and Christian devotion. They will take the same action concerning works that offend true religious feeling either by their corrupt forms or by their lack of art, their mediocrity or their meretricious character.

In the construction of sacred buildings good care will be taken to see that they are designed for the performance of liturgical functions and for the active participation of the faithful.

125. The practice of erecting in churches sacred images for the veneration of the faithful is to be maintained. However, they should not be too numerous and should be arranged in a fitting order, for they must not cause shock or surprise among the Christian people, or give encouragement to aberrant devotion.

126. In judging works of art local Ordinaries will consult their diocesan Commission on Sacred Art and, if the case call for it, other experts, and also the commissions mentioned in Art. 44, 45 and 46.

Ordinaries will keep careful watch to see that sacred furnishings or precious objects, since they are ornaments of God's house, are neither disposed of nor wantonly destroyed.

127. Bishops, either in person or through suitable priests endowed with the necessary skill and a love of art, will take a careful interest in instructing artists in the spirit of sacred art and of the Liturgy.

In addition, it is recommended that schools or academies of sacred art for the education of artists should be established in those places in which it may seem advisable.

All artists who, following their natural bent, intend to serve the glory of God in Holy Church, should always remember that they are dealing with something like a sacred imitation of God the Creator, that their work is with things made for Catholic worship, the edification and devotion of the faithful and their religious instruction.

128. The canons and ecclesiastical statutes concerning the making of external objects that have their place in divine worship, particularly those affecting the due and worthy construction of sacred buildings, the form and fashioning of altars, the nobility, situation and security of the eucharistic tabernacle, the suitability of and the honour due to the baptistry, the appropriate norms for sacred images, decorations and fittings—all these things together with the liturgical books (see Art. 25) will be revised as quickly as possible. Anything unsuited to the revised Liturgy will be corrected or deleted; anything useful will be kept or introduced.

In this domain, especially where the materials and design of sacred furnishings and vestments are concerned, the faculty of making adaptations to local needs and customs is granted to the territorial conferences of bishops, as in Art. 22 of this Constitution.

129. During their philosophical and theological studies, clerical students will receive instruction in the history and evolution of sacred art as well as in the right principles that should underlie the works of sacred art. In this way, they will be enabled to value and preserve the Church's venerable monuments and be ready with informed advice for artists in their work.

130. It would be well if the use of pontifical insignia were reserved to those ecclesiastical persons who enjoy either the episcopal character or some special jurisdiction.

A DECLARATION OF THE SACRED SECOND VATICAN ECUMENICAL COUNCIL ON THE REFORM OF THE CALENDAR

The Sacred Second Vatican Ecumenical Council attaches no little importance to the widespread wish that the feast of Easter should be assigned to a fixed Sunday and the calendar stabilized. Having considered carefully all the possible consequences of the introduction of a new calendar, it makes the following declaration.

1. The Sacred Council raises no objection to seeing the feast of Easter assigned to a fixed Sunday in the Gregorian calendar, provided the interested parties agree, above all those brethren who are separated from the communion of the Apostolic See.

2. Again, the Sacred Council declares that it does not oppose any efforts made in view of introducing a perpetual calendar in secular life.

However, of the various systems now under consideration for establishing and introducing in secular life a perpetual calendar, the Church does not oppose only those that keep and maintain the week of seven days with a Sunday and do not require the intercalation of any days falling outside the week. The point is that the unbroken succession of weeks should remain, unless the very gravest reasons to the contrary can be alleged, and of these the Apostolic See would be judge.

Each and every one of the matters set forth in this Constitution has been approved by the Fathers of the Sacred Council. And We, by the apostolic authority given Us by Christ, together with the Venerable Fathers, approve, decree and ordain its contents in the Holy Spirit, and order that what has been thus decided in council be promulgated to the glory of God.

✠ **PAUL**, *Bishop of the Catholic Church*
St Peter's, Rome, 18 November 1965
The signatures of the Fathers follow.

NOTE ON THE TRANSLATION

The Latin text of the Constitution on the Sacred Liturgy makes a great use of 'jussive subjunctives', i.e. the form literally rendered in English by 'let *x* be done' or '*x* is to be done'. In this translation, these renderings have been adopted very seldom, and, as a rule, the Latin subjunctives are represented by English futures: '*x* will be done'. However, when the Latin, instead of a simple *admittatur* (for example) has *admitti possit* or *admitti va leat*, an attempt has been made to reproduce this nuance.

The translator's aim has been to provide an accurate translation in something approaching readable English. He has not tried to present a word-for-word crib or an arsenal of weapons for controversialists.

Square brackets [ ] enclose words inserted by the translator. Linking expressions or repetitions necessitated by the breaking up of complex Latin sentences are not so marked.

DOGMATIC CONSTITUTION ON THE CHURCH

Lumen Gentium

INTRODUCTION
by Paul Cardinal Poupard

"I believe in One, Holy, Catholic and Apostolic Church."

The Creed

We live in an age of indifference. *Homo indifferens* is letting beauty and truth pass by with hardly the batting of an eye. Adherence to any kind of belief has given way to pragmatism in a disenchanted world. The fallout from belonging to religious organisations seems to run apace with the abandonment of the atheism of the past. And religious belief is going through some kind of identity crisis, with tiny but very visible pockets of fundamentalism on one side, widespread apathy and indifference on the other, and, in between the two, a whole range of new expressions of religiosity and the so-called "return of the sacred". But these are little more than the natural quest for truth misdirected into the glorification of subjective desire and a private satisfaction of self-centred spirituality. A far cry from the ordered, structured, timeless and revealed faith of the creed. God is often ignored and common indifference, errant belief and selfishness seem in our day to lead people to say yes to some sort of religious feeling, but no to God and no to the Church. The heresies of the past return under different guises. Yet the Church remains. It is God's chosen instrument to pass on the truth revealed in Jesus Christ. A truth that is historical and beautiful, that shares the joys and hopes, the griefs and anxieties of all the world, a truth that is safeguarded by the Church. And for this, faced with the apathy of our times, we are truly blessed to have that Church, a steadfast rock in times of change. It is a Church that orientates our belief in God and that we profess One, Holy, Catholic and Apostolic.

But when we express this article of the faith, what do we mean, why do we say it? What does the Church believe itself to be? What does it mean to be one of its members? Where has it come from and where is it going? What is its nature, its purpose, its end? Who are the people involved? An answer that is perennially valid lies in *Lumen Gentium*.

There is something misleading in this way of introducing *Lumen Gentium*, for its principle protagonist is not the Church, but Christ, the Son of God! The title *Lumen Gentium* comes from the opening two words of the text in Latin. They mean "light of humanity" and sit in the sentence "Christ is the light of humanity". Straightaway, then, the document avoids self-centredness and places the full accent on Christ. And note too, that Christ is not considered merely as light of the Church, but as light of the whole world. Next comes the reference to Church as sacrament, that is, by analogy to the seven sacraments, through the Church that same light is bestowed on all peoples uniting them with God and with one another. *Lumen Gentium* is about the light that is salvation, desired and brought about by God, and then about the Church as signpost to Christ, as means of salvation, as call to holiness, as pilgrim people, as hierarchical communion, as participators in the divine plan and fully depicted in Mary. And what are these if not God's plan for us?

I remember well the promulgation of *Lumen Gentium* on the 21st of November 1964 by Pope Paul VI, with whom as a young priest I collaborated closely. It was one of the key moments of the Second Vatican Council. Lest not all my readers have the benefit of age, permit me to recite a few key features of the last Council, a defining moment in the Church's recent history. At the invitation of Pope John XXIII, all the Bishops on every continent were invited to gather together in Rome over a period on and off for five years to consider a whole range of matters from the Virgin Mary to the Church, from Liturgy to Mission, from Religious Orders to Religious Freedom, from Revelation to Ecumenism. They were supported in prayer by the faithful, and closely followed by the world's media. It was a time of *ressourcement*. A wealth of pastoral talent and intellect flanked by academics and supporters who, in a massive meeting of minds under the guidance of the Holy Spirit, produced 16 major documents: two dogmatic constitutions, two pastoral constitutions, nine decrees and three declarations. As an event, the Council injected a stream of fresh vigour into the life of the Church, above all through *Lumen Gentium* the dogmatic (because it touches on dogma) constitution (a document with the highest authority) on the Church.

The text—which in its drafting phases was called *De Ecclesia*—was of course the fruit of years of commissions, sub-commissions, emendations, drafting and redrafting. Students can profit much from the ins-and-outs of the development of the text, the different people involved, the methods used and the theological themes which were rejected, altered or developed therein, but what is important is that at the end of the third period of the Council, in 1964, it received the moral approval of the gathered College of Bishops with 2144 voting *placet* and just 10 *non placet*. Two appendices, *nota explicativa praevia* and *nota bene*, were also added.

Those who read the text from the vantage point of theological and historical studies will appreciate the subtle and not so subtle changes, but I believe it is also accessible to all those who approach it with a charitable, ecumenical and prayerful attitude. Indeed during its drafting there was a deliberate effort not to be too academic in style, and although today's cultural milieu is not that of the 1960s and the theological vocabulary then used is not common today, the teaching of the document is timeless and is as relevant today as it was yesterday and will be tomorrow. Needless to say, in order to understand the document, you need to read it yourselves. Your understanding will be shaped by your culture. As a French Cardinal sitting at my desk in the Vatican writing a text that will be read in English, and reflecting on a document written forty years ago and officially promulgated in Latin, I am aware that various cultural boundaries exist. These are created by our language, our location, our times, our very cultures, our ways of thinking, our criteria of discernment, our mentalities. But the dynamic meeting between the Church and Cultures is for us an opportunity more than an obstacle.

Divided into eight chapters the document is a "statement to the faithful and to the whole world of the nature and universal mission of the Church" (LG 1), i.e. it says what the Church really is and her intentions concerning the world. Some might prefer to discover this by studying the document, underlining key passages, or learning by heart some key expressions. Others may use it as a source for meditation, prayer and discussion. Others may read it through as though it were a novel. No one however, should overlook its shape and perspective. Consider the titles of the eight chapters: The Mystery of the Church; The People of God; The Church is Hierarchical; The Laity; The Call to Holiness; The Religious; The Pilgrim Church; Our Lady. This overarching shape of the document outlines its dynamics: God-centred, it is descriptive of the Church in its intertwined theological, historical and hopeful dimensions; its call to holiness stems from the reality of creation, God's plan and intervention for His Church, and the hindered but natural inclination of man to assist in the bringing about of God's kingdom here on earth. Beginning with a description of salvation history, whose very author is God, it then develops a series of interrelated themes, identifying other protagonists in the Church: the laity, religious, priests, bishops, the papacy and of course the Virgin Mary herself.

The Church is but an instrument of God—a pencil in the hands of God as Mother Teresa of Calcutta would say. The actions of God for and through the Church are recounted in the actions of the three persons of the Trinity, that is the three divine persons to whom we dedicate ourselves in making the sign of the cross: Father, Son and Holy Spirit. *Lumen Gentium* speaks of each divine person's contribution to the life of the Church, from its creation and its animation to its future fulfilment. From this divine source, the nature of the Church receives its shape and form: the Church is seen to be "a people made one with the unity of the Father and Son and Holy Spirit" (LG 4).

Introduction—Cardinal Paul Poupard

The document draws heavily on what is known as the history of salvation. This biblical theme is far removed from the internal politics of a merely human society or business. It is the history of God's relationship with the people he created, a history which already in the beginning foresaw the Church. As God willed to make men holy and to save them not as individuals but as a people united in fearing him and serving him in holiness, He chose the Israelite race (LG 9) and established a covenant with it. On the backbone of that people He then built the Church, a messianic people, which will reach its fulfilment at the end of time; the eternal Father not only created us, but continues to love us, and, having sent His Son and calling us to be united in him, He sent the Holy Spirit to the Church—the People of God, chosen and called to come together from whatever their background—to nourish and sustain her.

The Church is the kingdom of Christ already present in mystery. Its beginning was symbolised in the blood and water that flowed from the open wound of Christ crucified. Baptised into this living water of new life, it is as priest, prophet and king that we are called to emulate him and to be his disciples. Having laid out Christ's foundational and originating activity for the Church in the early chapters, the same Second Adam is offered as model for our holiness. Like him we are called to be counter-cultural, to go against the tide when our culture carries us in the wrong direction. By our prophetic witness we evangelise it and inculturate the faith into it. The Church also has the august task of creating cultures, working continually to transform them to Christ.

God the Holy Spirit is the third member of the Trinity. The communion of the Trinity is a dynamic interchange marked by love and service and is the model for the New Communion of the Church. Indeed Love is another name for the Holy Spirit! The Church, filled with the Holy Spirit, the Paraclete, is also charity and is called to love both internally, i.e. love each member of the Church, and externally, i.e. love all men and women without exception. This Way of Love is the pathway that the Church is called to follow: "by this love you have for one another, everyone will know that you are my disciples"

(*Jn* 13:35). The road of Love necessitates justice and pardon, and is enabled by the recognition of the other and the very desire to forgive in the discipleship of Christ.

"She [The Church] was foreshadowed from the beginning of the world: she had a marvellous preparation in the history of Israel and the old covenant. In the latest era she has been founded and, by the outpouring of the Holy Spirit, made manifest. She will reach her glorious consummation at the end of the ages." (LG2). A people called to live in communion beyond cultural, racial and temporal boundaries it is a universal means of making known God's message here on earth. Already begun but not yet complete, it is a mystical communion, a People of God seeking to live in holiness and communion under the loving gaze of the Mother of God who looks on her with the same tenderness with which she looked on her crucified son, seeing in it the reflection of her offspring's life of sacrifice, devotion and celebration.

The Church unites around the Eucharist, "the source and the culmination of all christian life" (LG 11). Each local Church being made up of many elements seeking holiness and answering diverse vocations, gathers around the local bishop, who maintains communion with the other bishops in the college of bishops, itself in some way successor of the college of the apostles, and with the Holy Father, bishop of Rome, successor of Peter, who is "perpetual, visible, fundamental principle of unity" (LG 23) of the bishops and of the faithful. The Universal Church is fully present in the local Church, but is not a federation of local churches.

This Church is a sacrament; it gives witness to the reality of God's love for the human person. It is a sign of the coming of salvation and the presence of inter-Trinitarian love so fittingly depicted in Rublev's famous icon; her unity in charity gives witness, and—here is the key— it is by our witness, that the revealed-one, the incarnated-one is made real today! To be credible, such truth puts on the clothing of today's cultures. The unending love and charity which has its source in a devoted God is revealed through the Church's witness. This requires the holiness and exercise of the actual priesthood of all the members. My patron, St Paul the Apostle, wrote that we should present ourselves as a "sacrifice, living, holy and pleasing unto God" (*Romans* 12:1). The call to holiness, which receives a chapter in itself and is a recurring minor theme of the document, is a task for all people. It is a call to live lives worthy of our human dignity. All Christians are enabled by grace to attain it, but in a particular way those who embrace the religious life are the signs of the coming kingdom by their holiness. The call to holiness also extends to the priestly, prophetic and guiding duties also of the hierarchy: that is the priests and bishops who in the model of the suffering servant enjoin themselves to the people they serve and the God who gives them strength and protection to carry out their work.

A positive ecumenical outlook was one of the backbones of the Second Vatican Council and the biblical desire that "all may be one" remains a constant goal for the Church. The document describes the Church, reiterating the four attributes that come from a divine source:

It is *One* for it has a diversity within unity, a union in charity, and is a communion of those who profess the same faith, who worship together, and who share the apostolic succession in fraternal charity proper to the family of God.

It is *Holy* for the Son of God filled his spouse with holiness, a holiness which is given to the members, as the Church seeks to make herself and her members holy, for, as with all created things, its ultimate purpose is to sanctify and glorify God.

It is *Catholic* because she is fully whole, filled by Christ and possessing the full means of salvation. Each of the particular churches is Catholic in that, through its bishop it shares in the universal communion, presided over in charity by the Bishop of Rome.

It is *Apostolic* in that she is built on the foundation of the apostles, the teaching the deposit of faith heard by the apostles, and she continues to be guided by the college of Bishops who, as a body, are no less than the successors of the Apostles.

Since this document about the Church's relationship with God was written in the middle of the 20th Century, enormous cultural shifts have taken place: the Cold War, the spread of the threat of global

terrorism, growing misuse and exhaustion of the world's natural resources, the fall of almost all of the totalitarian atheist regimes, glo-
balisation with its good and bad effects, and rapid economic growth
across the world. It has been a period in which the human person has
been exalted and God either forgotten, ignored, or His name used and
abused. So it is providential to return to this document which teaches
so much about the Church, which is more than a mere society of people, and whose primary reference point is another person: God. For
if we seek to glorify man without understanding him as beloved of
God, we will—as history shows—once again create a society doomed
to failure (cf. GS 36).

I hope that you will forgive me if I have not paraphrased the document in this introduction, nor dwelt on certain issues which have
dominated academic writing on the text, instead my intention has
been to whet your appetite, and to have set you free from turgid pan-
demics to read the text for yourselves, alone or in your communities,
and to become familiar not so much with my interpretation, but with
the very mind of the Church who wrote it. If by sharing some of my
personal reactions to this document I have it more accessible and have
broken it open, I will have been the priest, prophet and king called for
by the text and true to my motto: "to be for you a bishop, and with
you a Christian", a text which incidentally appears in *Lumen Gentium*
demonstrating its *ressourcement* of ancient texts.

Finally, I commend this initiative of the CTS to create greater
awareness and understanding of the documents of the Second Vatican
Council [through these translations]. For overcoming ignorance is a
task for the Church as equally important as maintaining that embrace
of love that Holy Mother Church extends to all men and women, for
as good Pope John XXIII taught, the Church is not only our *Magistra*,
but also our *Mater*. Have a good read!

✝ **Paul Cardinal Poupard**
Feast of Saint Augustine of Canterbury

DOGMATIC CONSTITUTION
ON THE CHURCH

CHAPTER I

THE MYSTERY OF THE CHURCH

1. Christ is the light of the nations. It is, therefore, the eager desire of this sacred Council, assembled in the Holy Spirit, to enlighten all men with that brilliance of his which shines on the face of the Church, by preaching the gospel to the whole of creation (cf. *Mk* 16:15). The Church exists in Christ as a sacrament or instrumental sign of intimate union with God and of unity for the whole human race. The aim of the Council, therefore, is to make, with the support of evidence from earlier Councils, a clearer statement to the faithful and to the whole world of the nature and universal mission of the Church. The circumstances of our time lend an urgency to this duty of the Church if all men, who are already more closely united nowadays by the bonds of society, technology and culture, are to achieve also the fullness of unity in Christ.

2. The plan of the eternal Father's wisdom and goodness is utterly free; it is his secret: he created the whole world, decided to raise men to a share in the divine life. He did not abandon them when, in Adam, they fell, for he has continually offered them help to salvation having

Christ, the Redeemer, in view, 'who is the image of the invisible God, the first-born of all creation' (*Col* 1:15). All those the Father chose before time began, 'those whom he foreknew he also predestined to be conformed to the image of his Son, in order that he might be the first-born among many brethren' (*Rom* 8:29). He has resolved to assemble those who believe in Christ in the holy Church. She was foreshadowed from the beginning of the world: she had a marvellous preparation in the history of Israel and the old covenant.[1] In the latest era she has been founded and, by the outpouring of the Holy Spirit, made manifest. She will reach her glorious consummation at the end of the ages. Then, as we read in the Fathers of the Church, all the just from the time of Adam, 'from Abel, the just, to the last of the elect',[2] will be assembled in the Father's presence in the universal Church.

3. The Son came at the Father's sending, for the Father chose us in him before the foundation of the world and destined us to be his sons because it was his plan to unite all things in him (cf. *Eph* 1:4-5 and 10). In performance of the Father's will Christ has introduced the kingdom of heaven on earth. He has revealed the Father's mystery to us and brought about redemption by his obedience. The Church, or kingdom of Christ now present in a mystery, enjoys by the power of God a visible growth in the world. This introduction and this growth are seen symbolically in the blood and water which flowed out of the opening in the side of Jesus on the Cross (cf. *Jn* 19:34); they are proclaimed beforehand by what the Lord said of his death on the Cross: 'and I, when I am lifted up from the earth, will draw all men to myself' (*Jn* 12:32). In the sacrifice of the Cross 'Christ, our paschal lamb, has been sacrificed' (1 *Cor* 5:7). Whenever it is celebrated at the altar, the work of our redemption is being performed. The sacrament of the bread of the Eucharist symbolizes and gives reality to the unity of the

---

[1] Cf. St Cyprian, *Epist.* 64, 4: PL 3, 1017. CSEL (Hartel), III B, p. 720. St Hilary of Poit., in *Mt* 23:6; PL 9, 1047. St Augustine, *passim.* St Cyril of Alex., *Glaph. in Gen.* 2, 10: PG 69, 110 A.
[2] Cf. St Gregory the Great, *Hom. in Evang.* 19, 1: PL 76, 1154 B. St Augustine, *Serm.* 341,9, 11: PL 39, 1499 ff. St John Damascene, *Adv. Iconocl.* 11: PG 96,1357.

faithful, who make up one body in Christ (cf. 1 *Cor* 10:17). All men are invited to this unity with Christ; he is the light of the world, the source from which we come, the means whereby we live, the end to which we are moving.

4. On the completion of the work which the Father gave the Son to do on earth (cf. *Jn* 17:4) the Holy Spirit was sent on the day of Pentecost to be the perennial agent of the Church's sanctification; in this way believers were to have access to the Father in one Spirit through Christ (cf. *Eph* 2:18). He is the Spirit of life or the spring of water welling up to eternal life (cf. *Jn* 4:14; 7:38-39). By him the Father gives life to men, who are dead because of sin, until he shall raise their mortal bodies in Christ (cf. *Rom* 8:10-11). The Spirit has his dwelling in the Church and in the hearts of the faithful as in a temple (cf. 1 *Cor* 3:16; 6:19); that is where he prays and bears witness to the fact of adoption (cf. *Gal* 4:6; rom 8:15-16 and 26). He guides the Church into all the truth (cf. *Jn* 16:13): he makes her one in fellowship and service; he fits her out with gifts of different kinds, hierarchial* and charismatic†, and makes his fruits her adornment (cf. *Eph* 4:11-12; 1 *Cor* 12:4; *Gal* 5:22). By the power of the gospel he gives the Church youth and continual renewal, and he brings her safe to the consummation of union with her Bridegroom.[3] For the Spirit and the Bride say to the Lord Jesus: 'come' (*Rev* 22:17).

In this way the universal Church is clearly 'a people made one with the unity of the Father and Son and Holy Spirit'.[4]

5. There is a clear display of the mystery of the holy Church at its foundation: the Lord Jesus began his Church by preaching the happy news, the arrival of the kingdom of God which had been promised

---

*i.e. pertaining to the rule of bishops and priests.

†i.e. concerned with special divine gifts, e.g.: that of prophecy.

[3] Cf St Irenaeus, *Adv. Haer.* III, 24 1: PG 7, 966 B; Harvey 2, 131; ed. Sagnard, *Sources Chr.*, p. 398

[4] St Cyprian, *De Orat. Dom.* 23; PL 4, 553; Hartel, III A, p. 285 St Augustine *Serm.* 71, 20, 33; PL 38, 463 ff. St John Damascene, *Adv. Iconocl.* 12: PG 96, 1358 D.

ages ago in the Scriptures: 'The time is fulfilled and the kingdom of god is at hand' (*Mk* 1:15; cf. *Mt* 4:17). The light of this kingdom shines upon men in the speech, works and presence of Christ. The word of the Lord is compared to a seed which is sown in a field (*Mk* 4:14); when men hear it with belief and are counted in christ's little flock (*Lk* 12:32), it is the kingdom that they have accepted. The seed then sprouts and grows by its own power till harvest time (cf. *Mk* 4:26-29). Jesus' miracles too give confirmation of the arrival on earth of the kingdom: 'if it is by the finger of God that I cast out demons, then the kingdom of God has come upon you (*Lk* 11:20; cf. *Mt* 12:28). The supreme manifestation of the kingdom is in the very person of Christ, Son of God and Son of man, who came 'to serve and to give his life as a ransom for many' (*Mk 10:45*).

When Jesus rose again after undergoing the death of the cross for men, he made his appearance as Lord, Christ and Priest by appointment in perpetuity (cf. *Acts* 2:36; *Heb* 5:6; 7:17-21), and he poured out the Spirit that the Father had promised on his disciples (cf. *Acts* 2:33). Since then the Church, equipped with her founder's gifts, in loyal observance of the charity, humility and self-denial which he commanded, accepts her mission to proclaim the kingdom of Christ and God and to establish it among all nations; she is setting on earth the initial shoot of this kingdom's growth. In the meantime, as she gradually grows, she sighs for the kingdom's full achievement; she hopes and longs with all her strength to join her King in glory.

The various images of the Church

6. In the Old Testament the revelation of the kingdom was frequently put forward figuratively. Now the inner nature of the Church is made known to us in a similar way by various images. They may be taken from the life of a shepherd, from agriculture, from the process of building or even from the family and betrothal. Preliminary sketches of these are found in the books of the prophets.

The Church is the *sheepfold*, its single, obligatory entrance is Christ (*Jn* 10:1-10). She is the flock, and God himself proclaimed beforehand that he would be its shepherd (cf. *Is* 40:11; *Ez* 34:11 ff.); its sheep, while herded by human shepherds, are unfailingly guided and fed by Christ himself, the Good Shepherd, Chief Shepherd (cf. *Jn* 10:11; 1 *Pet* 5:4), who has laid down his life for the sheep (cf. *Jn* 10:11-15).

The Church is God's *tillage* or field (1 *Cor* 3:9). This is the field where the ancient olive grows; the patriarchs were its consecrated root. On this tree Jew and Gentile were reconciled and shall be reconciled (*Rom* 11:13-26). She has been planted by the heavenly vine-dresser as a choice vineyard (*Mt* 21:33-43; cf. *Is* 5:1 ff.). Christ is the true vine, he gives life and fruitfulness to us, the branches; we abide in him through the Church; apart from him, we can do nothing (*Jn* 15:1-5).

The Church is called, still more frequently, God's building (1 *Cor* 3:9). The Lord compared himself to the stone which the builders rejected yet it became the head of the corner (*Mt* 21: 42; cf. *Acts* 4:11; 1 *Pet* 2:7; *Ps* 117:22); this is the foundation on which the apostles built the Church (cf. 1 *Cor* 3:11), from it the Church receives its steadiness and cohesion. The structure is distinguished by many titles: 'God's household' (1 *Tim* 3:15), for in it dwells his family; 'dwelling place of God in the Spirit' (*Eph* 2:19-22), 'God's dwelling with men' (*Apoc* 21:3). In particular it is the consecrated temple which the Fathers of the Church praise when they find its image in sanctuaries made of stone. In the liturgy it is rightly likened to the holy city, the new Jerusalem.[5] In the Church we are being built up here on earth like living stones (1 *Pet* 2:5). This is the holy city that met John's gaze, coming down out of heaven from God when the earth was made new, prepared as a bride adorned for her husband (*Rev* 21:1 ff.).

The Church is also called 'the Jerusalem above' and 'our Mother' (*Gal* 4:26; cf. *Rev* 12:17). She is described as the unblemished bride of the unblemished Lamb (*Rev* 19:7; 21:2 and 9; 22:17). She is the bride

---

[5] Cf. ORIGEN, *in Mt.* 16, 21: PG 13, 1443 C; TERTULLIAN, *Adv. Marc.* 3, 7: PL 2, 357 C; CSEL 47, 3 p. 386. For liturgical documents, cf. *Sacramentarium Gregorianum:* PL 78, 160 B. or C. MOHLBERG, *Liber Sacramentorum Romanae Ecclesiae,* Rome, 1960, p. 111, XC: 'God, who foundest a dwelling place for thyself on the harmonious assembly of all the saints ...'. Hymn *Urbs Jerusalem beata* in the monastic Breviary, and *Coelestis urbs* Jerusalem in the Roman Breviary.

whom Christ 'loved and gave himself up for her, that he might sanctify her' (*Eph* 5:26). The covenant by which he has tied her to himself is indissoluble. He does not fail to 'nourish and cherish' her (*Eph* 5:29). He has wanted her to be cleansed and close to him, lovingly and loyally submissive (cf. *Eph* 5:24). He has loaded her for ever with the good things of heaven, to enable us to know what surpasses knowledge, the love of God and Christ for us (cf. *Eph* 3:19). The Church on this earth is away from the Lord (cf. 2 *Cor* 5:6). She has her being, as it were, in exile. Consequently she seeks and sets her mind on the things which are above, where Christ is, seated at the right hand of God; there the life of the Church is hid with Christ in God, until she shall appear in glory with her Bridegroom (cf. *Col* 3:1-4).

7. Man's ransom and transformation into a new creation was accomplished by the Son of God, in the human nature which he had taken to himself, when by his death and resurrection he conquered death (cf. *Gal* 6:15; 2 *Cor* 5:17). When he provides his brethren with his own Spirit after assembling them from all the nations, he is making them, as it were, his own body, in a mystical fashion.

This body is the setting in which the communication of Christ's life to believers takes place; the sacraments are the means of their union, hidden yet real, with Christ in his suffering and in his glory.[6] The work of baptism is to mould us to Christ's likeness: 'For by one Spirit we were all baptized into one body' (1 *Cor* 12:13). This sacred rite conveys the symbol and the reality of association with Christ's death and resurrection: 'we were buried with him by baptism into death'; but 'if we have been united with him in a death like his, we shall certainly be united with him in a resurrection like his' (*Rom* 6:4-5). At the breaking of the eucharistic bread we really do share the Lord's body and we are raised into fellowship with him and with each other. Because there is one bread, we who are many are one body, for we all partake of the one bread' (1 *Cor* 10:17). In this way we are all

---

[6] Cf. St Thomas, *Summa Theol.* III, q. 62, a. 5, ad 1.

made members of this body (cf. 1 *Cor* 12:27), 'individually members one of another' (*Rom* 12:5).

The relation of the faithful with Christ is like that of the members and the human body: there may be a great number of them, but the body they make is one (cf. 1 *Cor* 12:12). In the structure of the body of Christ too, there is a diversity of members and functions. The Spirit is one and he dispenses his gifts in variety, for the Church's advantage, according to his wealth and the requirements of the ministries (cf. 1 *Cor* 12:1-11). Among these gifts the foremost place is taken by the grace of the apostles, for the Spirit himself makes even those with spiritual gifts subject to their authority (cf. 1 *Cor* 14). The same Spirit uses his own power and the interconnection of the members to make himself the unity of the body and, in so doing, he produces charity among the faithful and gives it impetus. Consequently if one member suffers, all suffer together; if one member is honoured, all rejoice together (cf. 1 *Cor* 12:26).

The head of this body is Christ. He is the image of the invisible God; in him all things were created. He is before all things and in him all things hold together. He is the head of the body, the Church. He is the beginning, the first-born from the dead, that in everything he might be pre-eminent (cf. *Col* 1:15-18). By his mighty power he has dominion over heaven and earth; his pre-eminent perfection and his activity enable him to fill the whole body with the wealth of his glory (cf. *Eph* 1:18-23).[7]

All the members must be moulded to his likeness until Christ be formed in them (cf. *Gal* 4:19). This is the reason that we are caught up in the mysteries of his life, made like to him, sharing his death and resurrection, until we shall share his reign (cf. *Phil* 3:21; 2 *Tim* 2:11; *Eph* 2:6; *Col* 2:12; etc.). Making our pilgrimage on earth until that time, we follow his footsteps through trouble and persecution. Our association with his sufferings is that of the body with its head: we share his sufferings in order to share his glory (cf. *Rom* 8:17).

---

[7] Cf. Pius XII. Encycl. *Mystici Corporis*, 29 June 1943: AAS 35 (1943) p. 208.

From him 'the whole body, nourished and knit together through its joints and ligaments, grows with a growth that is from God' (*Col* 2:19). In his body, the Church, he continually dispenses his gifts of service. With the help of these gifts we have his strength to offer each other services which help towards salvation, with the result that, speaking the truth in love, we are to grow up in every way into him who is our head (cf. *Eph* 4:11–16).

The purpose of his gift of the Holy Spirit is that we may have ceaseless renewal in him (cf. *Eph* 4:23). The Spirit is one and the same in the head and in the members. It is he that gives life, unity and motion to the whole body. As a result, the Fathers have found it possible to compare his work to the function which is fulfilled in the human frame by the principle of life, the soul.[8]

Christ loves the Church as his bride; he makes himself the model of the husband who loves his wife as if she were his own body (cf. *Eph* 5:25-28). The Church in her turn is submissive to her head (*ibid.* 23-24). 'In him the whole fullness of deity dwells bodily' (*Col* 2:9); he therefore gives the Church her fill of his divine gifts, for she is his body and his fullness (cf. *Eph* 1:22-23). He intends her thereby to reach towards and to arrive at all the fullness of God (cf. *Eph* 3:19).

8. Christ, the sole mediator, has founded and gives unfailing support to his holy Church, the community of faith, hope and charity. He has made her visible framework, as it were,[9] the dispenser of the grace and truth which he sheds over all mankind. She is a society equipped with hierarchical organs and the Mystical Body of Christ, a visible assembly and a spiritual fellowship. For all her earthly character and

---

[8] Cf. Leo XII, Encycl. *Divinum illud*, 9 May 1897: ASS 29 (1896-97) p. 650. Pius XII, Encycl. *Mystici Corporis, loc. cit.*, pp. 219-220; Denz. 2288 (3808). St Augustine, *Serm.* 268, 2: PL 38, 1232, and elsewhere. St John Chrysostom, *in Eph.* Hom. 9, 3: PG 62, 72. Didymus of Alex., *Trin.* 2, 1: PG 39, 449 ff. St Thomas, *in Col.* 1, 18, lect. 5: ed. Marietti, II, n. 46; 'As one body is founded on the unity of the soul so the Church on the unity of the Spirit ...'.

[9] Leo XIII, Encycl. *Sapientiae christianae*, 10 Jan. 1890: ASS 22 (1889-90) p. 392; Encycl. *Satis cognitum*, 29 June 1896; ASS 28 (1895-96) pp. 710 and 724 ff. Pius XII, Encycl. *Mystici Corporis, loc. cit.*, pp. 199-200.

heavenly wealth, we must not think of the Church as two substances, but a single, complex reality, the compound of a human and a divine element.[10] By a significant analogy she is likened to the mystery of the Word incarnate: the nature taken by the divine Word serves as the living organ of salvation in a union with him which is indissoluble; in the same way, the social framework of the Church serves the Spirit of Christ, her life-giver, for his bodily growth (cf. *Eph* 4:16).[11]

She is Christ's only Church and we acknowledge her unity, holiness, catholicity and apostolic nature in the Creed.[12] After his resurrection our Saviour made her over to Peter to feed (*Jn* 21:17); he gave him and the rest of the apostles the commission to spread and to rule her (cf. *Mt* 28:18 ff.); he erected her as the perpetual 'pillar and foundation of the truth' (1 *Tim* 3:15). This Church, founded and organized in this world as a society, has its existence in the Catholic Church under the government of Peter's successor and the Bishops in communion with him,[13] although outside her framework there are found many elements of holiness and truth, and they give an impetus to universal unity inasmuch as they are gifts which belong to Christ's Church.

Christ completed the work of redemption in poverty and under persecution. In the same way, the Church is called to tread the same path if she is to provide men with the harvest of salvation. 'Though he was in the form of God', Christ Jesus 'emptied himself, taking the form of a servant' (*Phil* 2:6); 'though he was rich, he became poor' (1 *Cor* 8:9) for our sake. Just so the Church, while she may need human wealth to carry out her mission, is not erected to seek earthly glory, but to spread humility and self-denial by the example she must give. Christ was sent by the Father 'to preach good news to the poor ... to

---

[10] Cf. Pius XII, Encycl. *Mystici Corporis, loc. cit.*, p. 221 ff.; Encycl. *Humani generis*, 12 Aug. 1950: AAS 42 (1950) p. 571.

[11] Leo XII, Encycl. *Satis cognitum, loc. cit.*, p. 713.

[12] Cf. *Apostles' Creed*: Denz. 6-9 (10-13); *Creed of Nicaea-Constantinople*: Denz. 86 (150); contained in *Prof. fidei Trid.*: Denz. 994 and 999 (1862 and 1868).

[13] She is called 'The Holy (catholic apostolic) Roman Church': in *Prof. fidei Trid., loc. cit.* and Vatican Council I, Sess. III, Const. dogm. *de fide cath.*: Denz. 1782 (3001).

restore the broken-hearted' (*Lk* 4:18), 'to seek and to save the lost' (*Lk* 19:10). In like manner the Church has a loving embrace for all who are afflicted by human weakness; she goes further: in the poor and the suffering she recognizes the likeness of her founder, a poor man and a sufferer. She makes the relief of their poverty her business, the service of Christ in them her aim. Christ 'holy, blameless, unstained' (*Heb* 7:26) knew no sin (2 *Cor* 5:21), it was only for the sins of the people that he came to make expiation (cf. *Heb* 2:17). The Church, however, with sinners clasped to her bosom, is at once holy and in constant need of cleansing; thus she pursues a ceaseless course of penance and renewal.

'The Church proceeds on her pilgrim's course between the persecutions of the world and God's consolations';[14] she proclaims the cross and death of the Lord until he shall come (cf. 1 *Cor* 11: 26). She has the strength she draws from her risen Lord to enable her patience and love to overcome her trials and difficulties, those from within and those from without. With loyalty she is to reveal his mystery in the world, albeit in darkness, until at the end it shall be made manifest in the fullness of light.

---

[14] St Augustine, *City of God*. XVIII, 51, 2: PL 41.61.

CHAPTER II

THE PEOPLE OF GOD

9. In every age and in every nation anyone who fears God and does what is right is acceptable to him (cf. *Acts* 10:35). It has not been God's resolve to sanctify and save men individually with no regard for their mutual connection, but to establish them as a people who would give him recognition in truth and service in holiness. Thus he chose the Israelites for his people. He made a covenant with them and gave them gradual formation by making himself and the design of his will manifest in their history and by consecrating it to himself. All this came about to prepare and foreshadow the making of the new and perfect covenant in Christ and the delivery of a more complete revelation through the very Word of God made flesh. 'Behold, the days are coming, says the Lord, when I will make a new covenant with the house of Israel and the house of Juda ... I will put my law within them, and I will write it in their hearts; and I will be their God, and they shall be my people ... for they shall all know me, from the least of them to the greatest, says the Lord' (*Jer* 31:31-34). This is the new alliance that Christ established, the new covenant in his blood (cf. 1 *Cor* 11:25), when he called up a people out of Jews and Gentiles. This people's unity was not to be brought about according to the flesh but in the Spirit; it was to be the new People of God. Believers in Christ have been born anew, not of perishable seed but of imperishable, through the word of the living God (cf. 1 *Pet* 1:23), not of flesh but of water and the Holy Spirit (cf. *Jn* 3:5-6). They are established as 'a chosen race, a royal priesthood, a holy nation, God's own people ... Once (they were) no people but now (they are) God's People' (1 *Pet* 2:9-10).

This messianic People has for its head Christ 'who was put to death for our trespasses and raised for our justification' (*Rom* 4:25); now he is in possession of the name that is greater than any other name and reigning in glory in heaven. For rank it has the dignity and freedom of God's sons, whose hearts are like a temple, the dwelling-place of the Holy Spirit. For law it has the new commandment of loving as

Christ has loved us (cf. *Jn* 13:34). For goal it has the kingdom of God; it has had its beginning at the hands of God himself on earth, it must be spread further until it shall have its consummation from him at the end of the ages, when Christ, who is our life, appears (cf. *Col* 3:4) and 'creation itself will be set free from its bondage to decay and obtain the glorious liberty of the children of God' (*Rom* 8:21). Although this messianic People does not in fact embrace all men, and more than once has had the appearance of a tiny flock, for all that, it has the toughness of the rising shoot of unity, hope, and salvation for the whole human race. It is founded by Christ for a fellowship of life, charity and truth. It is taken up by him as the instrument of salvation for all men. It is sent on a mission to the world at large as the light of the world and the salt of the earth (cf. *Mt* 5:13-16).

Israel according to the flesh, on pilgrimage in the desert, already had the name of God's 'Church' (assembly) (2 *Neh* 13:1; cf. *Num* 20:4; *Deut* 23:1 ff.). Just so, the new Israel, making its way through the present age and in search of the lasting city that is to come (cf. *Heb* 13:14), is also called the 'Church' of Christ (cf. *Mt* 16:18). Christ it was who obtained it with his own blood (cf. *Acts* 20:28), who filled it with his own Spirit and fitted it out with the appropriate means to the visible union of a society. God has convened the assembly of those who fix their eyes, in belief, on Jesus, the author of salvation, the principle of unity and peace, and he has erected the Church to be for each and all the visible sacrament of this saving unity.[15] She is to extend to all lands; she enters human history, yet she transcends the ages and the boundaries of nations. On her progress through temptations and troubles the strength of God's grace that the Lord promised her, gives her the courage not to fall away from perfect loyalty through weakness of nature, but to persist as a bride worthy of her Lord, to renew herself by the activity of the Holy Spirit without intermission until, by way of the cross, she reaches the light which knows no nightfall.

---

[15] Cf. St Cyprian, *Epist.* 69, 6: PL 3, 1142 B; Hartel, 3 B, p. 754: 'The inseparable sacrament of unity'.

The universal priesthood

10. Christ the Lord, the High Priest chosen from among men (cf. *Heb* 5:1-5), has made the new people 'a kingdom, priests to his God and Father' (*Rev* 1:6; cf. 5:9-10). Through their rebirth and the Holy Spirit's anointing the baptized receive consecration as a spiritual house, a holy priesthood. It is their task, in every employment, to offer the spiritual sacrifices of a christian man; theirs to declare the wonderful deeds of him who called them out of darkness into his marvellous light (cf. 1 *Pet* 2:4-10). As a consequence all Christ's disciples must devote themselves to prayer, must praise God (cf. *Acts* 2:42-47), must present themselves as a living sacrifice, holy and acceptable to God (cf. *Rom* 12:1); must carry their witness of Christ all over the world; must make a defence to anyone who calls them to account for the hope of eternal life that is in them (cf. 1 *Pet* 3:15).

There is an essential difference between the faithful's priesthood in common and the priesthood of the ministry or the hierarchy, and not just a difference of degree. Nevertheless, there is an ordered relation between them: one and the other has its special way of sharing the single priesthood of Christ.[16] The ministerial priest, by the sacred power that he enjoys, is responsible for the formation and government of the priestly people; in the person of Christ he makes the eucharistic sacrifice and offers it in the name of the whole of God's People. The faithful, in virtue of their royal priesthood, concur in the offering of the Eucharist,[17] and they practise their priesthood in the reception of the sacraments, in prayer and thanksgiving, the witness of a holy life, self-denial and active charity.

11. The priestly community's sacred character and organic structure are carried into effect by means of the sacraments and the virtues. The faithful are incorporated into the Church by baptism; they are assigned by its character a place in the worship of the Christian religion;

---

[16] Cf. Pius XII, Alloc. *Magnificate Dominum,* 2 Nov. 1954: AAS 46 (1954) p. 669; Encycl. *Mediator Dei,* 20 Nov. 1947: AAS 39 (1947) p. 555.
[17] Cf. Pius XI, Encycl. *Miserentissimus Redemptor,* 8 May 1928: AAS 20 (1928) p. 171 ff. Pius XII. Alloc. *Vous nous avez,* 22 Sept. 1956: AAS 48 (1956) p. 714.

they are reborn as sons of God and obliged to profess before men the faith which they have received from God through the Church.[18] The bond that ties them to the Church is made more complete by the sacrament of confirmation. It enriches them with the special strength of the Holy Spirit and gives them a stricter obligation to act as true witnesses of Christ by spreading and defending the faith by word and deed.[19] When they share the eucharistic sacrifice, the source and the culmination of all Christian life, they offer the divine Victim to God and themselves with him.[20] Thus with no confusion, but each in his own way, they all play their own part in the liturgical action at the sacrificial offering and holy communion. Moreover, when they have had Christ's body for their refreshment at the sacred gathering, they are a concrete demonstration of the unity of God's People, of which this august sacrament is the appropriate sign and the marvellously effective instrument.

Those who approach the sacrament of penance win, by God's mercy, pardon for the offence done to him; at the same time they are reconciled with the Church, which their sin had injured and which, with charity, good example and prayers, is working for their conversion. In the holy anointing of the sick with the prayer of the priests, the whole Church recommends the sick to the Lord, who suffered and has been glorified, asking him to give them relief and salvation (cf. *Jas* 5:14-16). She goes further and calls upon them to associate themselves freely with the passion and death of Christ (cf. *Rom* 8:17; *Col* 1:24; 2 *Tim* 2:11-12; 1 *Pet* 4:13) and in this way to make their contribution to the good of God's People. Those among the faithful who are marked by holy order are appointed in the name of Christ to feed the Church with God's word and his grace. Finally, the sacrament of matrimony makes Christian couples the sign of the mystery of the unity and the fertile love existing between Christ and the Church, and gives them

---

[18] Cf. St Thomas, *Summa Theol.* III, q. 63, a. 2.

[19] Cf. St Cyril of Jerus., *Catech.* 17, *de Spiritu Sancto*, II, 35-37: PG 33, 1009-1012. Nic. Cabasilas, *De vita in Christo*, lib. III, *de utilitate chrismatis*: PG 150, 569-580. St Thomas, *Summa Theol.* III q. 65, a. 3 and q. 72, a. 1 and 5.

[20] Cf. Pius XII, Encycl. *Mediator Dei,* 20 Nov. 1947: AAS 39 (1947) especially p. 552 ff.

a share in it (cf. *Eph* 5:32). By its power they are a help to each other in their married life, in the acceptance of children and giving them an education in holiness. Thus they have their special gift among the People of God, in their own station of life and their own rank (cf. 1 *Cor* 7:7).[21] This married life is the starting-point of the family. In the family human society's new citizens are born, whom baptism, by the power of the Holy Spirit, makes into children of God to provide for the perpetuation of God's People throughout the ages. It is, as it were, a church in the home, where parents have, by word and example, to be the first preachers of the faith that their children hear, and where they must foster each child's individual vocation, taking special care in the case of a sacred vocation.

With the protection of all these great means of salvation, all Christ's faithful, no matter what their individual circumstances or status, have the vocation from the Lord to make each his own way to perfection, which consists in the holiness which constitutes the perfection of the Father himself.

The universality of the People of God

12. The consecrated People of God have a share too in Christ's prophetic office, chiefly by spreading a live witness to him by means of a life of faith and charity, and by offering God a sacrifice of praise, the tribute of lips that acknowledge his name (cf. *Heb* 13:15). The universal body made up of the faithful, whom the Holy One has anointed (cf. 1 *Jn* 2:20 and 27), is incapable of being at fault in belief. This is a property which belongs to the people as a whole; a supernatural discernment of faith is the means by which they make this property manifest, when, 'from Bishops to the last layman',[22] they show universal agreement in matters of faith and morals. This discernment of faith,

---

[21] 1 Cor 7:7: 'Each of us has his own special gift (*idion charisma*) from God, one of one kind and one of another'. Cf. St Augustine, *De Dono Persev.* 14, 37: PL 45, 1015 ff.: 'Not only continence but also the chastity of married people is a gift from God'.
[22] Cf. St Augustine, *De Praed. Sanct.* 14, 27: PL 44,980.

which is roused and maintained by the Spirit of truth, is the cause of the unfailing adherence of the People of God to the faith that was once for all delivered to the saints (cf. *Jude* 3); the cause too of the deeper entry that it makes into the faith by right judgment and of a more complete application of the faith to life. This all takes place under the guidance of the sacred magisterium, when the People of God, in loyal submission to it, accepts not the word of men but what really is the word of God (cf. 1 *Thess* 2:13).

It is not only by means of the sacraments and ministries that the Holy Spirit makes the People of God holy, gives it guidance and adorns it with virtues. He also 'apportions' his gifts 'to each one individually as he wills' (1 *Cor* 12:11). Among the faithful of every order he makes a distribution of special graces, by which he gives them an aptitude and a readiness to undertake the variety of works and duties which advance the renewal and the extension of the building of the Church: 'to each is given the manifestation of the Spirit for the common good' (1 *Cor* 12:7). These spiritual gifts may be very distinctive; they may be rather simple and widespread; they are all primarily adapted and useful to the needs of the Church. They are therefore to be accepted with thanksgiving and a sense of relief. There must be no rash ambition for extraordinary gifts, nor any presumptuous expectation of the fruits of apostolic services from them. The decision on their genuineness and on the organization of their exercise rests with the men who are over the Church, and whose specific competence lies, not in quenching the Spirit, but in testing everything and in holding fast what is good (cf. 1 *Thess* 5:12; 19-21).

13. All men have a vocation to the new People of God. And so this people, while remaining one and unique, is to expand all over the world throughout the ages to fulfil the design of God's will. He founded human nature originally as a unity, and he has resolved to gather into one, God's children who are scattered far and wide (cf. *Jn* 11:52). This was the errand on which God sent his Son, whom he appointed

the heir of all things (cf. *Heb* 1:2), to be Master, King and Priest of all, head of the new, universal people of God's children. This was the errand on which God sent his Son's Spirit, the Lord and life-giver, the principle of unified association, for the whole Church, and for each and every believer, in the apostles' teaching, their fellowship, breaking of bread and prayers (cf. *Acts* 2:42).

The one People of God exists among all the nations of the earth, for it takes its citizens from all nations; yet the kingdom is not earthly in character but heavenly. All the faithful, scattered all over the earth, are in communion in the Holy Spirit. Thus 'the man who is settled in Rome knows that the Indian is a member (of his own body)'.[23] Since the kingship of Christ is not of this world (cf. *Jn* 18:36), the Church, or People of God, which introduces this kingdom, does not detract from the temporal good of any nation. On the contrary, she encourages all the good that there is in the resources, wealth and customs of the nations; she takes it over and purifies it, strengthens and elevates it. She bears in mind that she must harvest with the King to whom the nations have been given for an inheritance (cf. *Ps* 2:8), who possesses the city to which the nations bring presents and gifts (cf. *Ps* 71 (72):10; *Is* 60:4-7; *Rev* 21:24). This characteristic universality is the adornment of the People of God; it is the gift of the Lord. It is the means whereby the Catholic Church is effective and constant in her aim to resume the whole of humanity, possessions and all, under the head, Christ, in the unity of his Spirit.[24]

Because of this universality the individual parts contribute their own gifts to the other parts and to the whole Church. The result is growth for the whole and for the individual parts, from the provision they all make for each other and their unified effort towards plenitude. The People of God, consequently, is not only assembled out of different nations, it is in itself an amalgam of different ranks. There is variety

---

[23] Cf. St John Chrysostom, *in Io.* Hom. 65, 1: PG 59, 361.
[24] Cf. St Irenaeus, *Adv. Haer.* III, 16,6; III, 22, 1-3: PG 7,925 C-926 A and 955 C-958 A; Harvey 2, 87 ff. and 120-123; Sagnard, ed. *Sources Chrét.* pp. 290-292 and 372 ff.

in its members: variety of duties, for some discharge the sacred ministry to the advantage of their brethren; variety of condition and rule of life, for a considerable number in the religious state stimulate their brethren by their example in striving towards perfection by a path of greater restriction. Thus, within the ecclesiastical fellowship particular Churches, with their own traditions, have a lawful existence and no damage is done to the primacy of the Chair of Peter. The Chair of Peter presides over the whole loving assembly;[25] it is the safeguard of legitimate variety, on the watch to see that in particular cases it supports unity and does it no harm. Finally, the different parts of the Church are bound in intimate fellowship with regard to spiritual wealth, apostolic labourers and temporal assistance. The vocation of the members of God's People requires them to put their goods in common; the words of the Apostle are valid also in the case of individual Churches: 'As each has received a gift, employ it for one another, as good stewards of God's varied grace' (1 *Pet* 4:10).

All men are called to this Catholic unity of the People of God. It is the sign which precedes and promotes universal peace. All in different ways belong to this unity or are orientated to it—the Catholic faithful, other believers in Christ and the whole of mankind, for all, by God's grace, are called to salvation.

The Catholic faithful

14. The sacred Council's attention is chiefly directed to the Catholic faithful. It relies on sacred Scripture and Tradition in teaching that this pilgrim-Church is necessary for salvation. Christ alone is the mediator of salvation and the way of salvation. He presents himself to us in his Body, which is the Church. When he insisted expressly on the necessity for faith and baptism (cf. *Mk* 16:16; *Jn* 3:5), he asserted at the same time the necessity for the Church which men enter by the gateway of baptism. This means that it would be impossible for men to be saved

---

[25] Cf. St Ignatius, Martyr, *Ad Rom.*, Praef.: ed. Funk, 1, p. 252.

if they refused to enter or to remain in the Catholic Church, unless they were unaware that her foundation by God through Jesus Christ made her a necessity.

Full incorporation in the society of the Church belongs to those who are in possession of the Holy Spirit, accept her order in its entirety with all her established means to salvation, and are united to Christ, who rules her by the agency of the Supreme Pontiff and the Bishops, within her visible framework. The bonds of their union are the profession of faith, the sacraments, ecclesiastical government and fellowship. Despite incorporation in the Church, that man is not saved who fails to persevere in charity, and remains in the bosom of the Church 'with his body' but not 'with his heart'.[26] All the Church's children must be sure to ascribe their distinguished rank to Christ's special grace and not to their own deserts. If they fail to correspond with that grace in thought, word and deed, so far from being saved, their judgment will be all the more severe.[27]

Catechumens are those who have been moved by the Holy Spirit explicitly to desire and to take steps to obtain incorporation in the Church. They are joined to her by this very desire and receive the embracing love and care of Mother Church.

15. The Church has come to recognize several reasons for her close connection with those who are baptized and have the honour of the name of Christian, yet do not profess the faith in its entirety, or maintain union in fellowship under Peter's successor.[28] There are a great number who honour the sacred Scripture as the norm of belief and

---

[26] Cf. St Augustine, *Bapt. c. Donat.* V, 28, 39: PL 43, 197: 'It is certainly clear, as is said, that in the Church "inside" and "outside" must be thought of in terms of the heart, not the body.' Cf. *ibid.*, III, 19, 26: col. 152; V, 18, 24: col. 189; *in Io.* Tr. 61,2: PL 35, 1800, and elsewhere frequently.

[27] Cf. Luke 12:48: 'Every one to whom much is given, of him will much be required'. Cf. also *Matt* 5:19-20; 7:21-22; 25:41-46; *James* 2:14.

[28] Cf. Leo XII, Apost. Letter *Praeclara gratulationis*, 20 June 1894: ASS 26 (1893-94) p. 707.

life and who show sincere religious zeal. They have a loving faith in God the Father almighty and in Christ, his Son, the Saviour.[29] They are marked by baptism and thereby joined to Christ; they acknowledge other sacraments too and receive them in their own Churches or ecclesiastical communities. Several of them possess the episcopate, celebrate the holy Eucharist and encourage piety towards the Virgin Mother of God.[30] They also have a fellowship in prayer and in other spiritual benefits, and a real union in the Holy Spirit, for he is at work among them too with his power of sanctification in gifts and graces: he has given some of them strength to the extent of shedding their blood. So it is that the Spirit is rousing in all Christ's disciples desire and action, in the hope that all men may be united peacefully, in the manner that Christ appointed, in one flock under one shepherd.[31] To obtain this union, Mother Church is incessantly praying, hoping and taking action, and she is exhorting her children to purification and renewal, so that the mark of Christ may shine more clearly on the face of the Church.

Non-Christians

16. Lastly there are those who have not yet accepted the gospel; their relationships with the People of God are varied.[32] In the first place stand the people that was given the covenants and the promises; they are the stock from which Christ took his origin according to the flesh (cf. *Rom* 9:4-5), the people as regards the election beloved for the sake of their fathers: for the gifts and the call of God are irrevocable (cf. *Rom* 11:28-29). But the design of salvation also includes those who

---

[29] Cf. Leo XIII, Encycl. *Satis cognitum*, 29 June 1896: ASS 28 (1895-96) p. 738. Encycl. *Caritatis studium*, 25 July 1898: ASS 31 (1898-99) p. 11. Pius XII, Broadcast *Nell' alba*, 24 Dec. 1941: AAS 34 (1942) p. 21.
[30] Cf. Pius XI, Encycl. *Rerum Orientalium*, 8 Sept. 1928: AAS 20 (1928) p. 287. Pius XII, Encycl. *Orientalis Ecclesiae*, 9 April 1944: AAS 36 (1944) p. 137.
[31] Cf. Instr. of Holy Office, 20 Dec. 1949: AAS 42 (1950) p. 142.
[32] Cf. St Thomas, *Summa Theol.* III, q. 8. a. 3, ad 1.

recognize the Creator, and among them especially the Moslems; it is their avowal that they hold the faith of Abraham, they join us in adoring the single, merciful God who will judge mankind at the last day. Then there are men who are seeking the God they do not know, in shadowy imaginings; God is not far from men of this kind, for he gives to all men life and breath and everything (cf. *Acts* 17:25-28), and he, the Saviour, desires all men to be saved (cf. 1 *Tim* 2:4). There are men who are in ignorance of Christ's gospel and of his Church through no fault of their own and who search for God in sincerity of heart; they attempt to put into practice the recognition of his will that they have reached through the dictate of conscience. They do so under the influence of divine grace; they can attain everlasting salvation.[33] Nor does divine Providence deny the necessary helps to salvation to men who, through no fault of their own, have not yet reached an express acknowledgment of God, yet strive with the help of divine grace to attain an upright life. Any good or any truth found among them has value in the Church's eyes as a preparation for the gospel;[34] it is a gift from him who enlightens every man so that they may end by possessing life. It is more frequently the case, however, that men have been deceived by the devil, they have become futile in their thinking, they have exchanged the truth about God for a lie and served the creature rather than the Creator (cf. *Rom* 1:21 and 25). Alternatively, since they live and die without God in this world, they are exposed to the extreme of despair. This is the reason that the Church aims to promote the glory of God and the salvation of them all, by taking care to encourage the missions. She remembers the Lord's commandment, when he said, 'preach the gospel to the whole creation' (*Mk* 16:15).

---

[33] Cf. Letter of HOLY OFFICE to Archbishop of Boston: DENZ. 3869-72.
[34] Cf. EUSEBIUS OF CAES., *Praeparatio Evangelica*, 1, 1: PG 21, 28 AB.

The missionary character of the Church

17. Just as the Son was sent on a mission by the Father, he sent the apostles on a mission himself (cf. *Jn* 20:21) with the words, 'Go therefore and make disciples of all nations, baptizing them in the name of the Father and of the Son and of the Holy Spirit, teaching them to observe all that I have commanded you; and lo, I am with you always, to the close of the age' (*Mt* 28:18-20). This solemn commandment of Christ to proclaim the saving truth the Church has received from the apostles; it must be carried out to the end of the earth (cf. *Acts* 1:8). Consequently, she takes to herself the Apostle's words, 'Woe to me if I do not preach the gospel' (1 *Cor* 9:16). She continues to send out preachers without fail until new Churches are fully created and themselves continue the work of preaching the gospel. She is under the compulsion of the Holy Spirit to co-operate in giving effect to the design of God, who set up Christ as the principle of salvation for the whole world, and in bringing that design to completion. When she preaches the gospel, the Church draws her hearers to belief and to a confession of faith, she gives them the disposition for baptism, she saves them from the tyranny of error, she incorporates them in Christ so that they may, through love, grow in him to full size. Her effort brings it about that all the good seed found in the mind and heart of men, or national rites and culture, should escape destruction, be made wholesome, raised and brought to fulfilment to the glory of God, the confusion of the devil and the happiness of man. The burden of spreading the faith according to his ability weighs on every disciple of Christ.[35] Anyone may baptize those who believe, but it belongs to the priest to complete the building of the Body with the eucharistic sacrifice in fulfilment of the message God spoke through the prophet, 'From the rising of the sun to its setting my name is great among the

---

[35] Cf. BENEDICT XV, Apost. Letter *Maximum illud*: AAS 11 (1919) p. 440. especially p. 451 ff. PIUS XI, Encycl. *Rerum, Ecclesiae*: AAS 18 (1926) pp. 68-69. PIUS XII, Encycl. *Fidei Donum*, 21 April 1957: AAS 49 (1957) pp. 236-237.

nations, and in every place sacrifice is offered to my name, and a pure offering' (*Mal* 1:11).[36] It is the purpose of the Church's prayer and work that the fullness of the whole world should pass over to join the People of God, the Lord's Body and the Temple of the Holy Spirit, and that all honour and glory be paid in Christ, the Head of all, to the Creator and Father of all.

---

[36] Cf. *Didachè*, 14: ed. FUNK, I. p. 32. ST JUSTIN, *Dial*. 41: PG 6, 564. ST IRENAEUS, *Adv. Haer.* IV, 17, 5: PG 7, 1023; HARVEY, 2, p. 199 ff. COUNCIL OF TRENT, Sess. 22, cap. 1: DENZ. 939 (1742).

CHAPTER III

THE HIERARCHICAL CONSTITUTION OF THE CHURCH AND THE EPISCOPATE IN PARTICULAR

18. So that the People of God might have tending and continual growth, Christ the Lord established in his Church different ministries. They are aimed at the good of the whole body. The ministers, invested with sacred power, are at the service of their brethren; for all who belong to the People of God, and enjoy in consequence the real dignity of Christians, are to arrive at salvation by uniting to the same end freely yet in order.

This sacred Council is following in the footsteps of the First Vatican Council, when it joins it in teaching and proclaiming that Jesus Christ, the eternal Shepherd, built his holy Church by sending his apostles, as he too had been sent by the Father (cf. *Jn* 20:21); and he wanted their successors, the Bishops, to be the pastors in his Church until the end of the world. To ensure the indivisible unity of the episcopate, he set Saint Peter over the other apostles. In him he established the fundamental principle of unity of faith and communion, a principle which would be perpetual and visible.[37] The sacred Council once again sets out for the strong belief of all the faithful this doctrine of the institution, the perpetuity, the power and the nature of the sacred primacy of the Roman Pontiff, and of his infallible magisterium. To continue this undertaking a stage further, it has resolved to make a universal profession and proclamation of the teaching on the Bishops, successors of the apostles, who control the household of the living God, and, in so doing, act in conjunction with Peter's successor, the Vicar of Christ,[38] and visible head of the Church in its entirety.

---

[37] Cf. Vatican Council I, Sess. IV, Const. Dogm. *Pastor aeternus*: Denz. 1821 (3050 ff.).
[38] Cf. Council of Florence, *Decretum pro Graecis*: Denz. 694 (1307) and Vatican Council I. *ibid.*: Denz. 1827 (3059).

19. The Lord Jesus, after entreating the Father in prayer, called to him those whom he desired and he appointed twelve, to be with him and to be sent out to preach the kingdom of God (cf. *Mk* 3:13-19; *Mt* 10:1-42). These were the apostles (cf. *Lk* 6:13) whom he established as a college, that is to say a group on a permanent footing, and among them he chose out Peter and put him at its head (cf. *Jn* 21:15-17). He sent them to the children of Israel in the first place and to all races (cf. *Rom* 1:16). With their share of his power, they were to make all nations his disciples, to sanctify and govern them (cf. *Mt* 28:16-20; *Mk* 16:15; *Lk* 24:45-48; *Jn* 20:21-23). In this way they were to propagate the Church and tend it by their ministry under the Lord's guidance through all the days that were coming, to the close of the age (cf. *Mt* 28:20). They received full confirmation in this mission on the day of Pentecost (cf. *Acts* 2:1-26), as the Lord had promised: 'You shall receive power when the Holy Spirit has come upon you; and you shall be my witnesses in Jerusalem and in all Judaea and in Samaria and to the end of the earth' (*Acts* 1:8). By preaching the gospel everywhere (cf. *Mk* 16:20)—and the welcome given it by their hearers is the work of the Holy Spirit—the apostles gather together the universal Church which the Lord founded on the apostles, built upon Saint Peter, their prince, while the chief corner-stone of it is Jesus Christ himself (cf. *Rev* 21:14; *Mt* 16:18; *Eph* 2:20).[39]

Bishops as successors of the apostles

20. This divine mission, entrusted to the apostles by Christ, is going to last until the end of the world (cf. *Mt* 28:20), since the gospel which they have to transmit is the principle of all life for the Church for all time. This is the reason that in this society with its hierarchical arrangement, the apostles took care to arrange the appointment of successors.

---

[39] Cf. *Liber sacramentorum* St Gregory, Preface on the feast of St Matthias and of St Thomas: PL 78, 51 and 152; cf. Cod. Vat. lat. 3548, f. 18. St Hilary. *in Ps.* 67, 10: PL 9, 450; CSEL 22, p. 286, St Jerome, *Adv. Iovin* 1, 26: PL. 23, 247 A. St Augustine, in Ps. 86, 4: PL 37, 1103. St Gregory the Great, *Mor. in Job,* XXVIII, V: PL 76, 455-456. Primasius, *Comm. in Apoc.*, V: PL 68, 924 BC. Paschasius Radb., *in Mt.* L. VIII, cap. 16: PL 120, 561 C. Cf. Leo XIII, Epist. *Et sane,* 17 Dec. 1888: ASS 21 (1888) p. 321.

They had various assistants in their ministry.[40] But in addition, for the continuance of their accredited mission after their own death, they bequeathed to their immediate fellow-workers as a legacy the task of completing and consolidating the work which they had begun.[41] They charged them to give their attention to the whole flock in which the Holy Spirit had set them to tend the Church of God (cf. *Acts* 20:28). They appointed such men, and then gave them the order that, on their decease, other approved men should take up their ministry in succession.[42] Among the different ministries which have been exercised in the Church from the very earliest times, on the evidence of tradition, a pre-eminent position is accorded to the office of the men who, on appointment to the episcopate, have a life-giving contact with the original apostles[43] by a current of succession which goes back to the beginning.[44] In this way, as St Irenaeus testifies, the apostolic tradition is demonstrated all over the world,[45] and safeguarded,[46] by the men who were appointed Bishops by the apostles and their successors to our own day.

The Bishops, then, with the assistance of priests and deacons, have undertaken the service of the community.[47] They preside over the flock in God's place,[48] for they are its pastors, as the masters of teaching, priests of sacred worship, ministers of government.[49] Office was given to Peter, the first of the apostles, by the Lord, by an individual commission, and was to be handed on to his successors. This office is

---

[40] Cf. *Acts* 6:2-6; 11:30; 13:1; 14:23; 20:17; 1 *Thess* 5:12-13; *Phil* 1:1; *Col* 4:11 *et passim*.

[41] Cf. *Acts* 20:25-27; 2 *Tim* 4:6 ff.; in conjunction with 1 *Tim* 5:22; 2 *Tim* 2:2; *Tit* 1:5; St Clement of Rome, *Ad Cor.* 44, 3: ed. Funk, I, p. 156.

[42] St Clement of Rome, *Ad Cor.* 44,2: ed. Funk, I, p. 154 ff.

[43] Cf. Tertullian, *Praescr. Haer.* 32: PL 2, 53.

[44] Cf. Tertullian, *Praescr. Hoer.* 32: PL 2, 52 ff.; St Ignatius, Martyr, *passim*.

[45] Cf. St Irenaeus, *Adv. Haer.* III, 3, 1: PG 7, 848 A: Harvey 2, 8; Sagnard, p. 100 ff.: '*manifestatam*'.

[46] Cf. St Irenaeus, *Adv. Haer.* III, 2, 2: PG 7, 847: Harvey 2, 7; Sagnard. p. 100: '*custoditur*', cf. *ibid.* IV, 26, 2; col. 1053; Harvey 2, 236, and IV, 33. 8; col. 1077; Harvey 2, 262.

[47] St Ignatius, Martyr, *Philad.*, Praef.: ed. Funk, I, p. 264.

[48] St Ignatius, Martyr, *Philad.*, 1, 1; *Magn.* 6, 1: ed. Funk, pp. 264 and 234.

[49] St Clement of Rome, loc. cit., 42, 3-4; 44, 3-4; 57, 1-2: ed. Funk, I, 152, 156, 171 ff. St Ignatius, Martyr, *Philad.* 2; *Smyrn.* 8, *Magn.* 3; *Trall.* 7: ed. Funk, I, p. 265 ff.; 282; 232; 246 ff. etc; St Justin, *Apol.*, 1, 65: PG 6, 428; St Cyprian, *Epist.*, *passim*.

permanent. The same permanence characterizes the apostles' office of tending the Church; the continuity of its exercise is to be ensured by the sacred order of Bishops.[50] Consequently the sacred Council teaches that it is by divine institution that Bishops have succeeded to the place of the apostles,[51] as the pastors of the Church, whose hearers are listening to Christ, while he who rejects them, rejects Christ and him that sent Christ (cf. *Lk* 10:16).[52]

21. It is in the Bishops, with the assistance of the priests, that the Lord Jesus Christ, the High Priest, is in the midst of the faithful. Seated at the right hand of God the Father, he is no absentee from the assembly of his Bishops.[53] It is chiefly by means of their expert service that he preaches the word of God to all races, that he administers without ceasing the sacraments of faith to believers. It is by their fatherly office (cf. 1 *Cor* 4:15) that he gives heavenly rebirth and incorporation in his Body to new members. By their wisdom and prudence he gives direction and order to the pilgrimage of the people of the New Testament towards their eternal happiness. They are the pastors, chosen for the purpose of tending the Lord's flock; they are Christ's servants and stewards of God's mysteries (cf. 1 *Cor* 4:1); theirs is the accredited testimony to the good news of God's grace (cf. *Rom* 15:16; *Acts* 20:24) and the dispensation of the Spirit and of righteousness in splendour (cf. 2 *Cor* 3:8-9).

For the fulfilment of these great functions, the apostles were enriched by Christ with the special outpouring of the Holy Spirit, who came upon them (cf. *Acts* 1:8; 2:4; *Jn* 20:22-23); with the laying on of hands they handed on the spiritual gift to their helpers (cf. 1 *Tim* 4:14; 2 *Tim* 1:6-7), and this gift has been passed on to our day by episcopal

---

[50] Cf. Leo XIII, Encycl. *Satis cognitum.* 29 June 1896: ASS 28 (1895-96) p. 732.

[51] Cf. Council of Trent, Sess. 23, *Decr. de sacr. Ordinis,* cap. 4: Denz. 960 (1768); Vatican Council I, Sess. 4. Const. Dogm. 1 *De Ecclesia Christi,* cap. 3: Denz. 1828 (3061). Pius XII, Encycl. *Mystici Corporis,* 29 June 1943; AAS 35 (1943) pp. 209 and 212. *Code of Canon Law* [1917], c. 329 § 1.

[52] Cf. Leo XIII, Epist. *Et sane,* 17 Dec. 1888: ASS 21 (1888) p. 321 ff.

[53] Cf. St Leo the Great, *Serm.* 5, 3: PL 54, 154.

consecration.[54] It is the teaching of the sacred Council that the fullness of the sacrament of order is conferred by episcopal consecration,
for the episcopate is truly named, by the Church's liturgical custom
and the statements of the Fathers of the Church, the high priesthood,
the height of the sacred ministry.[55] Together with the office of sanctification, episcopal consecration confers the offices of teaching and
ruling; but they, of their nature, can only be exercised in hierarchical
communion with the head and members of the college. It is evident
from tradition—and this is expressed particularly in the liturgical rites
and practice of the Eastern and the Western Church—that, with the
imposition of hands and the words of consecration, the bestowal of
the grace of the Holy Spirit[56] and the imprint of the sacred character[57]
are such, that the Bishops sustain, eminently and patently, the role of
Christ himself, Master, Pastor and Pontiff, and act in his person.[58] It is
the function of the Bishops to raise to the episcopal body by means of
the sacrament of order the new men who have been elected.

The college of Bishops and their head

22. By the Lord's establishment, St Peter and the other apostles con-
stitute a single apostolic college. In like manner, the Roman Pontiff,
Peter's successor, and the Bishops, successors of the apostles, are linked

---

[54] COUNCIL OF TRENT, Sess. 23, cap. 3, quotes the words of 2 *Tim* 1: 6-7 to show that order is a true sacrament:
DENZ. 959 (1766).

[55] In *Trad. Apost.* 3, ed. BOTTE, *Sources Chr.*, pp. 27-30, a 'primacy of the priesthood' is attributed to the
Bishop. Cf. *Sacramentarium Leonianum*, ed. C. MOHLBERG, *Sacramentarium Veronense*, Rome, 1955, p. 119: 'to
the ministry of the high priesthood ... Make the height of your mystery complete in your priests' ... the
same point is made in *Liber Sacramentorum Romanae Ecclesiae*, Rome, 1960, pp. 121-122: 'Assign them the
episcopal throne, Lord, to rule your Church and all the people'. Cf. PL 78, 224.

[56] *Trad. Apost.* 2, ed. BOTTE, p. 27.

[57] COUNCIL OF TRENT, Sess. 23, cap. 4, teaches that the sacrament of order imprints an indelible character:
DENZ. 960 (1767). Cf. JOHN XXIII, Alloc. *Jubilate Deo*, 8 May 1960: AAS 52 (1960) p. 466. PAUL VI,
Homily in Vatican, 20 Oct. 1963: AAS 55 (1963), p. 1014.

[58] ST CYPRIAN, *Epist.* 63, 14: PL 4, 386; HARTEL, III B, p. 713: 'The priest truly performs in the place of
Christ'. ST JOHN CHRYSOSTOM, *in 2 Tim*, Hom. 2,4: PG 62, 612: The priest is 'symbolon' of Christ. ST AM-
BROSE, *in Ps.* 38, 25-26: PL 14,1051-52: CSEL 64, 203-204. AMBROSIASTER, *in 1 Tim.* 5, 19: PL 17, 479 C and
in Eph. 4:11-12: col. 387 C. THEODORE OF MOPS., *Hom. Catech.* XV, 21 and 24: ed. TONNEAU, pp. 497 and 503.
HESYCH. OF JERUS., *in Lev.* L. 2, 9, 23: PG 93, 894 B.

together. The collegiate character and nature of the episcopal order is indicated by the ancient practice whereby Bishops, established all over the world, maintained communion with each other and with the Roman Pontiff in the bond of unity, charity and peace;[59] indicated too by the assembling of Councils,[60] so that deeper matters could be decided in common,[61] and weight given to their decision by the deliberation of a greater number.[62] It receives manifest approval from the ecumenical Councils which have been held in the course of the centuries. It is shown too by the practice, dating back to antiquity, of summoning several Bishops to take part in the elevation of a Bishop-elect to the ministry of the high priesthood. A man is made a member of the episcopal body by dint of sacramental consecration and hierarchical communion with the head of the college and with its members.

The college or body of Bishops has no authority, if the meaning of the term excludes its connection with the Roman Pontiff, the successor of Peter, as its head, and unless the power of his primacy over all, pastors or faithful, be maintained in its entirety. In virtue of his office, as Vicar of Christ and Pastor of the whole Church, the Roman Pontiff possesses full, supreme, universal power over the Church, and he is always able to exercise it without impediment. The order of Bishops is the successor to the college of the apostles in magisterium and pastoral direction; or rather, in the episcopal order, the apostolic body is continuing without a break. Together with its head, the Roman Pontiff—and never without this head—it also exists as a subject of supreme, plenary power over the universal Church.[63] But this power cannot be exercised except with the agreement of the Roman Pontiff. It was Simon alone whom the Lord appointed as the rock and the key-bearer of the Church (cf. *Mt* 16:18-19). It was Simon whom he established

---

[59] Cf. EUSEBIUS, *Hist. Eccl.*, V. 24. 10: GCS II, 1, p. 495: ed. BARDY, *Sources Chr.* II, p. 69. DIONYSIUS, in EUSEBIUS, *ibid.* VII, 5, 2: GCS II. 2, p. 638 ff.: BARDY, II, p. 168 ff.

[60] Cf. EUSEBIUS, *Hist Eccl.,* concerning the ancient Councils, V. 23-24: GCS II, 1, p. 488 ff.; BARDY, II, p. 66 ff. *et passim.* COUNCIL OF NICAEA, Can. 5: *Conc. Oec. Decr.* p. 7.

[61] TERTULLIAN, *De Ieiunio,* 13: PL 2. 972 B; CSEL 20, p. 292. lin. 13-16.

[62] ST CYPRIAN, *Epist.* 56, 3: HARTEL, III B, p. 650; BAYARD, p. 154.

[63] Cf. ZINELLI's *Relatio* in VATICAN COUNCIL I: MANSI 52, 1109 C.

as pastor of his whole flock (cf. *Jn* 21:15 ff.). It is clear that this office of binding and loosing, given to Peter (*Mt* 16:19), was given also to the college of apostles in conjunction with its head (*Mt* 18:18; 28:16-20).[64] This college, in its multiple composition, is the expression of the variety and universality of the People of God; in its collection under one head, it expresses the unity of Christ's flock. In the college, Bishops, while they faithfully observe the primacy and leadership of their head, employ their own power for the good of their faithful, or rather, for the good of the whole Church, while the Holy Spirit continues to strengthen its organic structure and its harmony. The solemn exercise of the supreme power over the universal Church, which this college enjoys, takes place in an ecumenical Council. An ecumenical Council is never possible, if it has not been confirmed as such or at least accepted by Peter's successor. It is the prerogative of the Roman Pontiff to summon these Councils, to preside over them, to confirm them.[65] The exercise of this collegiate power in union with the Pope is possible although the Bishops are stationed all over the world, provided that the head of the college gives them a call to collegiate action, or, at least, gives the unified action of the scattered Bishops such approval, or such unconstrained acceptance, that it becomes truly collegiate action.

23. The collegiate bond can also be seen in the reciprocal relations of individual Bishops with particular Churches and with the universal Church. As Peter's successor, the Roman Pontiff is the perpetual, visible, fundamental principle of unity, both of the Bishops and of the multitude of the faithful.[66] Individual Bishops are the visible, fundamental principle of unity in their particular Churches.[67] These Churches are moulded to the likeness of the universal Church; in

---

[64] Cf. Vatican Council I, *Schema* of the dogm. Const. II, *De Ecclesia Christi*, c. 4: Mansi 53, 310. Cf. Kleutgen's *relatio* on the revised *Schema*: Mansi 53, 321 B-322 B and Zinelli's *declaratio:* Mansi 52, 1110 A. See also St Leo the Great, Serm. 4, 3: PL. 54, 151 A.

[65] Cf. Code of Canon Law, c. 227.

[66] Cf. Vatican Council I, Const. Dogm. *Pastor aeternus:* Denz. 1821 (3050 ff.).

[67] Cf. St Cyprian, *Epist.* 66, 8: Hartel III, 2, p. 733: 'The Bishop in the Church and the Church in the Bishop'.

them, and of them, consists the one, sole Catholic Church.[68] For this reason individual Bishops represent their own Church; all, together with the Pope, represent the whole Church linked by peace, love and unity.

Individual Bishops, set over particular Churches, exercise their pastoral control over the section of the People of God entrusted to them, not over other Churches, nor over the universal Church. But, as members of the episcopal college and lawful successors of the apostles, they have individually a concern for the universal Church. This concern is an obligation deriving from Christ's institution and precept;[69] it makes a supreme contribution to the benefit of the universal Church, even if it is not put into practice by active jurisdiction. All Bishops have to be promoters and guardians of the unity and discipline of the faith which is common to the whole Church. They must educate the faithful in the love of the whole Mystical Body of Christ, especially of its poor members, the suffering and those who are persecuted for righteousness' sake (cf. *Mt* 5:10). They must promote every activity which is common to the whole Church, especially the increase of faith and the rising of the light of the fullness of truth over all men. There is, too, the contribution of holiness which they make effectively to the good of the whole Mystical Body, which is the body of the Churches, by their good rule of their own Church as a section of the universal Church.[70]

The charge of proclaiming the gospel all over the world belongs to the body of Pastors. Christ gave the injunction to all of them in common, when he established a common office, as Pope Celestine pointed out to the Fathers of the Council of Ephesus.[71] As a result, individual Bishops, as far as the performance of their own duty allows, are obliged to unite in a fellowship of labour with each other, and

---

[68] Cf. St Cyprian, *Epist.* 55, 24: Hartel, p. 642, lin. 13: 'One Church through out the world divided into many members'. *Epist.* 36, 4: Hartel, p. 575. lin. 20-21.

[69] Cf. Pius XII, Encycl. *Fidei Donum,* 21 April 1957: ASS 49 (1957) p. 237.

[70] Cf. St Hilary of Poit., *in Ps.* 14, 3: PL 9, 206; CSEL 22, p. 86. St Gregory the Great, *Moral.* IV, 7, 12: PL 75, 643 C. Ps.-Basil, *in Is.* 15, 296: PG 30, 637 C.

[71] St Celestine, *Epist.* 18, 1-2, to the Council of Ephesus: PL 50, 505 AB; Schwartz, *Acta Conc. Oec.* I, 1, 1, p. 22. Cf. Benedict XV, Apost. Letter *Maximum illud:* AAS 11 (1919) p. 440. Pius XI Encycl. *Rerum, Ecclesiae,* 28 Feb. 1926: AAS 18 (1926) p. 69. Pius XII, Encycl. *Fidei Donum, loc. cit.*

with Peter's successor, who is entrusted in a unique fashion with the task of propagating the Christian name.[72] They must put all their strength into supplying the missions with harvesters, and with spiritual and material help as well, by their own direct efforts as much as by appeals to the faithful for ardent cooperation. Bishops must be willing, in a universal fellowship of charity, to offer the assistance of a brother to other Churches after the admirable example of antiquity, to neighbouring Churches particularly and to those in greater need.

It is by divine Providence that Churches, established in different places by the apostles, have come to form several groups with organic union. These groups, without prejudice to the unity of faith and the sole, divine constitution of the universal Church, enjoy their own discipline, their own liturgical practice and their own theological and spiritual heritage. Some of them, notably the ancient patriarchates, as mothers in the faith, have given birth to daughter Churches, with whom they are more closely bound up by ties of love and have retained to our own time their connection in sacramental life and in mutual respect for rights and duties.[73] This agreement in diversity on the part of local Churches is a brighter demonstration of the catholicity of the undivided Church. Similarly, episcopal conferences can nowadays contribute manifold and fruitful help towards the concrete application of the idea of collegiality.

The office of Bishop

24. All power in heaven and on earth is entrusted to the Lord; from him, the Bishops, as successors of the apostles, receive the mission of teaching all nations and preaching the gospel to the whole creation, to enable all men to attain salvation by faith, baptism and the fulfilment

---

[72] LEO XIII, Encycl. *Grande Munus.* 30 Sept. 1880: ASS 13 (1880) p. 145. Cf. Code of Canon Law, c. 1327; c. 1350 §2.
[73] On the rights of patriarchal Sees, cf. COUNCIL OF NICAEA, can. 6 concerning Alexandria and Antioch, can. 7 on Jerusalem: *Conc. Oec. Decr.*, p. 8. LATERAN COUNCIL IV in the year 1215, Constit.V: *De dignitate Patriarcharum: ibid.* p. 212. COUNCIL OF FERR.-FLORENCE: *ibid.* p. 504.

of the commandments (cf. *Mt* 28:18; *Mk* 16:15-16; *Acts* 26:17 ff.). For the accomplishment of this mission, Christ the Lord promised the apostles the Holy Spirit and sent him from heaven on the day of Pentecost; by the power of the Spirit, they were to be his witnesses before the Gentiles, nations and kings, to the end of the earth (cf. *Acts* 1:8; 2:1 ff.; 9:15). This office, entrusted by the Lord to the pastors of his people, is the genuine service to which, in sacred literature, is given the meaningful name of 'diakonia', or ministry (cf. *Acts* 1:17 and 25; 21:19; *Rom* 11:13; 1 *Tim* 1:12).

The mission of Bishops can come into being canonically by lawful custom, which the supreme, universal power of the Church has not revoked, by laws enacted or recognized by the same authority, or directly by the personal action of Peter's successor; but should he deny or refuse communion with the apostolic See, Bishops cannot be admitted to office.[74]

25. Outstanding among the foremost functions of Bishops, is the preaching of the gospel.[75] Bishops are heralds of the faith—they bring new disciples to Christ. They are authentic teachers, teachers authorized by Christ—they preach the faith to the people entrusted to them, for their belief and for application to morals; they clarify the faith in the light of the Holy Spirit, they bring out of the treasure of Revelation what is new and what is old (cf. *Mt* 13:52) and they make the faith bear fruit; they keep their flock from error by their watchful attention (cf. 2 *Tim* 4:1-4). When Bishops engage in teaching, in communion with the Roman Pontiff, they deserve respect from all, as the witnesses of divine, catholic truth; the faithful must agree with the judgment of their Bishop on faith and morals, which he delivers in the name of Christ; they must give it their adherence with religious

---

[74] Cf. Code of Canon Law for the Oriental Church, c. 216-314: on Patriarchs; c. 324-339: on major Archbishops; c. 362-391: on other dignitaries; in particular, c. 238 § 3; 216; 240; 251; 255: on the nomination of Bishops by the Patriarch.

[75] Cf. COUNCIL OF TRENT. Decr. de reform., Sess. V. c. 2, n. 9, and Sess. XXIV, can. 4; *Conc. Oec. Decr.* pp. 645 and 739.

allegiance of the mind. The offering of this religious allegiance of mind and will is singularly owed to the authentic magisterium of the Roman Pontiff, even when he is not speaking ex cathedra; it must be offered in such a way, that his supreme magisterium receives respectful acknowledgment. The result should be a sincere adherence to the judgments which he has delivered that complies with his manifest meaning and intention, and this is conveyed chiefly by the character of the documents, by the frequency with which the same teaching is put forward, or by the style of the utterance.

Individual Bishops do not enjoy the prerogative of infallibility. Nevertheless, when, in the course of their authentic teaching on faith or morals, they agree on a single opinion to be held as definitive, they are proclaiming infallibly the teaching of Christ. This happens when, though scattered throughout the world, they observe the bond of fellowship tying them to each other and to Peter's successor.[76] This occurs more obviously when, united in an ecumenical Council, they are the teachers and judges of faith and morals for the universal Church, and an obedient adherence must be given to their definitions of faith.[77]

The divine Redeemer wanted his Church to be equipped with this infallibility in the definition of doctrine on faith and morals. It is commensurate with the deposit of divine Revelation, which is to be sacredly guarded and faithfully expounded. In virtue of his office, the Roman Pontiff, head of the college of Bishops, enjoys this infallibility, when he makes a definitive pronouncement of doctrine on faith or morals, as the supreme pastor and teacher of all the faithful, who strengthens his brethren in faith (cf. *Lk* 22:32).[78] His definitions deserve, in consequence, to be called unalterable of themselves, and not by reason of the Church's agreement; for they are delivered with the Holy Spirit's assistance, which was promised to him in the person

---

[76] Cf. Vatican Council I, Const. dogm. *Dei Filius*, 3: Denz. 1712 (3011). Cf. the note added to Schema I *De Eccl.* (taken from St Rob. Bellarmine): Mansi 51, 579 C; also the revised Schema of Const. II *De Ecclesia Christi*, with Kleutgen's commentary: Mansi 53, 313 AB. Pius IX, Letter *Tuas libenter*: Denz. 1683 (2879).

[77] Cf. Code of Canon Law, c. 1322-1323.

[78] Cf. Vatican Council I, Const. dogm. *Pastor aeternus*: Denz. 1839 (3074).

of St Peter. Consequently they stand in no need of approval on the part of others, and they admit of no appeal to another court. On such occasions, the Roman Pontiff is not pronouncing judgment as a private person; but he is expounding or safeguarding the doctrine of the Catholic faith, as supreme master of the universal Church, in whom the Church's own charism of infallibility exists in a unique fashion.[79] The infallibility promised to the Church, exists also in the body of Bishops, when it exercises supreme magisterium in combination with Peter's successor. The assent of the Church can never fail to be given to these definitions, because of the action which the Holy Spirit takes to keep the whole flock of Christ in the unity of faith, and to make it advance.[80]

When either the Roman Pontiff, or the body of Bishops in conjunction with him, make a definitive statement, their pronouncement is made in relation to Revelation. Everyone is obliged to abide by Revelation and to be in conformity with it. In its written form and in tradition, Revelation is transmitted in its entirety by means of the lawful succession of Bishops, and in particular, through the care of the Roman Pontiff. In the light of the Spirit of truth Revelation is guarded in the Church as a sacred trust, and faithfully expounded.[81] The Roman Pontiff and the Bishops, in proportion to their office and the seriousness of the matter, expend their care and pains on submitting it to due scrutiny, and announcing it in a fitting manner, making use of suitable media.[82] They do not accept a new, public revelation as belonging to the divine deposit of faith.[83]

---

[79] Cf. GASSER's *explicatio* in VATICAN COUNCIL I: MANSI 52, 1213 AC.

[80] GASSER, *ibid.*: MANSI 1214 A.

[81] GASSER, *ibid.*: MANSI 1215 CD, 1216-1217 A.

[82] GASSER, *ibid.*: MANSI 1213.

[83] VATICAN COUNCIL I, Const. dogm. *Pastor aeternus*, 4: DENZ. 1836 (3070).

26. The Bishop, distinguished by the fullness of the sacrament of order, is 'the steward of the grace of the high priesthood'.[84] This is particularly the case with the Eucharist, which he offers himself, or whose offering is his concern,[85] and the Eucharist is the direct source of life and growth for the Church. This Church of Christ is truly present in all lawful, local congregations of the faithful. These congregations, in attachment to their pastors, themselves have the name of Churches in the New Testament.[86] They are, for their own locality, the new people called by God, in the Holy Spirit and with full conviction (cf. 1 *Thess* 1:5). In these Churches the faithful are gathered together by the preaching of Christ's gospel; in them, the mystery of the Lord's Supper is celebrated 'so that the whole brotherhood is linked by the flesh and blood of the Lord's body'.[87] Any fellowship of the altar, under the ministry of the Bishop,[88] is the setting in which the symbol is shown of that charity and 'that unity of the Mystical Body, without which salvation is impossible'.[89] Christ is present in these communities, though they are often small in number and resources, or widely dispersed, and by his power, the One, Holy, Catholic and Apostolic Church is drawn together;[90] for 'the precise effect of the sharing of Christ's body and blood, is that we pass over into what we are taking'.[91]

Every lawful celebration of the Eucharist is directed by the Bishop; for his is the commission to offer to the divine Majesty, and to administer, the worship of the christian religion, in accordance with the Lord's commands and the Church's laws, which receive further determination for the diocese from the Bishop's particular judgment.

---

[84] Prayer of episcopal consecration in the byzantine rite: *Euchologion to mega*, Rome, 1873, p. 139.
[85] Cf. St Ignatius, Martyr, *Smyrn.* 8, 1: ed. Funk, 1. p. 282.
[86] Cf. Acts 8:1; 14:22-23; 20:17 *et passim*.
[87] Mozarabic prayer: PL 96, 759 B.
[88] Cf. St Ignatius Martyr, *Smyrn.* 8, 1: ed. Funk, I, p. 282.
[89] St Thomas, *Summa Theol.,* III, q. 73, a. 3.
[90] Cf. St Augustine, *C. Faustum*, 12, 20: PL 42, 265; *Serm.* 57,7: PL 38, 389, etc.
[91] St Leo the Great, *Serm.* 63. 7: PL 54, 357 C.

Bishops, then, when they pray and toil for the people, bring about a manifold and abundant outpouring of the fullness of Christ's holiness. By the ministry of the word, they provide believers with God's strength for salvation (cf. *Rom* 1:16). By the sacraments—and Bishops arrange their regular, fruitful distribution on their own authority[92]—they sanctify the faithful. They control the bestowal of baptism, which grants a share in the kingly priesthood of Christ. They are the original ministers of confirmation, the dispensers of holy orders and the directors of the penitential discipline. Their solicitude makes them give their people exhortation and instruction to play their part with faithful reverence in the liturgy, and, in particular, in the sacred sacrifice of the Mass. Finally, they have to benefit those in their charge, by the example of their life, keeping their own behaviour clear of evil and as far as they can, by the help of God, converting it to good, so that they may reach everlasting life together with the flock entrusted to them.[93]

27. Bishops rule the particular Churches entrusted to them, as vicars and legates of Christ,[94] by counsel, persuasion, example; and also by authority and sacred power, which they only employ for the purpose of building up their flock in truth and holiness; for they are mindful that the greatest must become as the youngest, the leader as one who serves (cf. *Lk* 22:26-27). This power, which, in the name of Christ, they employ personally, is their own, it is ordinary, it is immediate, for all that its exercise is ultimately controlled by the supreme authority of the Church, and may be circumscribed within fixed limits, with a view to the Church's or the faithful's advantage. In virtue of this power, Bishops have the sacred right and duty before the Lord, of enacting laws for their subjects, passing judgment, and directing everything connected with the arrangement of worship and the apostolate.

---

[92] *Traditio Apostolica* of Hippolytus. 2-3: ed. BOTTE, pp. 26-30.
[93] Cf. the text of the *examen* at the beginning of the consecration of Bishops, and the *Prayer* at the end of the Mass of the same consecration, after the *Te Deum*.
[94] BENEDICT XIV Br. *Romana Ecclesia*, 5 Oct. 1752, § 1: *Bullarium Benedicti XIV*, t. IV, Rome, 1758, 21: 'A Bishop bears the likeness of Christ, it is his office that he is performing'. PIUS XII, Encycl. *Mystici Corporis, loc. cit.*, p. 211: 'They feed and rule the flocks assigned to each individually'.

They are fully committed to a pastoral office, that is to say, to the habitual daily care of their sheep. They are not to be thought of as vicars of the Roman Pontiffs, because the power which they wield is their own, and they are truly called 'Antistites'—Presidents—of the peoples they rule.[95] Their power is not eliminated by the supreme, universal power; on the contrary, it receives from it assertion, strength and vindication,[96] since the Holy Spirit unfailingly preserves the form of government that Christ the Lord established in his Church.

Commissioned by the Father to govern his household, the Bishop must keep before his eyes the example of the Good Shepherd, who comes not to be served but to serve (cf. *Mt* 20:28; *Mk* 10:45), and to lay down his life for his sheep (cf. *Jn* 10:11). Chosen from among men and beset with weakness, he can deal gently with the ignorant and the wayward (cf. *Heb* 5:1-2). He must not refuse to listen to his subjects, whom he cherishes as true sons and encourages to cheerful co-operation with him. He is to give an account to God of their souls (cf. *Heb* 13:17). He must take care of them by prayer, preaching and every charitable endeavour; and not only of them, but of those too, who are not yet of the one flock, but whom he must consider as entrusted to him by the Lord. Since, like the Apostle Paul, he is under obligation to everyone, he must be eager to preach the gospel to all (cf. *Rom* 1:14-15), and encourage his faithful to apostolic and missionary activity. The faithful must cleave to their Bishop as the Church does to Jesus Christ, and Jesus Christ to the Father, so that they may have general agreement through unity[97] and may increase to the glory of God (cf. 2 *Cor* 4:15).

---

[95] Leo XIII, Encycl. *Satis cognitum*, 29 June 1896: ASS 28 (1895-96) p. 732; Letter *Officio sanctissimo*, 22 Dec. 1887: ASS 20 (1887) p. 264. Pius IX Apost. Letter to Bishops of Germany, 12 March 1875 and Consist. Alloc., 15 March 1875: Denz. 3112-3117, only in new edition.

[96] Vatican Council I, Dogm. Const. *Pastor aeternus*, 3: Denz. 1828 (3061). Cf. Zinelli's *relatio*: Mansi 42, 1114 D.

[97] Cf. St Ignatius, Martyr, *Ad Ephes.* 5,1: ed. Funk, I, p. 216.

The ministers in the Church

28. The Father sanctified Christ and sent him into the world (*Jn* 10:36). Christ, by the agency of his apostles, has made their successors, the Bishops, have a share in his consecration and mission;[98] they, in turn, have lawfully handed on the office of their ministry, in varying degree, to various subjects in the Church. In this way the divinely instituted ministry of the Church is practised in different orders by men who, from ancient times, have had the names of Bishops, Priests and Deacons.[99] Priests do not possess the high dignity of the pontificate; they are dependent on Bishops for the exercise of their power. They are nevertheless united with them in priestly honour.[100] In virtue of the sacrament of order,[101] they are consecrated, in the likeness of Christ, high and eternal priest (*Heb* 5:1-10; 7:24; 9:11-28), as genuine priests of the New Testament,[102] for the work of preaching the gospel, tending the faithful and celebrating divine worship. They do share, at their own level of the ministry, the office of Christ, the sole mediator (1 *Tim* 2:5) and they proclaim the divine word to all. Their mightiest exercise of their sacred office is at the eucharistic worship or assembly. There, acting in the person of Christ,[103] they make the proclamation of his mystery; they unite the aspirations of the faithful to the sacrifice of their head; in the sacrifice of the Mass, until the coming of the Lord (cf. 1 *Cor* 11:26), they present and apply the sole sacrifice of the New Testament, the single offering Christ makes of himself as an unblemished victim to the Father[104] (cf. *Heb* 9:11-28). The ministration of

---

[98] Cf. St Ignatius, Martyr, *Ad Ephes.* 6, 1: ed. Funk, I, p. 218.

[99] Cf. Council of Trent, Sess. 23, *De sacr. Ordinis*, cap. 2: Denz. 958 (1765), and can. 6: Denz. 966 (1776).

[100] Cf. Innocent I, *Epist. ad Decentium:* PL 20, 554 A; Mansi 3, 1029; Denz. 98 (215): 'Presbyters, although they are priests of the second rank, do not possess the *high degree* of the pontificate'. St Cyprian, *Epist.* 61, 3: ed. Hartel, p. 696.

[101] Cf. Council of Trent, loc. cit., Denz. 956a-968 (1763-1778), and specifically can. 7: Denz. 967 (1777). Pius XII, Const. Apost. *Sacramentum Ordinis:* Denz. 2301 (3857-61).

[102] Cf. Innocent I, loc. cit. St Gregory Naz., Apol. II, 22: PG 35, 432 B. Ps.-Dionysius, *Eccl. Hier.*, 1, 2: PG 3, 372 D.

[103] Cf. Council of Trent, Sess. 22: Denz. 940 (1743). Pius XII, Encycl. *Mediator Dei,* 20 Nov. 1947: AAS 39 (1947) p. 553; Denz. 2300 (3850).

[104] Cf. Council of Trent, Sess. 22: Denz. 938 (1739-40). Vatican Council II, Const. *De Sacra Liturgia*, n. 7 and n. 47.

reconciliation and relief is their high function on behalf of penitent or sick faithful. They convey the needs of the faithful and their prayers to God the Father (cf. *Heb* 5:1-4). Their exercise of the office of Christ, Pastor and Head, is proportionate to their share in authority.[105] It consists in gathering together the household of God as a brotherhood with a single mind[106] and bringing it through Christ, in the Spirit, to God the Father. In the midst of their flock they worship him in spirit and truth (cf. *Jn* 4:24). In conclusion, they labour in preaching and teaching (cf. 1 *Tim* 5:17); they believe what they have read and pondered in the law of the Lord; they teach what they have come to believe; whatever they teach, they practise.[107]

Priests, as prudent co-operators of the episcopal order,[108] its help, its instrument, are called to the service of the People of God. They make a single priesthood[109] with their Bishop, though there is a difference in the duties by which it is carried into effect. They render the Bishop present, in a way, in individual local communities. Their association with him is marked by confidence and generosity. To the best of their ability they shoulder his tasks and anxiety and make the exercise of them their own daily care. Under the authority in the Bishop, they sanctify the part of the Lord's flock ascribed to them and govern it, they enable the universal Church to be seen in their locality, and they lend stout help in the building up of the whole Body of Christ (cf. *Eph* 4:12). They must always be attentive to the good of the children of God and ready to contribute their exertions to the pastoral work of the whole diocese, or rather, of the whole Church. Because of this share that they have in his priesthood and mission, priests must recognize the Bishop truly as their father and show him respect and obedience. The Bishop, in turn, must regard the priests who work with him as his sons and friends, in the same way that Christ calls his disciples

---

[105] Cf. Pius XII, Encycl. *Mediator Dei, loc. cit.*, under n. 67.

[106] Cf. St Cyprian, *Epist.* 11, 3: PL 4, 242 B; Hartel, II, 2, p. 497.

[107] *Order of priestly consecration*, at the clothing with the vestments.

[108] *Order of priestly consecration*, the Preface.

[109] Cf. St Ignatius, Martyr, *Philad.* 4: ed. Funk, I, p. 266. St Cornelius I, in St Cyprian, *Epist.* 48, 2: Hartel, III, 2, p. 610.

servants no longer, but friends (cf. *Jn* 15:15). By reason of order and ministry, all priests, diocesan and religious as well, are attached to the body of Bishops and serve the good of the whole Church according to the demands of their vocation and grace.

In virtue of the sacred ordination and mission which they have in common, all priests are bound together in the intimacy of brotherhood, which should be spontaneously and cheerfully demonstrated in mutual help, spiritual and material alike, pastoral and personal; shown too in reunions and a fellowship of life, work and charity.

They must, like fathers in Christ, take care of the faithful, by baptism and instruction (cf. 1 *Cor* 4:15; 1 *Pet* 1:23). Being examples to the flock (1 *Pet* 5:3) they must take charge of their local community and serve it in such a way that it may deserve to be given the title of the Church of God (cf. 1 *Cor* 1:2; 2 *Cor* 1:1 *et passim*), which is the title that distinguishes the one People of God in its entirety. They must be mindful of their obligation truly to show the face of the priest's and pastor's ministry to believers and unbelievers, to Catholics and non-Catholics, by their daily life and care; to bear witness to all of truth and life; as good shepherds, to search out even those (cf. *Lk* 15:4-7), who after baptism in the Catholic Church have fallen away from sacramental practice, or, worse still, from belief.

The human race is uniting more and more nowadays on a civic, economic and social basis. It is all the more necessary, therefore, that priests combine their responsibility and their resources, under guidance of the Bishops and the Supreme Pontiff, to eliminate every form of separation, so that the whole human race may be brought into the unity of God's family.

29. On a lower level of the hierarchy are situated the deacons: hands are laid on them 'not for the priesthood, but for the ministry'.[110] With the strength of sacramental grace they serve the People of God, in

---

[110] *Constitutions of the Egyptian Church,* III, 2: ed. FUNK, *Didascalia,* II, p. 103. *Statuta Eccl. Ant.* 37-41: MANSI 3, 954.

fellowship with the Bishop and his body of priests, in the service of the liturgy, the word and charity. The function of the deacon is proportionate to the assignment granted him by the competent authority. It consists in the solemn administration of baptism, the reservation and distribution of the Eucharist, being in attendance in the Church's name and giving the blessing at matrimony, taking viaticum to the dying, reading the sacred Scripture to the faithful, giving the people instruction and exhortation, presiding over the faithful's worship and prayer, the administration of sacramentals, taking charge of funeral and burial rites. In their devotion to the duties of charity and administration, deacons must remember the advice of St Polycarp: 'Men of mercy and industry, proceeding in accordance with the truth of the Lord, who became the servant of all'.[111]

These functions are supremely necessary to the life of the Church, but, in the discipline of the Latin Church now in force, it is difficult for them to be fulfilled in many districts. For this reason, it is to be possible, for the future, for the diaconate to be restored as a proper and permanent grade of the hierarchy. It is for the competent regional conferences of Bishops, which vary in kind, to decide, with the personal approval of the Supreme Pontiff, whether it is opportune to have deacons of this kind appointed for the care of souls and exactly where. With the Roman Pontiff's consent it will be possible for this diaconate to be conferred on older men, even if they are living in matrimony, and on younger men of the right sort too, but in their case the law of celibacy must remain in force.

---

[111] St Polycarp, *Ad Phil.* 5, 2: ed. Funk, I, p. 300: It is said that Christ 'became the "diaconus" of all'. Cf. *Didachè*, 15, 1: *ibid.*, p. 32. St Ignatius, Martyr, *Trall.* 2, 3: *ibid.*, p. 242. *Constitutiones Apostolorum* 8, 28, 4: ed. Funk, *Didascalia*, I, p. 530.

CHAPTER IV

THE LAITY

30. After its declaration of the duties of the Hierarchy, the sacred Council is glad to turn its attention to the status of the members of Christ's faithful who are called the laity. All the statements it made about the People of God are directed equally to layfolk, religious, and clerics. Nevertheless a number of these statements have special reference to the laity, men and women, in view of their situation and their mission. The special circumstances of our time demand that these statements receive further basic consideration. The sacred Pastors are well aware of the great contribution layfolk make to the good of the whole Church. They are aware that they were not instituted by Christ to take on themselves in isolation the whole of the Church's mission of salvation to the world. They know on the contrary that it is their glorious task so to tend the faithful, so to appreciate their services and spiritual gifts, as to secure the unanimous co-operation of everyone in his own way in the common task. It is required that all of us, 'speaking the truth in love, are to grow up in every way into him who is the head, into Christ, from whom the whole body, joined and knit together by every joint with which it is supplied, when each part is working properly, makes bodily growth and upbuilds itself in love' (*Eph* 4:15-16).

What constitutes the laity

31. The title of layfolk in this context embraces all of Christ's faithful apart from members of the sacred order and those in the religious state which has the Church's approval. It embraces the members of Christ's faithful who are engaged, in the Church and in the world, in their allotted role in the mission of the whole christian people, because they have been incorporated in Christ by baptism, established in the People of God and have their own way of sharing the priestly, prophetic and kingly office of Christ.

Layfolk have their own special, secular character. Members of the sacred order may at times be involved in worldly matters, may even practise a worldly profession, nevertheless, by reason of their particular vocation, they are orientated chiefly and expressly to the sacred ministry. Religious by their state of life bear a glorious and remarkable witness to the truth that it is impossible for the world to be transformed and offered to God without the spirit of the beatitudes. The duty of the laity, which springs from their own vocation, is to seek the kingdom of God in the transaction of worldly business and the godly arrangement they give it. Their life is lived in the world. It is lived in each and all of the world's occupations and employments and in the ordinary situations of the life of the family and society. This is the context of their existence. This is where they have their call from God to make their contribution to the sanctification of the world from the inside, as a leaven, by tackling their own job with the spirit of the gospel as their guide. This is the principal way in which Christ is to be shown to others, by their life's witness, in the glow of their faith, their hope and their charity. It is their especial concern to bring such light and order to all worldly business, in which they are deeply involved, that it may be performed and developed in Christ's way, and may give glory to the Creator and the Redeemer.

32. As a result of its divine institution, the holy Church is remarkably varied in its order and government. 'As in one body we have many members, and all the members do not have the same function, so we, though many, are one body in Christ, and individually members one of another' (*Rom* 12:4-5).

There is then one chosen People of God: 'one Lord, one faith, one baptism' (*Eph* 4:5); the dignity the members have from their rebirth in Christ is common to all, so too is the grace of sonship, and the call to perfection; their salvation is the same, their hope is the same, and there is no division in charity. There is no room in Christ and in the Church for inequality on the grounds of race, nationality, social status or sex;

for 'there is neither Jew nor Greek, there is neither slave nor free, there is neither male nor female; for you are all one in Christ Jesus' (*Gal* 3:28; cf. *Col* 3:11).

In the Church we do not all walk the same path, yet we are all called to holiness and we have obtained a faith of equal standing in the righteousness of God (cf. 2 *Pet* 1:1). A certain number are appointed by Christ's will as teachers, stewards of the mysteries and pastors for the sake of the others, yet all are on a truly equal footing when it comes to the dignity and action common to all the faithful with regard to the building of Christ's Body. The very distinction the Lord has made between the sacred ministers and the rest of God's People involves a connection, since Pastors and the rest of the faithful are bound together by their common obligation: the Church's Pastors must follow the example of the Lord and render service to each other and to the rest of the faithful; the faithful have to be ready to offer their associated effort to the Pastors and teachers. All in this way bear witness in their variety to the remarkable unity in the Body of Christ. The very diversity of gifts, of service, of working, makes a single body of the sons of God, for 'all these are inspired by one and the same Spirit' (1 *Cor* 12:11).

As a result of God's goodness, the laity have Christ for their brother: for, though he is Lord of all, he did not come to be served, but to serve (cf. *Mt* 20:28). Just so, they have for brothers too the men who are appointed to the sacred ministry, the men who exercise such pastoral care that the new commandment of charity is carried out by all; this they do by teaching, sanctifying, governing the household of God with Christ's authorization. St Augustine has a splendid comment on this relationship: 'If my belonging to you frightens me, my being with you brings consolation. I belong to you as bishop, I am with you as a Christian. The first title represents a duty, the second a favour; the first represents a risk, the second, salvation.[112]

---

[112] St Augustine, *Serm.* 340. 1: PL 38, 1483.

33. The laity are assembled in the People of God, and established under one head in the single Body of Christ. They have the vocation, whoever they are, to contribute, as living members, to the growth of the Church and its continual sanctification, all the strength they have received from the kindness of the Creator and from the Redeemer's grace.

The apostolate of the laity is a share in the Church's mission of salvation. By baptism and confirmation all are assigned to this apostolate by the Lord himself. The life of the apostolate is charity towards God and man; it is communicated and nourished by the sacraments, especially by the holy Eucharist. The specific vocation of the laity is to make the Church actively present in those places and situations where the very salt of the earth can only be spread by their efforts.[113] Thus, by reason of the gifts given him, the existence of every layman is at the same time a witness and a living instrument of the Church's mission 'according to the measure of Christ's gift' (*Eph* 4:7).

This apostolate is the concern of all Christ's faithful without exception. There are, further, different ways in which layfolk may receive a call to a more direct co-operation with the apostolate of the Hierarchy,[114] after the fashion of the men and women who worked for the gospel at the side of the Apostle Paul, working hard for the Lord (cf. *Phil* 4:3; *Rom* 16:3 ff.). In addition, they are capable of being assigned by the Hierarchy to certain ecclesiastical offices, the performance of which has a spiritual object in view.

On all the laity, then, falls the glorious burden of toiling to bring the divine offer of salvation ever more and more into the reach of all men of all times and all over the world. They must have every path opened to a whole-hearted personal participation, as their strength and the needs of the time allow, in the saving work of the Church.

---

[113] Cf. Pius XI, Encyclical *Quadragesimo anno*, 15 May 1931: AAS 23 (1931) p. 221 ff. Pius XII, Alloc. *De quelle consolation*, 14 Oct. 1951: AAS 43 (1951) p. 790 ff.

[114] Cf. Pius XII, Alloc. *Six ans se sont écoulés*, 5 Oct. 1957: AAS 49 (1957) p. 927.

The layman's task

34. Christ is the supreme and everlasting Priest. It is his will that lay-folk too should be the agents whereby his witness and his service are maintained. For this reason he gives them life by his Spirit and an unfailing impetus to every good and perfect work.

He gives them an intimate association with his life and mission he also gives them a share in his priestly office for the performance of spiritual worship, so that God may have glory, and men salvation. This is the reason that layfolk, since Christ has consecrated and the Spirit anointed them, have their marvellous vocation and equipment so that the fruits of the Spirit may be produced in them in ever greater abundance. All their activity is turned into spiritual sacrifices acceptable to God through Jesus Christ (cf. 1 *Pet* 2:5). Their apostolic works, prayers and undertakings, their married life, their family life, their daily work, their mental and physical recreation, if it is taken in the Spirit, even life's troubles, if they are borne with patience—they are all offered with great piety to the Father, with the offering of the Lord's body in the celebration of the Eucharist. This is the way in which the laity too consecrate the world to God by their holy action as worshippers in all parts of the world.

35. Christ is the great prophet who has issued the proclamation of his Father's kingdom by his life's witness and the power of his word. The Hierarchy teaches in his name and by his power, but it is not the only agency through which he performs his prophetic task until the full manifestation of glory. He uses the laity too, and therefore he appoints them as witnesses and equips them with the discernment of faith and the grace of speech (cf. *Acts* 2:17-18; *Apoc* 19:10). He wants the power of the gospel to shine through their daily life in the family and in society. They show themselves as sons of the promise, if they make the most of the present moment with strong faith and hope (cf. *Eph* 5:16; *Col* 4:5), and if they wait with patience for the glory that is to come (cf. *Rom* 8:25). This hope must not be buried in the recesses of their

heart, it must find expression in the framework of their secular life through their continual conversion and struggle 'against the world rulers of the present darkness, against the spiritual hosts of wickedness' (*Eph* 6:12).

The sacraments of the New Law are the food of the life and apostolate of the faithful, and they foreshadow the new heaven and the new earth (cf. *Rev* 21:1). Just so, the laity go out as stout heralds of faith in things we must hope for (cf. *Heb* 11:1), if they do not shrink from combining a declaration of faith with a life based on faith. This evangelization is the pronouncement of Christ's message by life's witness and by speech. It acquires a specific characteristic and a particular effectiveness from the fact that it is carried out in ordinary worldly situations.

In this prophetic office great value is clearly attached to the state of life which is sanctified by a special sacrament—the life of marriage and of the family. It is the glorious training school of the apostolate of the laity, for there the whole arrangement of life is pervaded by the Christian religion, and undergoes daily a greater transformation. There the married have their own vocation: they must be witnesses to each other and to their children of the faith and of the love of Christ. The Christian family makes a loud proclamation of the present virtues of the kingdom of God and of hope in a life of blessedness. In this way, by the example it gives and the witness it bears, it convicts the world of sin and brings light to men in search of truth.

Consequently layfolk have the ability and the obligation to engage in valuable activity for the evangelization of the world, even when they are busy with worldly occupations. A number of them, when sacred ministers are lacking, or obstructed under a persecuting government, supply certain sacred duties to the best of their ability. A greater number expend all their efforts in apostolic work. It is still necessary for all the laity to co-operate towards the spread and increase of Christ's kingdom. Because of this, layfolk ought to apply their skill to deepening their understanding of revealed truth, and to win from God by urgent prayer the gift of wisdom.

36. Christ became obedient unto death and therefore God has highly exalted him (cf. *Phil* 2:8-9). He has entered the glory of his kingdom. All things are in process of being made subject to him, until he shall make himself, and all created things, subject to the Father, so that God may be everything in everyone (cf. 1 *Cor* 15:27-28). He has imparted this authority of his to his disciples so that they too may be set in a royal freedom, may overpower the reign of sin in themselves (cf. *Rom* 6:12), by self-denial and a life of holiness; or rather, so that they may serve Christ in others, and by their humility and their patience bring their brethren to the King, to serve whom is to have a kingdom. The Lord wants his kingdom to spread by the efforts of the faithful laity. It is the kingdom of truth, of life, the kingdom of holiness and grace, the kingdom of justice, love, peace.[115] It is the kingdom in which the creation itself will be set free from its bondage to decay and obtain the glorious liberty of the children of God (cf. *Rom* 8:21). It is a great promise that is given to the disciples, a great commandment: 'All things are yours; and you are Christ's; and Christ is God's' (1 *Cor* 3:23).

There is an obligation on the faithful to recognize the inner nature of the whole of creation, its value, its orientation to the praise of God. They must help each other to greater holiness of life even by means of their secular occupations. The result to be achieved is the drenching of the world in the spirit of Christ, the surer attainment of its goal through justice, charity and peace. The chief position in the wholesale fulfilment of this duty is held by the laity. Their competence in the secular sphere and their activity have been raised intrinsically by grace to a higher level. By these means they must make vigorous efforts to see that the resources of human labour, technology, civilization, are deployed in accordance with the Creator's plan and the light shed by his Word. In this case all men without exception will benefit from the cultivation of the goods of creation, these things will be more equitably distributed and will make their own contribution to universal progress in human and christian freedom. In this way Christ will use

---

[115] From the *Preface* of the Feast of Christ the King.

the members of the Church to increase the shining of his saving light over the whole of human society.

Moreover, where there is customary encouragement to sin, layfolk must use their strength to make the world's standards and conditions sound, to bring them all into conformity with the norms of justice, to the support and not the obstruction of the practice of the virtues. By such action they will steep human culture and activity in moral value. This is the way in which the field, which is the world, is better prepared for the seed, which is the divine word, and the gates of the Church opened wider to enable the preaching of peace to make its entry into the world.

The economy of salvation demands that the faithful should learn to make a careful distinction between the rights and duties they have undertaken as members of the Church's flock, and those which belong to them as members of human society. They must make efforts to harmonize both sets of rights and duties, bearing in mind that they must be guided by the Christian conscience, no matter what the temporal activity in which they are involved, for not even in temporal business can any human activity be removed from God's control. In our day there is the greatest need that this distinction and this harmony should be seen in the clearest possible light in the manner in which the faithful act, if the Church's mission is to be able more fully to correspond to the special conditions of the world today. While it must be recognized that the State which is rightly devoted to secular care has its own principles of government, it is right to reject the disastrous doctrine which strives to construct society without taking any account of religion, and which impugns the religious liberty of citizens and destroys it.[116]

---

[116] Cf. Leo XIII, Encycl. *Immortale Dei*, 1 Nov. 1885: ASS 18 (1885) p. 166 ff. Encycl. *Sapientiae christianae*, 10 Jan. 1890: ASS 22 (1889-90) p. 397 ff. Pius XII Alloc. *Alla vostra filiale*, 23 March 1958: AAS 50 (1958) p. 220: '*la legittima sana Iaicità dello Stato*'.

The laity and the hierarchy

37. The laity, as indeed all of Christ's faithful, have the right to receive abundant help from the sacred Pastors from the spiritual benefits of the Church, especially the help of the word of God and the sacraments.[117] They have the right too of making known to the sacred Pastors their needs and desires with the confident liberty which suits them as children of God and brothers in Christ. Their powers of knowledge, competence, position, give them the proportionate means, or rather duty, at times, of making known their opinion on matters which envisage the good of the Church.[118] It should be done, if the case allows, through the channels established by the Church for this purpose. It should be done in every case in a spirit of sincerity, courage and prudence, combined with a respectful charity towards the men who sustain the role of Christ by reason of their sacred office.

The laity, as indeed all of Christ's faithful, should be prompt to welcome in a spirit of Christian obedience the decisions the sacred Pastors make as leaders and directors in the Church, for they are the representatives of Christ. They must follow in this the example of Christ: he opened to all men the blessed road to the liberty enjoyed by the sons of God, by an obedience which brought him to death. They should not forget to recommend to God in their prayers those who have charge of them, for they are keeping watch as men who will have to give account for our souls. The laity's prayer should be that they may do this joyfully, and not sadly (cf. *Heb* 13:17).

Sacred Pastors must acknowledge and advance the dignity and responsibility of the laity in the Church. They must be willing to make use of their prudent advice, confidently to entrust them with functions in the service of the Church, to leave them freedom and scope for action; better still, to give them heart to approach the work of their own accord. With the love of a father they should give considerate

---

[117] Code of Canon Law, can. 682.
[118] Cf. Pius XII, Alloc *De quelle consolation*, 1.c., p. 789: 'In decisive battles, the happiest initiatives sometimes come from the front line ...' Alloc. *L'importance de la presse catholique*, 17 Feb. 1950: AAS 42 (1950) p. 256.

attention in Christ to the undertakings, the wishes, the wants the laity put before them.[119] Pastors will be on the watch to acknowledge the freedom which is everyone's due in the earthly city.

Many good results for the Church may be expected from this familiar exchange between layfolk and Pastors. On the side of the laity, this is the way to strengthen a sense of responsibility, to encourage alacrity, to facilitate the association of the laity's strength with the work of the Pastors. With the help of the laity's experience, Pastors are able to make clearer and more appropriate judgments in spiritual and temporal matters alike, and so the whole Church may draw strength from all its members for the more effective accomplishment of its mission for the life of the world.

38. Each individual layman has an obligation to be a witness before the world to the resurrection and life of the Lord Jesus, and a sign of the living God. All of them together and each for his part has an obligation to feed the world on the fruits of the Spirit (cf. *Gal* 5:22) and to spread in the world the spirit which is the life of the poor, the patient, the peacemakers, whom the Lord declared blessed in the gospel (cf. *Mt* 5:3-9). In a word, 'Christians must be in the world what the soul is in the body'.[120]

---

[119] Cf. 1 *Thess* 5:19; 1 *Jn* 4:1.
[120] *Epist. ad Diognetum*, 6: ed. FUNK, I, p. 400. Cf. ST JOHN CHRYSOSTOM *in Mt.* Hom. 46 (47), 2: PG 58, 478, on the leaven in the Mass.

Chapter V

THE UNIVERSAL VOCATION TO HOLINESS
IN THE CHURCH

39. The mystery of the Church is the subject matter of the sacred Council's present statements, and her unfailing holiness is part of our belief. Christ is the Son of God. Together with the Father and the Spirit he is acclaimed as 'uniquely Holy'.[121] He showed love for the Church as his bride, when he gave himself up for her, that he might sanctify her (cf. *Eph* 5:25-26); he joined her to himself as his body; he crowned her with the gift of the Holy Spirit; all this for the glory of God. Consequently all in the Church, whether they belong to the hierarchy or are under its pastoral care, have a vocation to holiness according to the Apostle's statement: 'This is the will of God, your sanctification' (1 *Thess* 4:3; cf. *Eph* 1:4). The holiness of the Church is shown continuously, it must be shown, in the harvest of grace which the Spirit brings forth in the faithful. It has many forms of expression among individuals, who so order their lives that they strengthen others and make the perfection of charity their aim. It is seen in a distinctive way in the practice of the counsels which have come to be called evangelical. This practice of the counsels is adopted, under the impetus of the Holy Spirit, by many Christians. Whether they do so in private life or in a condition or state which has the Church's authorization, it produces, and must produce, a glorious witness in the world to this holiness and a glorious example.

40. The Lord Jesus is the divine master and exemplar of all perfection. It is he who initiates and he who puts the finishing touches to holiness of life. He preached it to each and all of his disciples, no matter what their rank: 'You, therefore, must be perfect, as your heavenly father

---

[121] Roman Missal, *Gloria in excelsis*. Cf. *Lk* 1:35; *Mk* 1:24; *Lk* 4:34; *Jn* 6:69 (*ho hagious tou Theou*); *Acts* 3:14; 4:27 and 30; *Heb* 7:26; 1 *Jn* 2:20; *Rev* 3:7.

is perfect' (*Mt* 5:48).[122] He sent them all the Holy Spirit to stir them from within to love God with all their heart, all their soul, all their mind, and with all their strength (cf. *Mk* 12:30) and to love one another even as Christ has loved them (cf. *Jn* 13:34; 15:12). The followers of Christ have received their vocation from God not for their achievements but in accordance with his plan and his grace; they have been justified in the Lord Jesus; in the baptism of faith they have been made sons of God and partakers of the divine nature, and thereby saints in very truth. They are obliged consequently to retain the holiness they have received as God's gift in the life they lead, to bring it to perfection. They are advised by the Apostle to live 'as is fitting among saints' (*Eph* 5:3); 'as God's chosen ones, holy and beloved', to put on 'compassion, kindness, lowliness, meekness and patience' (*Col* 3:12); to possess the fruit of the Spirit for sanctification (cf. *Gal* 5:22; *Rom* 6:22). Since we all commit many faults (cf. *Jas* 3:2), we have a continual need of the mercy of God; our daily prayer must be: 'And forgive us our trespasses' (*Mt* 6:12).[123]

It is obvious then to all that all of Christ's faithful, no matter what their rank or station, have a vocation to the fullness of the christian life and the perfection of charity[124] and that this sanctity results in the promotion of a more humane way of life even in society on earth. The faithful must exert all the strength they have received, in the measure in which Christ makes his gift, so that they may acquire this perfection. They must follow Christ's footsteps, be moulded to his likeness, be attentive to the will of the Father in all things, be whole-heartedly devoted to the glory of God and the service of their neighbour. This is the way in which an abundant harvest will grow from the holiness of God's People, as is shown brilliantly in the history of the Church by the lives of so many saints.

---

[122] Cf. Origen. *Comm. Rom.* 7, 7: PG 14. 1122 B. Ps.-Macarius, *De Oratione*, II: PG 34. 861 AB. St Thomas. *Summa Theol.* II-II, q. 184, a. 3.

[123] Cf. St Augustine, *Retract.* II, 18: PL 32, 637 ff. Pius XII, Encycl. *Mystici Corporis*, 29 June 1943: AAS 35 (1943) p. 225.

[124] Cf. Pius XI, Encycl. *Rerum omnium*, 26 Jan. 1923: AAS 15 (1923) p. 50 and pp. 59-60. Encycl. *Casti Connubii*, 31 Dec. 1930: AAS 22 (1930) p. 548. Pius XII, Apostolic Constitution *Provida Mater*, 2 Feb. 1947: AAS 39 (1947) p. 117. Allocution *Annus sacer,* 8 Dec. 1950: AAS 43 (1951) pp. 27-28. Allocution *Nel darvi*, 1 July 1956: AAS 48 (1956) p. 574 ff.

The various ways of practising holiness

41. Though there are different ways of life and different duties, it is the same holiness which is cultivated by all who are led by God's Spirit, obey the Father's voice, adore God the Father in spirit and in truth, follow Christ in his poverty, his humility, his shouldering of the cross, and so earn a share in his glory. Each man, according to his gifts, his duties, must tread without hesitation the path of a lively faith, and a lively faith awakens hope and is set to work by charity.

For the Pastors of Christ's flock the chief obligation is holiness, promptness, humility and courage in carrying out their service, in the likeness of the supreme, eternal Priest, Pastor and Bishop of our souls. Such a fulfilment of their ministry will be an excellent means of sanctifying themselves. They have been selected for the fullness of the priesthood, endowed with the grace of the sacrament to enable them to pray, sacrifice, preach and so perform to perfection their office of pastoral charity by episcopal care and service of every form.[125] They must not be afraid to lay down their life for their sheep. They must be examples to the flock (cf. 1 *Pet* 5:3) and encourage the Church to a holiness which increases day by day.

Priests make up the Bishops' spiritual crown;[126] they have a share in their grace of office through Christ, the eternal, sole mediator. After the fashion of the episcopal order, they must grow in love of God and their neighbour by means of their daily performance of their duty. They must safeguard the bond of priestly fellowship, must overflow in all spiritual good, must present all men with a living witness to God,[127] must rival the priests who in the course of the centuries have bequeathed a glorious pattern of holiness in a service which was frequently lowly and hidden. Theirs is the glory in God's Church. They

---

[125] Cf. St Thomas, *Summa Theol.* II-II, q. 184, a. 5 and 6. *De perf. vitae spir.*, c. 18. Origen, *in Is.* Hom. 6, 1: PG 13, 239.

[126] Cf. St Ignatius, Martyr, *Magn.* 13, 1: ed. Funk, I, p. 241.

[127] Cf. St Pius X, Exhortation *Haerent animo*, 4 Aug. 1908: ASS 41 (1908) p. 560 ff. Code of Canon Law, can. 124. Pius XI., Encycl. *Ad catholici sacerdotii*, 20 Dec. 1935: AAS 28 (1936) p. 22 ff.

must pray, in duty bound, for their own people and for the whole of God's People; must offer sacrifice with awareness of what they are about, modelling themselves on the object they handle,[128] and so their apostolic responsibilities, risks, worries, so far from being an obstacle, must be the means of their rising to greater heights of sanctity, as they feed their activity and warm it on the overflow of their contemplation, for the delight of the whole of God's Church. All priests, and particularly those who have the special title of diocesan priests from their ordination, must bear in mind the great contribution which a loyal union and generous co-operation with their Bishop makes to their own sanctification.

There are also in a lower order of the ministry men who have a special way of sharing the supreme Priest's mission and grace. Chief among these are the deacons,[129] who must keep themselves free from every vice as servants of the mysteries of Christ and the Church, must be pleasing to God, and take every precaution to gain a good standing in the sight of men (cf. 1 *Tim* 3:8-10 and 12-13). Clerics have had their vocation from the Lord, have been reserved for his inheritance, and are making themselves ready for the duties of the ministry under the Pastors' watchful care. They are bound to give their minds and hearts a formation in conformity with the choice made of them and the distinction it carries. They must be persistent at prayer, fervent in love, their minds dwelling on everything that is true, just and held in esteem, the honour and glory of God the goal of all their actions. In close approximation to these is the select body of layfolk called by the Bishop to complete dedication to apostolic activity, whose labour in the Lord's field is very fruitful.[130]

---

[128] *Order of priestly consecration*, introductory Exhortation.
[129] Cf. St Ignatius, Martyr, *Trall.* 2, 3: ed. Funk. 1, p. 244.
[130] Cf. Pius XII, Allocution *Sous la maternelle protection*, 9 Dec. 1957: AAS 50 (1958) p. 36.

Married people and Christian parents have their own path to pursue. With a love that is loyal they must give each other support in grace throughout their lives. They must steep in Christian teaching and the virtues of the gospel, the children they have lovingly received from God. This is their way of presenting all men with an example of untiring, generous love, of building the brotherhood of charity, of being outstanding witnesses to Mother Church's fertility, of co-operating in it, to show and to share the love Christ has had for his bride, the love with which he gave himself up on her behalf.[131] Those who are widowed and those who have not married have another way of giving the same example, and they make no small contribution to the Church's holiness and activity. Their work is often hard; they must use their human occupations to bring themselves to perfection, to help their fellow countrymen, to improve the condition of the whole of society and creation. They must model themselves in active charity on Christ. His hands once were busy with tools and he is always at work with his Father for the saving of all men. Their hope must make them gay. They must shoulder each other's burdens and use their daily work to rise to greater heights of holiness, the holiness of an apostle.

Those who feel the weight of poverty, disability, disease and different troubles must realize that they are engaging in a special union with Christ in his suffering for the world's salvation; those too who suffer persecution in the cause of righteousness. The Lord proclaimed them blessed in the gospel, and after they 'have suffered a little while, the God of all grace, who has called us to his eternal glory in Christ Jesus, will himself restore, establish and strengthen' (1 *Pet* 5:10) them.

All Christ's faithful then will grow daily more holy in the conditions their life imposes, its duties and its circumstances. These things will be the means of their advance in holiness, if they combine their

---

[131] Pius XI, Encycl. *Casti Connubii,* 31 Dec. 1930: AAS 22 (1930) p. 548 ff. Cf. St John Chrysostom, *in Ephes.* Hom. 20, 2: PG 62, 136 ff.

faith with an acceptance of everything which comes from the hand of their heavenly Father and if they are co-operative with the divine will, making in the very service of this life a demonstration to all men of the charity with which God has loved the world.

42. 'God is love; and he who abides in love abides in God, and God abides in him' (1 *Jn* 4:16). God has poured out his love in our hearts by the Holy Spirit who has been given to us (cf. *Rom* 5:5). Consequently the first, the most necessary, gift is the charity which enables us to love God above all things and our neighbour for God's sake. Charity is to grow like good seed in the soul and bear fruit. Each individual believer then must give the word of God a willing hearing, with the help of his grace do God's will, partake of the sacraments, especially the Eucharist, and take part in the sacred actions, apply himself steadily to prayer, self-denial, active brotherly charity, the practice of all the virtues. Charity is the bond which binds us perfectly, the fulfilling of the law (cf. *Col* 3:14; *Rom* 13:10). Thus it controls all the means to sanctification, gives them their form and brings them to their goal.[132] And so the true disciple of Christ carries the mark of charity towards God and his neighbour.

Since Jesus, God's Son, has demonstrated his charity by laying down his life on our behalf, no man has greater love than he who lays down his life for Christ and his brethren (cf. 1 *Jn* 3:16; *Jn* 15:13). A number of Christians have had, from the very first age, the vocation to bear love's highest witness in the sight of all and of persecutors in particular; and this vocation will always exist. Martyrdom makes the disciple like his master in his unconstrained acceptance of death for the world's salvation; it models the disciple on him at the moment of shedding his blood. The Church values it as the choice gift, the highest test of charity. It may be given to few,

---

[132] Cf. St Augustine, *Enchir,* 121, 32: PL 40. 288. St Thomas. *Summa Theol.* II-II, q. 184, a. 1. Pius XII, Adhort. Apost. *Menti nostrae,* 23 Sep. 1950: AAS 42 (1950) p. 660.

but all must be ready to acknowledge Christ before men, to follow him on the way of the cross through the persecutions of which the Church is never free.

The Church's holiness is especially fostered by the numerous counsels which the Lord proposed for the observance of his disciples in the gospel.[133] A position of eminence among them is held by the Father's gift of divine grace to a certain number (cf. *Mt* 19:11; 1 *Cor* 7:7) to facilitate the devotion of their undivided heart to God alone in the state of virginity or celibacy (cf. 1 *Cor* 7: 32-34).[134] This complete continence for the sake of the kingdom of heaven has always been held in the highest esteem in the Church as a badge of charity, an encouragement to charity and a special source of spiritual fertility in the world.

The Church also reflects on the admonition which the Apostle uttered when he challenged the faithful to charity and urged them to have the same mind which Christ Jesus showed, for he 'emptied himself, taking the form of a servant ... and became obedient unto death' (*Phil* 2:7-8) and for our sake 'though he was rich, he became poor' (2 *Cor* 8:9). As there is a need for constant testimony on the part of disciples by imitation of this charity and humility of Christ, it is a matter of joy to Mother Church that there are to be found in her bosom men and women in considerable number who practise a closer following, a clearer showing of the Saviour's state of dispossession. They do this by accepting poverty with the freedom that belongs to the sons of God and by renunciation of their own will. In pursuit of perfection they go beyond the limit of what is laid down; they submit to man for the love of God so that their modelling of themselves on Christ in his obedience may be more complete.[135]

---

[133] On the counsels in general, cf. ORIGEN, *Commentary on Romans* X, 14: PG 14, 1275 B. ST AUGUSTINE, *De Sancta Virginitate* 15, 15: PL 40, 403. ST THOMAS, *Summa Theol.* I-II, q. 100, a. 2 C (in fine); II-II, q. 44, a. 4, ad 3.

[134] *On the pre-eminence of holy virginity*, cf. TERTULLIAN, *Exhort. Cast.* 10: 2, 925 C. ST CYPRIAN, *Hab. Virg.* 3 and 22: PL 4, 443 B and 461 A ff. ST ATHANASIUS (?), *De Virg.*: PG 28, 252 ff. ST JOHN CHRYSOSTOM, *De Virg.*: PG 48, 533 ff.

[135] *On spiritual poverty*, cf. *Mt* 5:3 and 19:21; *Mk* 10:21; *Lk* 18:22; *on obedience* Christ's example is presented in *Jn* 4:34 and 6:38; *Phil* 2:8-10; *Heb* 10: 5-7. Texts of the Fathers and founders of orders are abundant.

All Christ's faithful have an invitation, which is binding, to the pursuit of holiness and perfection in their own station of life. They must all make it their aim to keep a due control over their passions to avoid being impeded in their pursuit of perfect charity by a use of worldly possessions and an attachment to wealth which conflicts with the spirit of gospel poverty. The Apostle utters the warning: Those who deal with the world must not take their stand on it: for the form of this world is passing away (cf. 1 *Cor* 7:31).[136]

---

[136] On the effective practice of the counsels which is not a general obligation, cf. St John Chrysostom, *in Mt.* Hom. 7, 7: PG 57, 81 ff. St Ambrose, *De Viduis*, 4, 23; PL 16, 241 ff.

CHAPTER VI

RELIGIOUS

43. The evangelical counsels, chastity dedicated to God, poverty, and obedience, are a divine gift which the Church has received from her Lord and always preserves by his grace, for they have their foundation in the Lord's words and example, they have the recommendation of the apostles, fathers, doctors of the Church and pastors. Under the guidance of the Holy Spirit, the Church's authority has looked to their elucidation, the control of their practice and the establishment of stable rules for living by them. The result has been as if a tree had grown from the seed God gave and sent out its branches in a striking manner in many sectors of God's field. There has come about the growth of different rules of life, solitary or in community, and of different families which multiply the resources for the improvement of their members and the good of the whole Body of Christ.[137] These families give their members support of the following kinds: greater stability in their way of life, well-tested teaching on the pursuit of perfection, fraternal fellowship in Christ's service, the strength which obedience brings to freedom. They are able, in consequence, to live up to their religious profession without anxiety and keep it loyally, while they make progress along the way of charity in a spirit of joy.[138]

When account is taken of the Church's divine, hierarchical constitution, the state here described is not an intermediate condition between the clerical and the lay. It is the case rather that a number of Christ's faithful are invited from the clerical and the lay states to enjoy a special gift in the life of the Church and to advance, each in his own way, the Church's mission of salvation.[139]

---

[137] Cf. ROSWEYDUS, *Vitae Patrum,* Antwerp, 1628. *Apophthegmata Patrum:* PG 65. PALLADIUS, *Historia Lausiaca:* PG 34, 995 ff.; ed. C. BUTLER, Cambridge, 1898 (1904). PIUS XI, Apost. Const. *Umbratilem,* 8 July 1924: AAS 16 (1924) pp. 386-387. PIUS XII, Alloc. *Nous sommes heureux,* 11 April 1958: AAS 50 (1958) p. 283.

[138] PAUL VI, Alloc. *Magno gaudio,* 23 May 1964: AAS 56 (1964) p. 566.

[139] Cf. Code of Canon Law: c. 487 and 488, 4°. PIUS XII, Alloc. *Annus sacer,* 8 Dec. 1950: AAS 43 (1951) p. 27 ff. PIUS XII, Apost. Const. *Provida Mater,* 2 Feb. 1947: AAS 39 (1947) p. 120 ff.

The profession of the evangelical counsels

44. A member of Christ's faithful binds himself to the three evangelical counsels with the help of vows or other sacred obligations which resemble vows in their nature. By these means he is completely dedicated to God who is loved above all things and he is involved in the service and honour of God on a new, special warrant. He is already dead to sin and consecrated to God by reason of his baptism. He makes profession in the Church of the evangelical counsels to enable him to gather a more abundant harvest from the grace of baptism. His aim thereby is freedom from the obstacles which might hold him back from a fervent charity, from perfection in divine worship, and he is more deeply consecrated to the service of God.[140] The perfection of the consecration is proportionate to the strength and stability of the bonds which enable Christ to be seen more clearly in his indissoluble union with his bride, the Church.

The evangelical counsels bring about a special union of their adherents with the Church and her mystery, by means of charity to which they are the guide.[141] The spiritual life of these adherents must therefore be devoted also to the good of the whole Church. This is the origin of their duty of working for the kingdom of Christ, so that it may put down its roots and gain strength in souls, and may be carried abroad to every land. This duty they have to fulfil according to their strength and the rule of their particular vocation, by prayer or by active service in addition. For this reason the Church keeps a watchful and encouraging eye on the particular character of the different religious Institutes.

The profession of the evangelical counsels is seen to be like a sign which has the power of effectively attracting all the Church's members to a lively performance of the duties of the Christian vocation.

---

[140] Paul VI, *loc. cit.*, p. 567.
[141] Cf. St Thomas, *Summa Theol.* II-II, q. 184. a. 3 and q. 188, a. 2. St Bonaventure, Opusc. XI, *Apologia Pauperum.* c. 3, 3: ed. Opera, Quaracchi, t. 8, 1898, p. 245 a.

It must do so. The People of God have here no abiding city; they are seeking rather the city that is to come. The religious state, while giving its followers greater independence of earthly cares, gives all believers a clearer demonstration of the good things of heaven which are already present in this age. It also bears a greater witness to the gaining of the new, eternal life which has come from Christ's redemption; it gives clearer notice of the resurrection to come and the glory of the kingdom in heaven. It is a closer imitation, a perpetual presentation in the Church of the way of life, which the Son of God took up on his entry into the world to do the Father's will, and which he proposed to the disciples, his followers. To sum up, it has a particular way of bringing to light the kingdom of God in its elevated position above all earthly goods and the supremacy of its requirements; it shows all men the supreme and massive dominance of Christ's rule, and the unlimited nature of the Holy Spirit's power at work in the Church in a remarkable way.

While it is true that the state constituted by profession of the evangelical counsels has no bearing on the hierarchical structure of the Church, it has an undeniable relevance to her life and holiness.

45. It is the task of the ecclesiastical Hierarchy wisely to regulate by its laws the practice of the evangelical counsels, which offer unique encouragement towards perfection in charity towards God and one's neighbour; for the function of the Hierarchy is to feed the People of God and to bring them to richer pastures (cf. *Ezech* 34:14).[142] In response to the urging of the Holy Spirit, the Hierarchy accepts the rules proposed by eminent men and women, and when they have been made more precise gives them authentic approval. Moreover, its vigilant, protective authority lends its presence to the Institutes set up

---

[142] Cf. VATICAN COUNCIL I, Schema *De Ecclesia Christi,* cap. XV, and Adnot. 48: MANSI 51, 549 ff. and 619 ff. LEO XIII, Letter *Au milieu des consolations,* 23 Dec. 1900: ASS 33 (1900-1901) p. 361. PIUS XII, Apost. Const. *Provida Mater, loc. cit.*, p. 114 ff.

in many places for the building up of Christ's Body, to see that they grow and flower in accordance with the spirit of their founders.

For the better provision of the needs of all the Lord's flock, any Institute of perfection and its members individually may be exempted by the Supreme Pontiff from the jurisdiction of the local Ordinary, and made subject to him alone; this by reason of his primacy over the whole Church and with a view to the general benefit.[143] Similarly it is possible for them to be left or entrusted to the authority of their own Patriarch. Members of such Institutes have a duty to fulfil towards the Church which arises from the special form their life takes. They are obliged in so doing to show respect and obedience to Bishops in accordance with Canon Law. This is owed to their pastoral authority in individual Churches and to the need of unity and harmony in apostolic work.[144]

Not only does the Church sanction the elevation of religious profession to the dignity of a canonical state, but her liturgical action holds it up as a state of consecration to God. It is the Church, by the authority entrusted to her by God, who accepts the vows of those making profession, wins help and grace for them by her public prayer, recommends them to God, gives them a spiritual blessing when she associates their offering with the eucharistic sacrifice.

46. Religious must make it their careful aim that their efforts improve the Church's real and daily presentation, to believers and non-believers, of Christ as he meditated on the hillside, proclaimed to the crowds the kingdom of God, healed the sick and the injured, turning sinners to repentance, blessing children, doing good to all, and continually obeying the will of the Father who sent him.[145]

---

[143] Cf. Leo XIII, Const. *Romanos Pontifices*, 8 May 1881: ASS 13 (1880-1881) p. 483, Pius XII, Alloc. *Annus sacer*, 8 Dec. 1950: AAS 43 (1951) p. 28 ff.

[144] Cf. Pius XII, Alloc. *Annus sacer, loc. cit.*, p. 28. Pius XII, Apost. Const. *Sedes Sapientiae*, 31 May 1956: AAS 48 (1956) p. 355. Paul VI, *loc. cit.*, pp. 570-571.

[145] Cf. Pius XII, Encycl. *Mystici Corporis*, 29 June 1943: AAS 35 (1943) p. 214 ff.

Religious

All must have a clear understanding of the fact that, although the profession of the evangelical counsels involves a renunciation of advantages which undoubtedly deserve to be highly valued, it is no obstacle to the true development of the human person; on the contrary it is, of its own nature, supremely advantageous to that development. The voluntary acceptance of the counsels in the light of a personal vocation makes no slight contribution to the heart's cleansing and to spiritual freedom; it is a continual incitement to fervent charity; it has the special value of bringing a Christian into greater conformity with the kind of virginal life of poverty which Christ the Lord chose for himself, and his virgin Mother embraced. There is proof of this in the example of holy founders in great number. No one should think that their consecration makes religious strangers to their fellow men or unprofitable citizens here on earth. Even if in some cases they have no direct contact with their contemporaries, they keep their company at a deeper level in the heart of Christ. They give them spiritual co-operation to ensure that the building, which is the State has its foundations in the Lord and is aligned on him, to prevent frustration in the work of those who are engaged in building it.[146]

For this reason the sacred Council gives its support and praise to the men and women, brothers and sisters, who combine in the adornment of Christ's bride by their steadfast, humble loyalty to the consecration under discussion, in monasteries, schools, hospitals or missions, and who offer a great variety of generous services to all men.

47. It must be the careful purpose of anyone called to the profession of the counsels, to remain in the vocation which he has from God, and to advance to greater excellence. He is thereby to enrich the holiness of the Church and to increase the glory of the one, undivided Trinity, which in Christ and through Christ is the original source of all holiness.

---

[146] Cf. Pius XII, Alloc. *Annus sacer, loc. cit.*, p. 30. Alloc. *Sous la maternelle protection*, 9 Dec. 1957: AAS 50 (1958) p. 39 ff.

CHAPTER VII

THE PILGRIM CHURCH'S CHARACTERISTIC ATTITUDE OF EXPECTANCY AND HER CONNECTION WITH THE CHURCH IN HEAVEN

48. We are all called to the Church in Christ Jesus, and in the Church we acquire holiness by the grace of God. She will not however reach her perfection in the glory of heaven until the time comes 'for establishing all' (*Acts* 3:21), and the whole universe, as well as the human race, will be completely united in Christ; for the universe has an intimate connection with the human race, and through him it reaches its destined end (cf. *Eph* 1:10; *Col* 1:20; 2 *Pet* 3:10-13).

Lifted up from the earth, Christ has drawn all men to himself (cf. *Jn* 12:32); rising from the dead (cf. *Rom* 6:9), he has sent his life giving Spirit among the disciples; through the Spirit he has established his Body, which is the Church, as the universal sacrament of salvation; sitting at the right hand of the Father, he is at work in the world without ceasing, to bring men to the Church, to join them more closely to himself through her, and to give them a share in his glorious life by feeding them on his own Body and Blood. The promised restoration to which we look forward has already had its beginning in Christ. It receives impetus on the sending of the Holy Spirit and is continued by his efforts in the Church, where we also receive instruction, by faith, in the significance of our earthly life. We meanwhile, in expectation of a good future, are bringing to completion the work in the world entrusted to us by the Father, and are working out our salvation (cf. *Phil* 2:12).

The end of the ages has already reached us (cf. 1 *Cor* 10:11) and the world is irrevocably set on the renewal which is anticipated in a real way in this life. Already the Church is marked on earth by a genuine, if imperfect, holiness. The Church is on pilgrimage until the coming of the new heavens and the new earth in which righteousness dwells (cf.

2 *Pet* 3:13). In her sacraments and organization, which belong to this life, she is wearing this age's fashion, a transient mode, and she spends her time surrounded by creatures who groan in travail, as they wait for the revealing of the sons of God (cf. *Rom* 8:19-22).

In the Church we have been joined to Christ and had a seal set on us by the Holy Spirit 'who is the guarantee of our inheritance' (*Eph* 1:14); we have the true name of sons of God, for so we are (cf. 1 *Jn* 3:1), but we have not yet appeared with Christ in glory (cf. *Col* 3:4). In glory we shall be like to God for we shall see him as he is (cf. 1 *Jn* 3:2). Thus 'while we are at home in the body, we are away from the Lord' (2 *Cor* 5:6); we have the first-fruits of the Spirit and we are groaning inwardly (cf. *Rom* 8:23), desirous to be with Christ (cf. *Phil* 1:23). The same love is the motive which urges us to live to a greater degree for him who for our sake died and was raised (cf. 2 *Cor* 5:15). We make it our aim in all things to please the Lord (cf. 2 *Cor* 5:9) and we put on the whole armour of God, so that we may be able to stand against the wiles of the devil and to withstand in the evil day (cf. *Eph* 6:11-13). Since, as the Lord told us, we do not know the day or the hour, we must be constantly on guard if, when our life has run its single course on earth (cf. *Heb* 9:27), we are deservedly to escort him to the wedding and be counted among the blessed (cf. *Mt* 25:31-46) and are not to be told, like wicked and slothful servants (cf. *Mt* 25:26), to depart into the eternal fire (cf. *Mt* 25:41), into the outer darkness where 'men will weep and gnash their teeth' (*Mt* 22:13 and 25:30). Before we begin our reign with Christ in glory, we shall all make an appearance 'before the judgment seat of Christ, so that each one may receive good or evil, according to what he has done in the body' (2 *Cor* 5:10). At the end of the world 'they will come forth, those who have done good, to the resurrection of life, and those who have done evil, to the resurrection of judgment' (*Jn* 5:29; cf. *Mt* 25:46). Since in our estimation 'the sufferings of this time are not worth comparing to the glory that is to be revealed to us' (*Rom* 8:18; cf. 2 *Tim* 2:11-12), our faith gives us the strength to await 'our blessed hope, the appearing of the glory of our great God and Saviour, Jesus Christ' (*Tit* 2:13) 'who will change our lowly body to be like his glorious body' (*Phil* 3:21).

135

He will come 'to be glorified in his saints and to be marvelled at in all who have believed' (2 *Thess* 1:10).

The union between the Church in heaven and the pilgrim Church
49. Until the Lord comes in his glory, and all the angels with him (cf. *Mt* 25:31), and death is destroyed and all things have been put in subjection under him (cf. 1 *Cor* 15:26-27), some of his disciples are pilgrims on earth, some, their life now over, are undergoing purification, others still are in their glory gazing 'clearsighted on God himself, three and one, as he is'.[147] Despite the difference of our degree and mode, all of us are in communion with the same love of God and of our neighbour; we all sing the same hymn to the glory of our God. All who belong to Christ and are in possession of his Spirit, combine to make one Church with a cohesion that depends on him (cf. *Eph* 4:16). The union of the living with their brethren who have fallen asleep in Christ, is not broken; the Church has rather believed through the ages that it gains strength from the sharing of spiritual benefits.[148] The greater intimacy of the union of those in heaven with Christ, gives extra steadiness in holiness to the whole Church. It gives distinction to the worship the Church is offering God on earth, and makes a manifold contribution to the extension of her building (cf. 1 *Cor* 12:12–27).[149] Now that they are welcomed in their own country and at home with the Lord (cf. 2 *Cor* 5:8), through him, with him and in him they intercede unremittingly with the Father on our behalf,[150] offering the merit they acquired on earth through Christ Jesus, the one

---

[147] COUNCIL OF FLORENCE, *Decretum pro Graecis:* DENZ. 693 (1305).

[148] Apart from documents of greater antiquity which oppose any form of summoning spirits, from the time of Alexander IV (27 Sept. 1258). Cf. Encycl. of the HOLY OFFICE, *De magnetismi abusu*, 4 Aug. 1856: ASS (1865) pp. 177-178. DENZ. 1653-1654 (2823-2825); reply of the HOLY OFFICE, 24 Apr. 1917: AAS 9 (1917) p. 268, DENZ. 2182 (3642).

[149] A synthesis and exposition of this Pauline doctrine is to be found in: PIUS XII, Encycl. *Mystici Corporis* AAS 35 (1935) p. 200 *et passim*.

[150] Cf., among others, ST AUGUSTINE. *Enarr. in* Ps. 85, 24: PL 37, 1099, ST JEROME, *Liber contra Vigilantium*, 6: PL 23, 344; ST THOMAS, *In 4m Sent.*, d. 45, q. 3, a. 2. ST BONAVENTURE, *In 4m Sent.*, d. 45, a.3, q. 2: etc.

and only mediator between God and man (cf. 1 *Tim* 2:5), when they were at God's service in all things, and in their flesh were completing what is lacking in Christ's afflictions for the sake of his Body, the Church (cf. *Col* 1:24).[151] Their brotherly care is the greatest help to our weakness.

50. In special recognition of the communion of the whole Mystical Body of Jesus Christ, the Church on earth, from the first ages of the christian religion, has cherished the memory of the dead with great piety,[152] and offered prayers for them, 'for it is a holy and wholesome thought to pray for the dead that they may be released from their sins' (2 *Mac* 12:46). The Church has always believed the apostles and martyrs of Christ, who shed their blood and gave the supreme witness of faith and charity, to have a closer union with us in Christ. She has joined them to the Blessed Virgin Mary and the holy angels in her especially affectionate respect.[153] She has piously implored the help of their intercession. To their number have later been added those who modelled themselves more closely on Christ's virginity and poverty,[154] and finally those recommended to the devout imitation of the faithful by their glorious practice of the christian virtues[155] and their spiritual gifts from God.[156]

When we fix our gaze on the life of men who have followed Christ faithfully, we have a new motive that impels us to seek the city which is to come (cf. *Heb* 13:14; and 11:10). At the same time we receive instruction in the safest route whereby we may arrive at perfect union

---

[151] Cf. Pius XII, Encycl. *Mystici Corporis*: AAS 35 (1943) p. 245.
[152] Cf. Innumerable inscriptions in the Roman catacombs.
[153] Cf. Gelasius I, Decretalis, *De libris recipiendis*, 3: PL 59, 160, Denz. 165 (353).
[154] Cf. St Methodius, *Symposium*, VII, 3: GCS (Bonwetsch), p. 74.
[155] Cf. Benedict XV, *Decree of the approval of virtues in the case of the beatification and canonization of the Servant of God, John Nepomucene Neumann*: AAS 14 (1922) p. 23. Many allocutions of Pius XI on saints: *Inviti all'eroismo*. Speeches ... t. I-III, Rome 1941-42, *passim*; Pius XII, *Speeches and Broadcasts*, t. 10, 1949, pp. 37-43.
[156] Cf. Pius XII. Encycl. *Mediator Dei.*: AAS 39 (1947) p. 581.

with Christ or perfect holiness—a route through the diversity the world offers, a route which suits each man in his condition and in his own circumstances.[157] In the life of men who share our human nature, yet become more completely changed into the likeness of Christ (cf. 2 *Cor* 3:18), God makes his presence, his countenance, vividly manifest to men. In their person he addresses us, he offers us the standard of his kingdom,[158] and we who are surrounded by so great a cloud of witnesses (cf. *Heb* 12:1), such a proof of the Gospel's truth, are powerfully attracted to it.

Their example is not the only warrant we have for cherishing the memory of those who are in heaven. A still greater motive is our hope that strength be given to the unity of the whole Church in the Spirit by the practice of brotherly love (cf. *Eph* 4:1-6). In the same way that the christian fellowship existing among members of the Church on earth brings us nearer to Christ, fellowship with the saints brings us union with Christ, and he is the well-spring and the head from which streams every grace and the very life of the People of God.[159] It is supremely fitting that we should show love for these friends and fellow-heirs of Christ; they are our brethren too and our outstanding benefactors. We have a debt of thanks to pay to God for them.[160] 'We must call upon them humbly, and throw ourselves on the resourceful aid of their prayers to win benefits from God through his Son Jesus Christ, our sole Redeemer and Saviour'.[161] Every genuine show of love on our part for those in heaven has of its nature Christ for its aim, and reaches its conclusion in Christ who is 'the crown of all the saints';[162] through him it reaches God, who is to be marvelled at in the saints and is called great among them.[163]

---

[157] Cf. Heb. 13:7; Ecclus 44-50; Heb 11:3-40. Cf. also Pius XII, Encycl. *Mediator Dei*: AAS 39 (1947) pp. 582-583.

[158] Cf. Vatican Council I, Const. *De fide catholica*, cap. 3: Denz. 1794 (3013).

[159] Cf. Pius XII, Encycl. *Mystici Corporis*: AAS 35 (1943) p. 216.

[160] For gratitude towards the saints, cf. E. Diehl, *Inscriptiones latinae christianae veteres*, I, Berlin, 1925. nn. 2008. 2382 *et passim*.

[161] Council of Trent, Sess. 25, *De invocatione … Sanctorum*: Denz. 984 (1821).

[162] Roman Breviary. *Invitatory on the feast of All Saints.*

[163] Cf. e.g. 2 *Thess* 1:10.

The Pilgrim Church and the Church in Heaven

The noblest motive of our attachment to the Church in heaven is realized when we are together transported with joy and jointly celebrate the praise of the divine Majesty,[164] especially in the sacred liturgy, where the power of the Holy Spirit works on us through sacramental signs. In the liturgy, all of us who have been ransomed with Christ's blood out of every tribe and tongue and people and nation (cf. *Rev* 5:9), and are assembled in the one Church, declare the greatness of God, one and three, with a single canticle of praise. We reach the highest degree of union with the worship of the Church in heaven at our celebration of the eucharistic sacrifice, as in the fellowship of communion we honour and remember first of all the glorious Mary ever virgin, then we recall the blessed Joseph and the blessed apostles, martyrs and all saints.[165]

51. This belief of our forebears concerning the vitality of our partnership with the brethren who are in the glory of heaven, or who are still undergoing purification after their death, deserves respect. This sacred Council accepts it in a spirit of piety and reiterates the propositions of the Second Council of Nicaea,[166] the Council of Florence[167] and that of Trent.[168] Its pastoral solicitude requires that it urge all concerned to take the necessary steps to restrain or correct any abuses, by excess or defect, which may have made inroads in places, and to make a complete restoration to a fuller praise of God and Christ. They must teach the faithful that the authentic cult of the saints consists not so much in the multiplication of exterior acts, as in the intense activity of our love, which makes us aim at our own, and the Church's, greater good by seeking 'the example of the saints in our way of life, their partnership in our fellowship and their support by our prayer'.[169] On the

---

[164] VATICAN COUNCIL II, Const. *De Sacra Liturgia*, cap. 5, n. 104.

[165] Canon of the Roman Mass.

[166] COUNCIL OF NICAEA II, Act. VII: DENZ. 302 (600).

[167] COUNCIL OF FLORENCE, *Decretum pro Graecis*: DENZ. 693 (1304).

[168] COUNCIL OF TRENT; Sess. 25, *De invocatione, veneratione et reliquiis Sanctorum et sacris imaginibus*: DENZ. 984-988 (1821-1824); Sess. 25, *Decretum de Purgatorio*: DENZ. 983 (1820); Sess. 6, *Decretum de iustificatione*, can. 30: DENZ. 840 (1580).

[169] *Preface* granted to some dioceses.

other hand, they must instruct the faithful that the converse we hold with those in heaven, provided that our conception of it is grounded on the fuller light of faith, does not diminish the cult of worship we give to God the Father through Christ in the Spirit; on the contrary, it enriches it enormously.[170]

We are all the children of God and we make up one family in Christ (cf. *Heb* 3:6). The communion we hold with each other in mutual love and the unified praise of the most Holy Trinity, is the mark of our correspondence with the deepest vocation of the Church and a foretaste of the liturgy celebrated when the consummation of glory is attained, and a share in it.[171] When Christ appears and the glorious resurrection of the dead takes place, God's glory will light up the heavenly city, and the Lamb will be its lamp (cf. *Rev* 21:24). Then the whole Church of saints at the summit of love's blessedness will adore God and 'the Lamb who was slain' (*Rev* 5:12). With a single voice she will cry out 'To him who sits upon the throne and to the Lamb be blessing and honour and glory and might for ever and ever!' (*Rev* 5:13-14).

---

[170] Cf. St Peter Canisius. *Catechismus Maior seu Summa Doctrinae christianae*, cap. III (ed. crit. F. Streicher), Pars I, pp. 15-16, n. 44 and pp. 100-101. n.49.
[171] Cf. Vatican Council II, Const. *De Sacra Liturgia*. cap. 1, n. 8.

CHAPTER VIII

THE BLESSED VIRGIN MARY, MOTHER OF GOD IN THE MYSTERY OF CHRIST AND THE CHURCH

1. INTRODUCTION

52. God, in his loving kindness and his wisdom, has wished to bring about the redemption of the world; 'when the time had fully come, he sent forth his Son, born of a woman ... so that we might receive adoption as sons' (*Gal* 4:4-5). It was the Son 'who for us men and for our salvation came down from heaven, and was incarnate by the Holy Ghost of the Virgin Mary'.[172] This is the divine mystery of salvation which is revealed to us and continued in the Church which the Lord set up as his own body, in which the faithful, in adherence to Christ, the head, and in fellowship with all his saints, must also venerate the memory 'first of all, of the glorious Mary ever virgin, Mother of Jesus Christ, our Lord and God'.[173]

53. The Virgin Mary, when the angel brought the news, welcomed the Word of God in her heart and in her body, and brought Life into the world. She is therefore recognized with honour as the real Mother of God the Redeemer. In view of her Son's merits, she was redeemed in a more exalted manner, she was tied to him tightly with a permanent bond, she is endowed with the supreme office and dignity of being the Mother of God the Son; she is therefore the daughter to whom the Father has shown surpassing love, she is the shrine of the Holy Spirit. This gift of outstanding grace makes her outstrip by far all other creatures in excellence, whether they are in heaven or on earth. At the same time she is to be found linked, in Adam's stock, to all men in

---

[172] Creed in the Roman Mass: Creed of Constantinople: Mansi 3, 566. Cf. Council of Ephesus, *ibid.* 4, 1130 (also *ibid.* 2, 665 and 4, 1071); Council of Chalcedon, ibid. 7, 111-116: Council of Constantinople 11, *ibid.* 9, 375-396.
[173] Canon of the Roman Mass.

need of salvation; or rather, she is 'clearly mother of the members (of Christ) ... for she has with love co-operated in the birth of the faithful in the Church, and they are the members of that head'.[174] She is hailed for this reason as eminent above all, and as a wholly unique member of the Church, as the type of the Church in her faith and charity and its most honoured model. The Catholic Church, under the instruction of the Holy Spirit, honours her as its most loving mother with all the affection of a son's love for his mother.

54. The sacred Council, in its exposition of doctrine on the Church, in which the divine Redeemer is busy with the work of salvation, has the deliberate intention of throwing light on the Blessed Virgin's function in the mystery of the Word made flesh and the Mystical Body, and on the duties of men who have been redeemed towards the Mother of God, Mother of Christ and Mother of men, especially the faithful. It has no intention, however, of proposing the doctrine of Mary in its fullness, or of setting a conclusion to questions which the labours of theologians have not yet brought fully into the light. Opinions which are freely put forward in Catholic theological schools on the subject of the woman who holds the loftiest position in the holy Church after Christ, and the nearest to us,[175] do not lose their right to be preserved.

2. THE FUNCTION OF THE BLESSED VIRGIN IN THE ECONOMY OF SALVATION

55. The sacred Literature of the Old and the New Testament, and venerable Tradition, show with increasing clarity the function of the Saviour's mother in the economy of salvation; they hold it up to view, so to speak. The history of salvation in the books of the Old Testament is the account of the slow preparation for the coming of Christ into the world. As these documents of early times are read in the Church and

---

[174] St Augustine, *De S. Virginitate*, 6: PL 40. 399.
[175] Cf. Paul VI, *Allocution in Council*, 4 Dec. 1963: AAS 56 (1964) p. 37.

understood in the light of the complete revelation which followed, they gradually bring more clearly into the light the outline of the woman, the Redeemer's mother. In this light it is she who is foreshadowed by prophecy in the promise of victory over the serpent, made to the first parents on their fall into sin (cf. *Gen* 3:15). In the same way, she is the virgin who is to be with child and is to bear a son, who shall be called Emmanuel (cf. *Is* 7:14; cf. *Mic* 5:2-3; *Mt* 1:22-23). She stands out among the lowly and the Lord's poor who have confident hope of salvation at his hands, and who receive it. The long waiting for the promise is finally over, the ages are brought to completion with the surpassing Daughter of Sion, and a new economy is inaugurated, when the Son of God has taken human nature from her to free man of sin by the mysteries of his flesh.

56. It was the merciful will of the Father that the Incarnation should be preceded by acceptance on the part of the predestined mother, so that, as a woman had contributed to death, a woman too should make a contribution to life. This is supremely true in the case of Jesus' mother who brought into the world the very Life which renews all things; she was also endowed by God with adequate gifts for this great office. It is not a matter for surprise, then, that the practice grew up among the Fathers of the Church of calling the Mother of God all-holy and free of every stain of sin, as though fashioned and formed by the Holy Spirit into a new creature.[176] From the first instant of her conception the Virgin of Nazareth was enriched with a unique, resplendent holiness. When the angel brought her tidings, on God's instructions, she was greeted as 'full of grace' (cf. *Lk* 1:28), and her reply to heaven's messenger was: 'Behold I am the handmaid of the Lord; let it be to me according to your word' (*Lk* 1:38). In this way Mary, daughter of

---

[176] Cf. St Germanus of Const., *Hom. in Annunt. Deiparae*: PG 98. 328 A; *in Dorm*. 2: col. 357. Anastasius of Antioch, *Serm.* 2 *de Annunt.*, 2: PG 89, 1377 AB; *Serm.* 3, 2: col. 1388 C. St Andrew of Crete, *Can, in B. V. Nat.* 4: PG 97,1321 B. ln *B. V. Nat.* 1:col.812 A. *Hom. in dorm.*,1 col. 1068 C. St Sophronius, *Or.* 2 *in Annunt.*, 18: PG 87 (3), 3237 BD.

Adam, by consent to the divine Word became Jesus' mother; with no sin to hamper her she whole-heartedly embraced God's will of salvation, made a complete dedication of herself as the Lord's handmaid to the person and work of her Son; in subordination to him and in company with him, by almighty God's grace, she entered the service of the mystery of the Redemption. The Fathers of the Church are right to consider Mary not as one passively made use of by God, but as one who co-operated with unconstrained faith and obedience in the salvation of man. As St Irenaeus says: 'In her obedience she became the cause of salvation for herself and for the whole human race'.[177] Consequently, many of the Fathers of antiquity join him with this assertion in their preaching. 'The knot of Eve's disobedience had its untying by means of Mary's obedience; what Eve the virgin tied with her unbelief, the Virgin Mary untied by faith';[178] comparing her with Eve, they give Mary the title 'mother of the living',[179] and frequently declare, 'Eve was the introduction of death, Mary of Life'.[180]

57. The mother's union with the Son in the work of salvation can be seen from the time of his virginal conception to his death. In the first place, when Mary rose up and went with haste to visit Elizabeth, she was hailed by her as blessed for her belief in the promise of salvation, and the precursor leaped in his mother's womb (cf. *Lk* 1:41-45). At the Nativity she, the Mother of God, joyfully showed the shepherds and the magi her Son, the first-born, who had brought no loss, but consecration to her virginal integrity.[181] When she made the offering of the poor and presented him to the Lord in the temple, she heard

---

[177] St Irenaeus, *Adv. Haer.* III, 22, 4: PG 7,959 A; Harvey, 2, 123.
[178] St Irenaeus. *ibid.*; Harvey 2, 124.
[179] St Epiphanius, *Haer.* 78, 18: PG 42, 728 CD-729 AB.
[180] St Jerome, *Epist.* 22, 21: PL 22, 408. Cf. St Augustine, *Serm.* 51, 2, 3: PL 38, 335; Serm. 232. 2: col. 1108. St Cyril of Jerus.. *Catech.* 12, 15: PG 33, 741 AB. St John Chrysostom. *in Ps.* 44, 7: PG 55. 193. St John Damascene, *Hom. 2 in dorm. B. M. V.,* 3: PG 96. 728.
[181] Cf. Lateran Council (in the Year 649), Can. 3: Mansi 10. 1151. St Leo the Great. *Epist. ad Flav.*: PL 54, 759. Council of Chalcedon: Mansi 7,462. St Ambrose, *De instit. virg.*: PL 16, 320.

Simeon foretell that her Son was to be a sign that is spoken against, and that a sword was to pierce the mother's soul, so that the thoughts out of many hearts should be revealed (cf. *Lk* 2:34-35). When Jesus was lost as a child and sought with sorrow, his parents found him in the temple busy with his Father's business; they did not understand the Son's remark. But his mother kept in her heart the memory of all this and pondered (cf. *Lk* 2:41-51).

58. His mother makes a signal appearance in Jesus' public life. At the outset, she was moved by pity at the marriage-feast at Cana in Galilee, and provoked with her plea the beginning of the signs of Jesus the Messiah (cf. *Jn* 2:1-11). In the course of his preaching, she heard the words with which he exalted the kingdom above the natural bonds of flesh and blood, when he proclaimed the blessedness of those who, as she did so faithfully (cf. *Lk* 2:19 and 51), hear the word of God and keep it (cf. *Mk* 3:35, *Lk* 11:27-28). This was the way in which the Blessed Virgin made progress on the pilgrimage of faith. She loyally maintained her union with her Son right up to the cross. There, by the divine plan, she took her stand (cf. *Jn* 19:25), grieved bitterly with her only child, joined with a mother's heart in his sacrifice by giving a loving consent to the offering of the victim who had taken birth from her. At the end, when Christ Jesus was dying on the cross, he gave her as mother to his disciple with the words, 'Woman, behold your son' (cf. *Jn* 19:26-27).[182]

59. It was God's resolve that the solemn manifestation of the sacrament of human salvation should not take place before he poured out the Spirit that Christ had promised. Before the day of Pentecost, therefore, we see the apostles 'with one accord devoting themselves to prayer, together with the women and Mary the mother of Jesus, and with his brethren' (*Acts* 1:14). We see Mary too at prayer beseeching the gift of the Spirit who had already overshadowed her at the Annunciation. Finally the immaculate Virgin, who had been kept free of

---

[182] Cf. Pius XII, Encycl. *Mystici Corporis*, 29 June 1943: AAS 35 (1943) pp. 247-248.

all stain of original sin,[183] completed the course of her life on earth and was raised, body and soul to the glory of heaven.[184] She has been exalted by the Lord as Queen of all, so as to be more fully modelled on her Son, the Lord of lords (cf. *Rev* 19:16), victor over sin and death.[185]

3. THE BLESSED VIRGIN AND THE CHURCH

60. In the words of the Apostle, our mediator is unique: 'there is one God, and there is one mediator between God and men, the man Christ Jesus who gave himself as a ransom for them all' (1 *Tim* 2:5-6). Mary's function as mother of men makes for no dimming or diminution of this unique mediation of Christ, but rather demonstrates its power. All the Blessed Virgin's salutary influence on men has its origin not in any real necessity, but in the divine decision, it streams from the overflow of Christ's merits, his mediation is its support; it is wholly dependent on that mediation, draws all its strength from it. It is no impediment to the immediate union of believers and Christ, but an encouragement.

61. The association of the Blessed Virgin as Mother of God with the Incarnation of the divine Word dates back in predestination to all eternity. By the plan of divine Providence she has been the divine Redeemer's attentive mother here on earth, the Lord's uniquely generous associate and humble handmaid. She conceived Christ, gave birth to him, reared him, offered him to the Father in the temple, shared her Son's sufferings as he died on the cross. This was her wholly unique co-operation in the Saviour's work for the restoration of supernatural life to souls; it was performed in obedience, faith, hope and burning charity. This is the reason why she has been our mother in the order of grace.

---

[183] Cf. Pius IX, Bull *Ineffabilis*. 8 Dec. 1854: Acts of Pius IX, 1,I, p. 616; Denz. 1641 (2803).

[184] Cf. Pius XII, Apost. Const. *Munificentissimus*, 1 Nov. 1950: AAS 42 (1950); Denz. 2333. (3903). Cf. St John Damascene, *Enc. in dorm. Dei genitricis*, hom. 2 and 3: PG 96, 721-761, especially col. 728 B. St Germanus of Constantinople, *In S. Dei gen. dorm.* Serm. 1: PG 98 (6), 340-348; Serm. 3: col. 361. St Modestus of Jerus., *In dorm. SS. Deiparae*: PG 86(2); 3277-3312.

[185] Cf. Pius XII, Encycl. *Ad caeli Reginam*, 11 Oct. 1954: AAS 46 (1954). pp. 633-636; Denz. 3913 ff. Cf. St Andrew of Crete, *Hom. 3 in dorm. SS Deiparae*: PG 97, 1089-1109. St John Damascene, *De fide orth.*, IV, 14: PG 94, 1153-1161.

62. Mary's motherhood in the economy of grace has no pause in its duration from the consent that she loyally gave at the Annunciation, and maintained without faltering at the foot of the cross, until the everlasting consummation of all the elect. Raised into heaven, she has not laid aside this saving office but she persists, with many pleas, in winning us the gifts of divine salvation.[186] Her motherly love makes her care for her Son's brethren still on their pilgrimage, still involved in dangers and difficulties until they shall be brought to the happiness of their fatherland. For this reason the Blessed Virgin is called upon in the Church under the titles of Advocate, Auxiliatrix, Adjutrix, Mediatrix.[187] Yet this practice is so understood that it represents no derogation from the dignity and efficacy of Christ, the sole mediator, nor any addition.[188]

No creature, of course, can ever be counted with the incarnate Word and Redeemer; but the priesthood of Christ is shared, in different ways, by ministers and the faithful people, the unique goodness of God is really spread in various ways among creatures; just so, the unique mediation of the Redeemer does not exclude, but rather stimulates among creatures a participation and cooperation which is varied but which originates from a single source.

The Church has no hesitation in admitting this subordinate office of Mary. It is the subject of her constant experience and she recommends to the faithful, for their heartfelt attention, that they should use the support of this mother's aid to gain a closer adherence to the Mediator and Saviour.

---

[186] Cf. KLEUTGEN, revised text *De mysterio Verbi incarnati*, cap. IV: MANSI 53, 290. Cf. ST ANDREW OF CRETE, *in nat. Mariae*, sermo 4: PG 97, 865 A. ST GERMANUS OF CONSTANTINOPLE, *In annunt. Deiparae*: PG 98, 321 BC. *In dorm. Deiparae*, III: col. 361 D. ST JOHN DAMASCENE, *In dorm. B. V. Mariae*, Hom. 1, 8: PG 96, 712 BC–713 A.

[187] Cf. LEO XIII, Encycl. *Adiutricem populi*, 5 Sept. 1895: ASS 15 (1895–96) p. 303. ST PIUS X, Encycl. *Ad diem illum*, 2 Feb. 1904: Acta I, p. 154; DENZ. 1978 a (3370). PIUS XI, Encycl. *Miserentissimus*, 8 May 1928: AAS 20 (1928) p. 178. PIUS XII, *Broadcast*, 13 May 1946: AAS 38 (1946) p. 266.

[188] ST AMBROSE, *Epist.* 63: PL 16, 1218.

63. The intimate connection of the Blessed Virgin with the Church is based on the gift, the office, of divine motherhood which unites her to her Son, the Redeemer, and on her singular graces and gifts. As St Ambrose taught long ago, the Mother of God is the type of the Church in the order of faith, charity and perfect union with Christ.[189] In the mystery of the Church, which is rightly called mother and virgin, the Blessed Virgin Mary has taken precedence because of the eminence and uniqueness of the example that she offers as virgin and mother.[190] By her belief and obedience she gave birth on earth to the very Son of the Father, and this with no knowledge of man, under the shadow of the Holy Spirit. She was like a new Eve presenting a faith unadulterated by doubt, not to the serpent of old but to God's messenger. She brought forth the Son whom God had appointed the first-born among many brethren (*Rom* 8:29), in other words, the faithful, and she co-operates in their generation and education with all the love of a mother.

64. Now the Church, with Mary's hidden holiness before her eyes, in imitation of her charity, fulfils faithfully the will of the Father: and the loyal reception that she gives to the word of God makes her a mother in her turn. With preaching and baptism she brings forth children, who have been conceived by the Spirit and born of God, to the new deathless life. She too is a virgin who keeps in its integrity and purity the faith pledged to the spouse. She is imitating her Lord's mother by the power of the Holy Spirit when she keeps a virginal guard on the integrity of her faith, the firmness of her hope, the sincerity of her love.[191]

65. In the most Blessed Virgin the Church already attains the perfection in which she is without stain or wrinkle (cf. *Eph* 5:27). Christ's

---

[189] St Ambrose, *Expos. Luke* 2:7; PL 15, 1555.
[190] Cf. Ps.-Peter Dam., *Serm.* 63: PL 144, 861 AB. Godfrey of St Victor, *In nat. B. M.*, Ms. Paris, Mazarine, 1002, fol. 109r. Gerhohus Reich., *De gloria et honore Filii hominis*, 10: PL 194, 1105 AB.
[191] St Ambrose. *loc. cit.* and *Expos. Luke* 10: 24-25; PL 15, 1810. St Augustine, *in Io.* Tr. 13, 12: PL 35, 1499. Cf. *Serm.* 191, 2, 3: PL 38, 1010; etc. Cf. also Ven. Bede, *In Lk. Expos.* I, cap. 2: PL 92, 330. Isaac of Stella. *Serm.* 51: PL 194, 1863 A.

faithful, in the meantime, are still striving to overcome sin and grow in holiness. They, therefore, raise their eyes to Mary who shines, as the exemplar of the virtues, on the whole community of the chosen. The Church dutifully reflects on her, contemplates her in the light of the Word made man, and so makes a reverent and more penetrating entry into the mystery of the Incarnation, and increases her conformity with her bridegroom. Mary has made an entry in depth into the history of salvation. She gathers in herself the greatest resolutions of faith and sets them reverberating. While she is the subject of preaching and cult, she is calling believers to her Son, to his sacrifice, and to the Father's love. The Church in the glory she gives to Christ is gaining a greater resemblance to her Type on high as she makes constant progress in faith, hope and charity, as she looks for the divine will in all things and shows it respect. Even in her apostolic work, then, the Church is right to look to the woman who gave birth to Christ. The purpose of his conception by the Holy Spirit and birth of the Virgin was to have birth and growth in the hearts of the faithful also, by means of the Church. In her life the Virgin has been the living example of the motherly affection which must animate all those who join in the Church's apostolic mission for the regeneration of mankind.

4. THE CULT OF THE BLESSED VIRGIN IN THE CHURCH

66. It is right that Mary should have from the Church the honour of a special cult. She has been raised by God's grace to a position second to her Son above all angels and men; she is the most holy Mother of God and has been involved in the mysteries of Christ. The cult of the Blessed Virgin under the title of the 'Mother of God', on whose protection the faithful throw themselves in prayer in every danger and need, dates from the most ancient times.[192] Especially since the Council of Ephesus there has been a remarkable growth in the cult of the

---

[192] 'To thy protection'.

People of God for Mary, by way of respect and love, invocation and imitation. It corresponds with her own prophetic words, 'all generations will call me blessed; for he who is mighty has done great things for me' (*Lk* 1:48). This cult, as it has always existed in the Church, is quite unique, yet essentially different from the cult of adoration rendered equally to the Word incarnate, the Father and the Holy Spirit, to which it gives strong support. The Church has approved, within the bounds of sound, orthodox doctrine, various forms of piety towards the Mother of God, having regard to circumstance of time and place, and the character and natural bent of the faithful. The effect of these forms of piety is that, while honour is paid to the mother, due recognition, love and glory is given to the Son on whose account all things exist (cf. *Col* 1:15-16), in whom it was the eternal Father's 'good pleasure to let all fullness dwell' (*Col* 1:19), and his commandments are kept.

67. The sacred Council is teaching this Catholic doctrine of set purpose. At the same time it reminds all the Church's children to give generous encouragement to the cult of the Blessed Virgin, especially to the liturgical cult, to value highly the practices and exercises of piety in her regard which have had, in the course of the ages, the recommendation of the magisterium, and religiously to observe the decrees of time gone by with regard to the cult of representations of Christ, the Blessed Virgin and the saints.[193] The Council strongly urges theologians and preachers of the divine word to be careful in their consideration of the Mother of God's unique dignity, to refrain as much from falsehood by way of superlatives as from narrow-mindedness.[194] They must develop the study of sacred Scripture, the Fathers and Doctors and the Liturgies of the Church, under the guidance of her magisterium, and throw a correct light on the functions and privileges of the

---

[193] Council of Nicaea II (in the year 787): Mansi 13, 378-379; Denz. 302 (600-601). Council of Trent, Sess. 25: Mansi 33, 171-172.
[194] Cf. Pius XII, *Broadcast*, 24 Oct. 1954: AAS 46 (1954) p. 679. Encycl. *Ad caeli, Reginam*, 11 Oct. 1954: AAS 46 (1954) p. 637.

Blessed Virgin, which are always relative to Christ, the origin of all truth, holiness and piety. They must be careful to exclude from their writings and their behaviour anything which might lead separated brethren, or others, into error over the Church's true teaching. The faithful must bear in mind that real devotion does not consist in sterile, transitory emotion nor in idle credulity but that it has its starting point in the true faith which brings us to recognize the excellence of God's Mother, and rouses us to a Son's love for our mother and to imitation of her virtues.

5. MARY, THE SIGN OF SURE HOPE AND OF COMFORT FOR THE PEOPLE OF GOD ON PILGRIMAGE

68. Jesus' mother, in the glory of body and soul she has attained already in heaven, is the image of the Church's attainment of glory in the age that is to come; she is the beginning of that attainment. Meanwhile, here on earth, until the day of the Lord comes (cf. 2 *Pet* 3:10), she is as certainly the resplendent sign of sure hope and comfort to the People of God on their pilgrimage.

69. It gives the sacred Council great joy and consolation to observe that among separated brethren also there are those who give due honour to the Lord and Saviour's mother, especially among Eastern Christians who assemble for the veneration of the ever virgin Mother of God with impulsive fervour and heart's devotion.[195] All Christ's faithful must issue urgent pleas to the Mother of God and Mother of men. She once assisted with her prayers at the beginnings of the Church. Now that she is placed high in heaven above all the blessed and the angels, they must plead with her to make intercession before her Son in the communion of all the saints, until all the families of

---

[195] Cf. Pius XI, Encycl. *Ecclesiam Dei*, 12 Nov. 1923: AAS 15 (1923) p. 581. Pius XII, Encycl. *Fulgens corona*, 8 Sept. 1953: AAS 45 (1953) pp. 590-591.

nations, whether they go under the name of Christian or are still without knowledge of their Saviour, shall have the happiness of assembling in peace and harmony in a single People of God to the glory of the most holy and undivided Trinity.

Each and all of the matters pronounced in this dogmatic Constitution have been approved by the Fathers. And We, by the apostolic authority given Us by Christ, together with the Venerable Fathers, approve, appoint and decree its contents in the Holy Spirit, and order that what has been decided in the Council be promulgated to the glory of God.

✛ **PAUL**, *Bishop of the Catholic Church*
St Peter's, Rome, 18 November 1964
The signatures of the Fathers follow.

'NOTIFICATIONES'

GIVEN BY THE SECRETARY GENERAL OF THE
COUNCIL AT THE ONE HUNDRED AND TWENTY-THIRD GENERAL
CONGREGATION 16 NOVEMBER 1964

A question has been raised as to the *precise theological note* to be attached to the teaching put forward in the *Schema de Ecclesia*, on which a vote is to be taken.

The Doctrinal Commission has given this answer to the question, in its assessment of the *Modi* in connection with the third chapter of the *Schema de Ecclesia*:

'As is self-evident, the Council's text must always be interpreted in accordance with the general rules which are known to all.'

On this occasion the Doctrinal Commission referred to its *Declaratio* of 6 March 1964, the text of which is given here:

'Taking conciliar custom into consideration and also the pastoral purpose of the present Council, the sacred Council is only defining as binding on the Church in matters of faith and morals, those statements which it has openly declared to be so.

'All the other statements that it proposes are the teaching of the supreme magisterium. They must therefore be welcomed and accepted by each and every one of Christ's faithful in the way in which the sacred Council intended. This intention is conveyed either by the subject matter or by the manner of utterance, according to the norms of theological interpretation.'

***

By higher authority, then, the Fathers are provided with a preliminary note of explanation attached to the *Modi* of Chapter III of the *Schema de Ecclesia*. The doctrine set out in the third chapter must always be explained and understood in the meaning stated in this note.

153

PRELIMINARY NOTE OF EXPLANATION

The Commission has decided to preface its assessment of the *Modi* with the following general observations.

1. The word "college" is not understood in its *strict, juridical* sense, i.e. a group of equals who bestow their power on their chairman, but as a group on a permanent footing, whose structure and authority can only be traced from Revelation. This is the reason that, in the reply to *Modus* 12, the express statement about the Twelve is that the Lord erected them "as a college or a *group on a permanent footing*". Cf. also *Modus* 53, c. The same reason explains the application, in places, of the terms "order" and "body" to the college of Bishops. The parallel between Peter with the rest of the apostles and the Supreme Pontiff with the Bishops, implies no transmission on the part of the apostles of their extraordinary power to their successors, nor, obviously, does it imply the existence of an *equality* between the head and the members of the college, but only a *proportion* between the two relationships: Peter-Apostles and Pope-Bishops. This made the Commission decide in Sec. 22 on the words "in like manner" and not "in the same way".

2. A man becomes a *member of the college* by dint of episcopal consecration and hierarchical communion with the head of the college and with its members. Cf. Sec. 22, end of par. 1.

An *ontological* share in the *sacred* functions is conveyed at the *consecration*; this is undoubtedly the teaching of Tradition, liturgical tradition included. Deliberate use is made of the word "function" in preference to "power", for the latter term might be interpreted as "power in readiness for action". The possession of "power in readiness for action" demands a further *determination, canonical* or *juridical*, by the channel of hierarchical authority. Such determination can consist in the appointment to a particular office or in the allotment of subjects; it is granted in accordance with the *norms* approved by the supreme

155

authority. The need for a further norm of this kind follows from the *nature of the case*: the functions in question have to be discharged by *more than one subject* acting in the co-operation which Christ willed. This "communion", it is evident, existed *in the life* of the Church in practice in accordance with the needs of the time, before it existed *in the law* as part of the Code.

This was the reason for making the clear statement that what is required, is *hierarchical* communion with the head of the Church and with the members. *Communion* is an idea which receives high respect in the ancient Church (and indeed today especially in the East). It does not carry the meaning of a vague *disposition*, but of an *organic reality* which demands a juridical shaping, and is quickened to life by charity. Thus the Commission, almost unanimously, agreed on the wording: "in *hierarchical* communion". Cf. *Modus* 40 and also the statements on *canonical mission* (Sec. 24).

The documents of recent Pontiffs which speak of the jurisdiction of Bishops, must be interpreted as referring to this necessary determination of powers.

3. The college, which does not exist without its head, is said "to exist as the subject of *supreme, plenary power* over the universal Church". This admission must be made without jeopardizing the fullness of power belonging to the Roman Pontiff. The meaning of college, of necessity, always includes its head, and *in the college the head preserves intact his function of Vicar of Christ and Pastor of the Universal Church*. In other words there is no distinction between the Roman Pontiff and the Bishops taken collectively. There is a distinction between the Roman Pontiff on his own and the Roman Pontiff in conjunction with the Bishops. Since the Roman Pontiff is the *head* of the Church there are certain actions which he alone can perform and in which the Bishops have no competence, e.g. the convening of the college, its direction, approval of its norms of action etc. Cf. *Modus* 81. The care of the whole of Christ's flock has been committed to the Roman Pontiff. It is for

his judgment to determine according to the needs of the Church (and they vary in the course of the ages) the appropriate manner, whether personal or collegiate, of exercising this care. The Roman Pontiff uses his own discretion in proceeding to arrangements for the exercise of collegiate activity, to promoting it or giving it approval, in view of the needs of the Church.

4. The Supreme Pontiff as Supreme Pastor of the Church can at any time exercise his power at will. This is demanded by his very function. The college, on the other hand, may always be in existence, but it is not permanently engaged in *strictly* collegiate activity, as the Church's tradition makes clear. In other words it is not always "fully active", or rather, it engages in strictly collegiate activity at intervals, but only *with the consent of the head* (nonnisi *consentiente Capite*). The phrase *"with the consent of the head"* (*consentiente Capite*) is used to avoid conveying the impression of a kind of *dependency* on an *outsider*. The phrase "with the consent of" (*consentiente*) suggests rather a *communion* between the head and the members; it implies the need of an *act* which is within the head's proper competence. The point is made explicitly in Sec. 22, par. 2, and it is explained at the end of the same section. The negative formula "only with" (*nonnisi*) includes all cases. It is evident from this that the *norms* approved by the supreme authority must always be observed. Cf. *Modus* 84.

It is clear throughout that the subject under discussion is the connection of the Bishops *with their head* and never of action on the part of Bishops *in independence* of their head. In such a case, in default of the head's action, the Bishops cannot be acting as a college. This is clear from the notion of "college". This hierarchical communion of Bishops with their head is certainly of long standing in Tradition.

N.B. Without hierarchical communion the "ontologico-sacramental" function (and this must be distinguished from its "juridico-canonical" aspect) *cannot* be discharged. It was the decision of the Commission not to enter into questions of *legality* and *Validity*. They are left to theologians to discuss, specifically as far as concerns the power exercised *de facto* among separated Eastern Christians; there are various opinions in existence as to how this is explained.

+ Pericles Felici, Titular Archbishop of Samosata
Secretary General of the Second Vatican Ecumenical Council

DOGMATIC CONSTITUTION ON DIVINE REVELATION

Dei Verbum

INTRODUCTION
by Archbishop Charles Chaput

Vatican II urges faithful to read the Bible

"It has pleased God in his goodness and wisdom to reveal himself and to disclose the mystery of his will" (cf. *Eph* 1:9).

So begins the Dogmatic Constitution on Divine Revelation (*Dei Verbum*), issued on November 18, 1965. *Dei Verbum*—which means "Word of God" in Latin—is one of the four foundational documents of the Second Vatican Council. And yet in some ways over the past 35 years, it's been a better-guarded secret than the "third secret of Fatima". Too many Catholics barely know it exists. And I hope we can begin to remedy that together.

Esteem for 'Word of God'

Many of you will remember that Vatican II produced 16 texts, divided into four major constitutions, plus various decrees and declarations. *Dei Verbum*, written as a constitution, showed the bishops' esteem for the Word of God and the reverence in which they hoped all Christian believers would hold that Word. *Dei Verbum* stands at a crossroad. On the one hand, it served as an official seal of approval on decades of biblical research by Catholic scholars, some of whom operated under a cloud of suspicion for much of their academic careers. At the same time, it launched everyday Catholics on a scriptural revival unparalleled in the history of the Church.

Dei Verbum opens by explaining the basic flow of the process of Divine Revelation, which comes to fruition in the life of Jesus Christ, who made revelation perfect by completing it, and confirming it by divine testimony (cf. no. 4). Since Jesus Christ is the definitive manifestation of God, the Council Fathers naturally say that "no other public revelation is to be awaited before the glorious manifestation of our Lord Jesus Christ" (no. 4).

Scripture and Tradition

Moreover, the bishops teach that "Sacred Tradition and holy Scripture form a single sacred deposit of the word of God entrusted to the Church" (no. 10). In doing so, the council bypasses the old Protestant Reformation debate about "Scripture versus Tradition" to a more useful discussion of the Lord's desire to reveal Himself fully to His People—a process carried forward by both Scripture and Tradition.

This makes sense. In reality, Tradition came before Scripture, and the Church came before them both, because the writing of the New Testament didn't begin until some fifteen to twenty years after the Lord's Death and Resurrection. The Gospel message was passed along through oral tradition first, and only later committed to written form. The means of transmission—whether oral or written—were secondary to the goal (revelation) and to the receiver of the revelation (God's People, the Church).

'Authentic Interpretation'

Obviously, the Scriptures didn't drop from heaven in final form. They took shape in and through the community of the Church, working under divine inspiration. And somewhat like the American Constitution, the Scriptures are not self-explanatory documents. They require an authentic interpretation—and that task "has been entrusted exclusively to the living voice of the Church's magisterium" (no. 10). The bishops stress that "sacred Tradition, holy Scripture and the Church's magisterium are by God's most wise decree so closely connected and associated together that one does not subsist without the other two, and that all of them, and each in its own manner, under the impulse of the one Spirit of God, contribute efficaciously to the salvation of souls" (*ibid.*).

Divine Inspiration

Dei Verbum therefore offers a middle way between Protestant fundamentalism and secular rationalism in interpreting the Bible. It clearly teaches the divine inspiration of the sacred authors and, therefore, the inerrant quality of their writings. It says "that the books of Scripture teach certainly, faithfully and without error the truth that God for our salvation willed to be recorded in holy Writ" (no. 11). In that qualifying phrase, "for our salvation," we hear the Catholic response to modern rationalism, which denies the inerrancy of Scripture and even the need for salvation. But *Dei Verbum* also avoids a simple-minded literalism.

In response to fundamentalists and biblical literalists, *Dei Verbum* stresses the need to "investigate what the sacred writers really intended to signify and God was pleased to manifest by their words" (no. 12). For Catholics, this comes through an analysis of "literary forms of expression. Truth is, in effect, set forth and enunciated in a diversity of fashions, in texts that are, in varying ways historical or prophetic or poetic, or that employ other modes of expression" (no. 12). *Dei Verbum*, then, follows the common sense wisdom of the great 16th century cardinal and historian Cesare Baronius, who reacted to the Galileo crisis of his day with the simple comment that, "The Scriptures tell us how to go to heaven—not how the heavens go."

God's Word leads us to fulfillment

Catholics hold that Scripture does not interpret itself. Obviously, it has great power and value for any reader. But to be fully understood, it needs both a scientific approach—the work of biblical scholars, along with experts in linguistics, history, archaeology and other fields—and also a final and authoritative voice. As *Dei Verbum* says, "all that has been said about the manner of interpreting Scripture is subject ultimately to the Church's judgment; she has the divine commission and the office of preserving and explaining the word of God" (no. 12).

In my experience, relatively few Catholics make the mistake of biblical literalism. But quite a few in recent years have bought into a kind of rationalism, which tends to deny the historical truth of the Gospels or the possibility of miracles, including even the virginal conception and bodily resurrection of Jesus. And yet the healthy response to today's skepticism is not a reactionary swing to fundamentalism, which simply doesn't fit with nineteen centuries of Catholic scholarship. Rather, the right path is the "middle road" of *Dei Verbum*, which gives proper weight to the scientific examination of Scripture, but insists that it be done from the perspective of faith and within the context of the Tradition of the Church.

Dei Verbum's most powerful passage may arguably be in its final chapter, which is devoted to the place of "Holy Scripture in the Life of the Church." It stresses that "the Church has always venerated the Body of Christ ... for she never fails, more especially in the sacred liturgy, to receive the bread of life, whether this comes from the table of the word of God or from that of Christ's Body" (no. 21). In other words, for Catholics, there is no conflict between Word and Sacrament. Just the opposite. The Word leads to the Sacrament, and the Sacrament presupposes and is actually made present by the Word.

Dei Verbum strongly encourages that the Scriptures "should lie wide open" to the faithful (no. 22). One way this has been done over the centuries, say the Council Fathers, has been through the rendering of the Bible into the various languages of the human family "from the very beginning" of Church history (no. 22). Some historians might have us believe that Martin Luther gave us the first modern-language vernacular Bible. But that's simply not true. Other German versions came first. Luther's claim to fame was that his translation was a very well polished, literary German. At any rate, with both practical and ecumenical concerns in mind, the bishops in *Dei Verbum* call for translations to be undertaken "by a common effort shared by our separated brethren," with ecclesiastical approval. One such successful effort has been the Common Bible, produced by a team of Protestant, Catholic and Eastern Orthodox scholars.

Another way the Church has listened to the Council's invitation to have the Scriptures open wide to the faithful is through the revised lectionary used for the liturgy. In this plan, the three Sunday readings rotate in a three-year cycle, covering all four Gospels, major passages from the epistles and significant portions of the Old Testament, especially the prophetical and historical books. The weekday lectionary is based on a two-year cycle, offering a broad exposure to portions of the Bible previously unread in the Liturgy. The arrangement is so good that a number of Protestant denominations have voluntarily adopted this lectionary. Not only are millions of Christians now being fed a very substantial diet at the table of God's Word, but it's happening to them at precisely the same moment, which suggests some hope for future unity.

Over the past thirty five years, the biblical revival sparked by Vatican II has been a source of blessing and vitality for the whole Church—and it will continue to renew the hearts of believers for many years to come. After all, if it "pleased God ... to reveal Himself" to us, shouldn't it equally please Him when we search the depths of that Revelation found in His Word and celebrated in His Church? Let me close this reflection with the words the Council Fathers used to conclude *Dei Verbum* 35 years ago:

So may it come that, by the reading and study of the sacred books the word of God may "'spread rapidly and be glorified' (2 *Thess* 3:1) and may the treasure of revelation entrusted to the Church more and more fill men's hearts. Just as persevering devotion to the eucharistic mystery augments the Church's life, so it is permissible to hope that a new impulse will be given to the spiritual life as a result of increased veneration for that word of God 'which endures for ever' (*Is* 40:8; 1 *Pet* 1:23-25)" (no. 26).

To which, I hope all of us throughout the Church, will always be able to give a heartfelt "Amen."

+Charles Chaput

PAUL, BISHOP
SERVANT OF THE SERVANTS OF GOD
TOGETHER WITH THE FATHERS
OF THE SACRED COUNCIL PUTS ON
PERMANENT RECORD THE

DOGMATIC CONSTITUTION
ON DIVINE REVELATION

INTRODUCTION

1. The sacred Council, devoutly attentive to the word of God and confident in proclaiming it, pays homage to the words of St John when he says: 'We declare unto you the life eternal which was with the Father and has appeared to us: that which we have seen and heard we declare unto you, that you also may have fellowship with us, and our fellowship may be with the Father, and with his son Jesus Christ' (1 *Jn* 1:2-3). For which cause, following in the footsteps of the Council of Trent, and of the First Vatican Council, this Council proposes to set forth the authentic doctrine of divine revelation and its transmission, so that the whole world may by hearing the message of salvation, come to believe it, by believing may hope, and by hoping may love.[1]

---

[1] Cf. St AUGUSTINE, *De catechizandis rudibus*, c. IV, 8: PL 40, 316.

CHAPTER I

REVELATION ITSELF

2. It has pleased God in his goodness and wisdom to reveal himself and to disclose the mystery of his will (cf. *Eph* 1:9), whereby men through Jesus Christ, the Word made flesh, have access to the Father in the Holy Spirit, and become partakers of the divine nature (cf. *Eph* 2:18; 2 *Pet* 1:4). By this revelation the invisible God (cf. *Col* 1:15; 1 *Tim* 1:17), out of the abundance of his love, speaks to men as to friends (cf. *Ex* 33:11; in 15:14-15) and is conversant with them (cf. *Bar* 3:38), that he may invite them to share his company and admit them to it. The divine plan of revelation is realised in deeds and words that are closely interconnected, so that the deeds wrought by God in the history of salvation manifest and reinforce the teaching and realities signified by the words, while the words proclaim the deeds and cast light upon the mystery contained in them. The profound truth conveyed by this revelation, whether it concerns God or man's salvation, shines forth for us in Christ who is at once the mediator and the fullness of revelation in its entirety.[2]

3. God who creates and keeps in existence all things by means of his Word (cf. *Jn* 1:3) offers to men in created things an abiding witness to himself (cf. *Rom* 1:19-20). Further, that he might open the way to heavenly salvation, he from the beginning made himself known to our first parents. Then, after their fall he raised them again by his promise of deliverance to the hope of salvation (cf. *Gen* 3:15) and without any intermission took loving care of the human race, so as to give eternal life to all who sought for salvation by patient endurance in the practice of good works (cf. *Rom* 2:6-7). In his own good time he called Abraham to make him the father of a great nation (cf. *Gen* 12:2), which, after the patriarchal era, he instructed through Moses and the Prophets, so that they might recognize him as the only living and true

---

[2] Cf. *Mt* 11:27; *Jn* 1:14, 17; 14:6; 17:1-3; 2 *Cor* 3:16, 4:6; *Eph* 1:3-14.

God, the beneficent Father and the just Judge, and might look for the promised Saviour; thus preparing through the centuries the way for the Gospel.

4. God having spoken diversely and in many ways by the Prophets 'last of all, in these days, has spoken to us by his Son' (*Heb* 1:1-2). He sent his Son, the eternal Word, who enlightens all men, that he might dwell among men, and interpret to them the divine secrets (cf. *Jn* 1:1-18). Jesus Christ, therefore, the Word made flesh, having been sent 'as man to men'[3] 'speaks the words of God' (*Jn* 3:34), and perfects the work of salvation that the Father gave him to perform (cf. *Jn* 5:36; 17:4). Wherefore he, to see whom is to see the Father also (cf. *Jn* 14:9), by the total fact of his presence and his public declaration of himself, by words and deeds, by signs and miracles, especially by his death and glorious resurrection from the dead, and, finally, by the sending of the Spirit of truth, made perfect by completing, and confirmed by divine testimony, the revelation that God is with us to deliver us from the shadow of sin and of death, and to raise us again to eternal life.

The Christian economy, then, as it is the new and definitive covenant, will never pass away, and no other public revelation is to be awaited before the glorious manifestation of our Lord Jesus Christ (cf. 1 *Tim* 6:14; *Tit* 2:13).

5. To God, as revealer, is to be given the 'obedience of faith' (*Rom* 16:26; cf. *Rom* 1:5; 2 *Cor* 10:5-6), whereby man abandons himself freely and entirely to God, yielding to him 'the entire submission of mind and will';[4] and voluntarily assenting to the revelation given by him. In order that this faith may be forthcoming there is need for God's prevenient and assisting grace, together with the inward aid of the Holy Spirit to move the heart and turn it towards God, open the eyes of the mind, and bestow upon all 'sweetness in consenting to and

---

[3] Epistle to Diognetus, c.VII, 4: FUNK, Apostolic Fathers, I, p. 403.
[4] VATICAN COUNCIL I, Dogmatic Constitution on the Catholic Faith, c. 3, on faith: DENZ. 1789 (3008).

believing the truth'.[5] And that the understanding of revelation may become more profound, the same Holy Spirit continues to perfect faith by his gifts.

6. By divine revelation God willed to make known and to communicate himself and the eternal decrees that are willed by him in regard to men's salvation 'that they may be sharers in those divine blessings which wholly surpass the understanding of the human mind'.[6]

The sacred Council declares that 'God, the beginning and end of all things, can certainly be known from created things by the natural light of human reason' (cf. *Rom* 1:20). It teaches, however, that one must attribute to his revelation that 'those matters relating to God which in divine affairs are not of themselves inaccessible to man's mind, may even in the present condition of the human race be known by all promptly, with firm certitude, and without any admixture of error.'[7]

---

[5] Council of Orange II, can. 7: Denz. 180 (377); Vatican Council I, *loc. cit.*: Denz. 1791 (3010).
[6] Vatican Council I, Dogmatic Constitution on the Catholic Faith, c. 2, on revelation: Denz. 1786 (3005).
[7] *Ibid.*: Denz. 1785 and 1786 (3004 and 3005).

CHAPTER II

THE TRANSMISSION OF DIVINE REVELATION

7. God in his supreme kindness so disposed that the truths he had revealed for the salvation of all peoples should persist for ever in their entirety, and should be handed on to all future generations. Therefore Christ our Lord, in whom the complete revelation of the most high God is fully accomplished (cf. 2 *Cor* 1:30; 3:16-4:6) gave command to his apostles that the Gospel, first promised by the Prophets, and later fulfilled by him and promulgated by his own lips, should be preached by them to all men as the source of all saving truth, and of all instruction in morals,[8] thus communicating the divine gifts to their hearers. This work was faithfully performed, first by the apostles, who by their oral preaching, their examples and their institutions handed on what they had received either from Christ's lips, from their association with him, and from his works or from what they had learned from the promptings of the Holy Spirit. Later, the work was carried on by those apostles and members of the apostolic circle who under the inspiration of the same Holy Spirit set down the message of redemption in writing.[9]

In order that the whole living Gospel might be for ever preserved in the Church, the apostles left as their successors, the bishops 'entrusting to them their own position as a teaching body'.[10] Hence sacred Tradition and the holy Scriptures of each of the two Testaments resemble a mirror in which the Church, during her journeying on earth, contemplates God, from whom she receives all things, until she may be brought to see him, face to face, as he is (cf. 1 *Jn* 3:2).

8. Thus the apostolic preaching, which is expressed in a special manner in the inspired books, had to be preserved by a continuous succession

---

[8] Cf. *Mt* 28:19-20, *Mk* 16:15; COUNCIL OF TRENT, Sess. IV, Decree on Scriptural Canons: DENZ. 783 (1501).

[9] Cf. COUNCIL OF TRENT, *loc. cit.*; VATICAN COUNCIL I, Sess. III, Dogmatic Constitution on the Catholic Faith, c. 2. on revelation: DENZ. 1787 (3006).

[10] ST IRENAEUS, *Adv. Haer.* III, 3, 1: PG 7, 848; HARVEY, 2, p. 9.

until the end of time. Hence the apostles, in handing on what they had themselves received, instruct the faithful to hold fast to the traditions they have learned, either by word of mouth or by letter (cf. 2 *Thess* 2:15) and to contend earnestly for the faith once and for all delivered to them (cf. *Jude* 3).[11] That which the apostles transmitted includes everything that contributes towards holiness of life in the People of God, and to the increase of their faith. And so the Church in her doctrine, her life and her worship perpetuates and hands on to all generations to come, all that she is and all that she believes.

This Tradition which comes from the apostles, progresses with the assistance of the Holy Spirit in the Church,[12] in so far as the understanding both of the events and of the words transmitted grows, both by reflection and study on the part of the faithful who ponder them in their hearts (cf. *Lk* 2:19, 51), and from a more profound experienced penetration of spiritual matters, as also through the preaching of those who have received with the episcopal succession an assured spiritual gift of truth. The Church, in the course of centuries, tends perpetually towards the fullness of divine truth, until the words of God shall find their complete expression in her.

The words of the holy Fathers bear witness to the vivifying presence of this Tradition, the riches of which are poured forth in the practice and life of the believing and praying Church. By means of this same Tradition the complete canon of holy Scripture is made known to the Church, and the sacred writings themselves are more profoundly understood and become unceasingly operative. In this manner God who spoke in times past continues without interruption to converse with the bride of his beloved Son, while the Holy Spirit, through whom the living voice of the Gospel resounds in the Church, and through her in the world, guides believers into all truth and makes the word of Christ dwell in them abundantly (cf. *Col* 3:16).

---

[11] Cf. COUNCIL OF NICAEA II: DENZ. 303 (602); COUNCIL OF CONSTANTINOPLE IV, Sess. X, can. 1: DENZ. 336 (650-652).

[12] Cf. VATICAN COUNCIL I, Dogmatic Constitution on the Catholic Faith. c. 4, on faith and reason: DENZ. 1800 (3020).

9. Sacred Tradition, then, and holy Scripture are closely joined and connected, each with the other. Both spring from the same divine fountain, and so in some manner merge into a unity, and tend towards the same end. For holy Scripture is the utterance of God, in so far as it was written down under the Holy Spirit's inspiration; while sacred Tradition hands on in its entirety the word of God, that was committed to the apostles, by Christ our Lord and the Holy Spirit to their successors, in order that being enlightened by the Spirit of Truth, they may in their preaching faithfully preserve, set forth and disseminate it. In this way it comes about that the Church does not derive from holy Scripture alone the certainty she possesses on all revealed truths. Therefore both Scripture and Tradition should be accepted with equal sentiments of devotion and reverence.[13]

10. Sacred Tradition and holy Scripture form a single sacred deposit of the word of God entrusted to the Church, holding fast to which the entire holy people, in union with their pastors, persevere in the apostles' teaching and the fellowship, in the breaking of bread and the prayers (cf. *Acts* 2:42, Gk), so that in their holding, practice and profession of the faith committed to them there is a wonderful unity between bishops and faithful.[14]

The office of interpreting authentically the word of God, whether scriptural or traditional,[15] has been entrusted exclusively to the living voice of the Church's magisterium,[16] whose authority is exercised in the name of Jesus Christ. This magisterium is not superior to the word of God, but ministers to the same word by teaching only what has been handed on to it, in so far as, by divine command and with the assistance of the Holy Spirit, the magisterium devoutly hears, religiously

---

[13] Cf. COUNCIL OF TRENT, Sess. IV, *loc. cit.*: DENZ. 783 (1501).
[14] Cf. PIUS XII, Apostolic Constitution, *Munificentissimus Deus,* 1 Nov. 1950: AAS 42 (1950), p. 756; compare with writings of ST CYPRIAN, Letter 66, 8: HARTEL, III, B, p. 733; 'The Church is the people united with the priest and the pastor together with his flock.'
[15] Cf. VATICAN COUNCIL I, Dogmatic Constitution on the Catholic Faith, c. 3 on faith: DENZ. 1792 (3011).
[16] Cf. PIUS XII, Encycl. *Humani Generis*, 12 Aug. 1950: AAS 42 (1950), pp. 568-69: DENZ. 2314 (3886).

keeps and faithfully explains the word, and from this one deposit of faith derives all those things which it proposes to us for acceptance as divinely revealed.

It is clear, therefore, that sacred Tradition, holy Scripture and the Church's magisterium are by God's most wise decree so closely connected and associated together that one does not subsist without the other two, and that all of them, and each in its own manner, under the impulse of the one Spirit of God, contribute efficaciously to the salvation of souls.

CHAPTER III

THE DIVINE INSPIRATION
AND INTERPRETATION OF HOLY SCRIPTURE

11. The divinely revealed truths that are contained and expressed in the books of holy Scripture were written under the inspiration of the Holy Spirit. Holy Mother Church from apostolic faith holds as sacred and canonical all the books of both the Old and the New Testaments with all their parts, because, having been written under the Holy Spirit's inspiration they have God for their author (cf. *Jn* 20:31; 2 *Tim* 3:16; 2 *Pet* 1:19-21; 3:15-16) and have been delivered as such to the Church herself.[17] For the composition of these books God chose and made use of men who employed in their task their natural capabilities and powers,[18] in order that through his action on them and by means of them[19] they should write, as true authors, all that he willed and only what he willed.[20]

Since therefore, all that the inspired authors or sacred writers assert is to be regarded as asserted by the Holy Spirit, it is also to be professed that the books of Scripture teach certainly, faithfully and without error the truth that God for our salvation willed to be recorded in holy Writ.[21] Hence, 'Every Scripture is inspired of God and profitable for teaching, for reproof, for correction and for training in justice; that the man of God may be perfect and fully equipped for every good work' (2 *Tim* 3:16-17 *Gk*).

---

[17] Cf. Vatican Council I, Dogmatic Constitution on the Catholic Faith, c. 2 on revelation: Denz. 1787 (3006); Biblical Commission, Decree 18 June 1915: Denz. 2180 (3629): EB (Enchiridion Bibl.) 420; Holy Office, Epistle 22 Dec. 1923: EB 499.

[18] Cf. Pius XII, Encycl. *Divino afflante Spiritu*, 30 Sept. 1943: AAS 35 (1943), p. 314: EB 556.

[19] *In and through man*: cf. *Heb* 1:1, 4:7; (in): 2 *Sam* 23:2; *Mt* 1:22 *et passim (through)*: Vatican Council I, Schema on Catholic Doctrine, note 9: Coll. Lac. VII, 522.

[20] Leo XIII, Encycl. *Providentissimus Deus*, 18 Nov. 1893: Denz. 1952 (3293); EB 125.

[21] Cf. St Augustine, *Gen. ad litt.* 2, 9, 20: PL 34, 270-271; Epistle 82, 3: PL 33, 277: CSEL 34, 2, p. 354. St Thomas, on Truth, q. 12, a. 2, C. Council of Trent, Sess. IV, Decree on Scriptural Canons: Denz. 783 (1501). Leo XIII, Encycl. *Providentissimus Deus:* EB 121, 124, 126-127. Pius XII, Encycl. *Divino afflante Spiritu:* EB 539.

12. Seeing that in holy Scripture God has spoken by means of men, and in a human manner,[22] the interpreter of holy Scripture in order to perceive what God willed to communicate to us, should investigate what the sacred writers really intended to signify and God was pleased to manifest by their words.

To discover the sacred writer's purpose one should pay attention, among other matters, to the literary forms of expression. Truth is, in effect, set forth and enunciated in a diversity of fashions, in texts that are, in varying ways historical or prophetic or poetic, or that employ other modes of expression. It behoves the interpreter to discover the sense which a sacred writer intended to express and did express, in certain definite circumstances, according to the conditions of his time and of his culture, and according to the classes of literature then in use.[23] For a correct understanding of what the sacred writer wished to assert in writing, due consideration should be paid to the habitual and ingrained methods of thinking, expressing oneself and narrating, that were current in the age of the sacred writer, and then to those usages that were customary in the relations between human beings, in that epoch.[24]

Since, however, holy Scripture is to be read and interpreted with the help of the Holy Spirit, by means of whom it was written,[25] it is necessary to have a right understanding of the sacred text, not least of the content and unity of all Scripture, taking account at the same time of the living Tradition of the whole Church and of the analogy of faith. It is the office of an interpreter to be at pains to penetrate with the help of these rules, to understand more fully, and to explain more deeply the sense of holy Scripture, and thus to provide the data where the Church's judgment maybe matured. All that has been said about the

---

[22] St Augustine, *City of God*, XVII, 6, 2: PL 41, 537: CSEL XL, 2, 228.

[23] St Augustine. *On Christian Doctrine,* III, 18, 26: PL 34, 75-76.

[24] Pius XII, *loc. cit.*: Denz. 2294 (3829-3830); EB 557-562.

[25] Cf. Benedict XV, Encycl. *Spiritus Paraclitus*, 15 Sept. 1920: EB 469. St Jerome, *In Galatians*, 5. 19-21: PL 26, 417 A.

manner of interpreting Scripture is subject ultimately to the Church's judgment; she has the divine commission and the office of preserving and explaining the word of God.[26]

13. In holy Scripture, therefore, God's truthfulness and holiness being always safeguarded, there is made known the wonderful "condescension" of the eternal Wisdom 'that we may be able to apprehend God's ineffable generosity whereby, in his providential care for human nature, he has adapted his speech to our needs'.[27] God's words expressed in human language are made like to human discourse, as formerly the eternal Father's Word, having taken upon himself the weakness of a human nature, was made like unto men.

---

[26] Cf. Vatican Council I, Dogmatic Constitution on the Catholic Faith, c. 2, on revelation: Denz. 1788 (3007).

[27] St John Chrysostom, In Gen. 3, 8 (Hom 17, 1): PG 53, 134. 'Attemperatio'; Gk synkatábasis.

Chapter IV

THE OLD TESTAMENT

14. God, when in his great love he willed and prepared the salvation of the human race, by a unique dispensation chose for himself a people to whom he would entrust his promises. Having made his covenant with Abraham (cf. *Gen* 15:18) and with the people of Israel through Moses (cf. *Ex* 24:8), he so revealed himself to that people by words and deeds as the one true God that Israel might learn by experience what were God's ways with men, and, when God himself spoke through the voice of the Prophets, might appreciate it with ever increasing depth and clarity, and might make it known to the Gentiles (cf. *Ps* 21:28-29; 95:1-3; *Is* 2:1-4; *Jer* 3:17). The economy of salvation which had been announced beforehand, described and expounded by the sacred writers, appears as the authentic word of God in the Old Testament books. For this reason these books, being divinely inspired, are of permanent value: 'Whatsoever things were written, were written for our learning; that through patience and the comfort of the Scriptures we might have hope' (*Rom* 15:4).

15. The Old Testament economy was above all devised to prepare for and to announce prophetically (cf. *Lk* 24: 44; *Jn* 5:39; 1 *Pet* 1:10) the coming of Christ, the world's redeemer, and the messianic kingdom, and to signify it by various types (cf. 1 *Cor* 10:11). Hence it is that the books of the Old Testament disclose to all, in accordance with the condition of the human race before the time of salvation instituted by Christ, the knowledge of God and of man and the manner in which a merciful and just God had dealings with men. These books, while containing also much that is imperfect and ephemeral, show clearly the manner in which God truly educated his people.[28] The faithful, then, should revere these books, which express a vivid perception of

---

[28] Pius XI, Encycl. *Mit brennender Sorge*, 14 March, 1937: AAS 29 (1937) p. 151.

God, and in which are stored up a sublime doctrine concerning God, saving wisdom on man's life, and rich treasures of prayer, in which moreover lies hidden the mystery of our salvation.

16. God then, the inspirer and author of the books of both the Testaments, has wisely provided that the New Testament should be concealed in the Old, and that the Old Testament should be made manifest in the New.[29] For though Christ established a new Covenant in his blood (cf. *Lk* 22:20; 1 *Cor* 11:25), the books of the Old Testament, taken up in their entirety as part of the Gospel message,[30] acquire and display their full signification in the New Testament (cf. *Mt* 5:17; *Lk* 24:27; *Rom* 16:25-26; 2 *Cor* 3:14-16) and, in their turn, make clear the latter and interpret it.

---

[29] St Augustine, *Quaest. in Hept.*, 2, 73: PL 34, 623.

[30] St Irenaeus, *Adv. Haer.* III, 21, 3: PG 7, 950; (Same as 25, 1: Harvey 2, p. 115). St Cyril of Jerusalem, *Catech.* 4, 35; PG 33, 497. Theodore of Mopsuestia, *In Soph.* 1; 4-6; PG 66, 452D-453A.

CHAPTER V

THE NEW TESTAMENT

17. The word of God, which is the power of God unto salvation to everyone who believes (cf. *Rom* 1:16), is made present and manifests its force in a sublime manner in the pages of the New Testament. When the fullness of time had come (cf. *Gal* 4:4) the Word was made flesh and dwelt among us, full of grace and truth (cf. *Jn* 1:14); Christ established on earth the kingdom of God, made known by work and by word his Father and himself, and completed the task by his death, resurrection and glorious ascension, and by sending the Holy Spirit. Being lifted up from the earth, he draws all men to himself (cf. *Jn* 12:32 Gk), since he alone has the words of eternal life (cf. *Jn* 6:68). This mystery was not made known to the sons of men in previous generations as it has now been revealed to his apostles and prophets by the Holy Spirit (cf. *Eph* 3:4-6 Gk), that they may preach the Gospel, stir up faith in Jesus Christ as Lord, and assemble the members of the Church. Of all this the New Testament writings remain as an enduring and divine witness.

18. It is common knowledge that among all the Scriptures, even those of the New Testament, the Gospels have a special pre-eminence, and this because they are the principal witness to the life and teaching of the Word Incarnate, our Saviour.

The Church has in every age held and holds that the four Gospels are of apostolic origin, in so far as the apostles preached by order of Christ, and later, under the inspiration of the Holy Spirit, this message was transmitted in writing by them and by men of their circle as a foundation of the faith, that is the fourfold Gospel of Matthew, Mark, Luke and John.[31]

19. Holy Mother Church has maintained and maintains with entire constancy and steadfastness that the four above-mentioned Gospels,

---

[31] Cf. St Irenaeus, *Adv. Haer.* III, 11,8: PG 7, 885; ed. Sagnard, p. 194.

whose historicity she affirms without hesitation, faithfully relate what Jesus the Son of God, while he passed his life among men, did and taught for their eternal salvation until the day when he was taken up into heaven (cf. *Acts* 1:1-2). The apostles after our Lord's ascension handed on to their hearers the things that he had said and done, in the light of the fuller understanding that they themselves, having been taught by the events of Christ's glorification and illumined by the Spirit of truth,[32] enjoyed.[33] The sacred writers, when they composed the four Gospels, made a selection of some of the many things that had been transmitted orally or in writing. Some of these they related in an abbreviated form or explained with due regard for the situation of the Churches. They retained the character of the original preaching, in such a way as always to impart to us an honest and true account of Jesus.[34] This was their intention when they wrote either from their own memory and recollection or from the testimony of others 'who from the beginning were eyewitnesses and ministers of the word': that we might know "the truth" of those words in which we have been instructed (cf. *Lk* 1:2-4).

20. The canon of the New Testament contains, besides the four Gospels, St Paul's epistles and other apostolic writings set down under the Holy Spirit's impulse, by which, according to God's wise counsel, the facts regarding Christ our Lord are confirmed, his true doctrine is more and more fully expounded, the saving power of his divine work is preached, the Church's beginnings and her wonderful extension are related, and her glorious consummation is foretold.

The Lord indeed, as he had promised, was present to his apostles (cf. *Mt* 28:20) and sent to them the Spirit of Truth who was to lead them into all the truth (cf. *Jn* 16:13).

---

[32] Cf. *Jn* 14:26; 16:13.

[33] *Jn* 2:22; 12:16; cf. 14:26; 16:12-13; 7:39.

[34] Cf. Instruction 'Holy Mother Church'. edited by the Pontifical Consilium for Promotion of Bible Studies: AAS 56 (1964), p. 715.

Chapter VI

HOLY SCRIPTURE IN THE LIFE OF THE CHURCH

21. Just as the Church has always venerated the Body of Christ, so she has always held in reverence the sacred Scriptures; for she never fails, more especially in the sacred liturgy, to receive the bread of life, whether this comes from the table of the word of God or from that of Christ's Body, and so to offer it to the faithful. She has ever considered, and considers, Holy Scripture to be, together with sacred Tradition, the supreme rule of her faith. Inspired as they are by God, and set down once and for all in writing, the Scriptures communicate unchangeably the word of God, and cause to resound in the words of prophets and apostles the voice of the Holy Spirit. All the Church's preaching, therefore, like the Christian religion itself, must be nourished and directed by holy Scripture. In the sacred books our Father who is in heaven most lovingly meets his children and speaks with them; such force and power are present in the word of God that it remains the Church's support and source of energy, and for her children a strengthening of the faith, a food of the soul, and a pure and never failing source of spiritual life. Hence one may admirably apply to holy Scripture the phrase: 'For the word of God is living and effectual' (*Heb* 4:12) which 'is able to build up and to give inheritance among all the sanctified' (*Acts* 20:32; cf. 1 *Thess* 2:13).

22. For Christ's faithful the approach to holy Scripture should lie wide open. Therefore the Church has from the very beginning accepted as her own that ancient Greek version known as the Septuagint; likewise she has always held in esteem other Eastern versions, and the Latin versions, especially that one which is styled the Vulgate. And since the word of God ought to be available at all times, the Church with motherly care provides that suitable and accurate versions are made in a variety of languages, and especially versions based on the original texts of holy Scripture. If, when occasion offers and leave is given by

182

the Church's authority, such versions are prepared by a common effort shared by our separated brethren, the resulting works can be used by all Christians.

23. The Church as the Bride of the incarnate Word, instructed by the Holy Spirit, is much concerned with the task of achieving an ever deeper understanding of holy Scripture, so that she may nourish her children unceasingly by the divine words; hence she rightly encourages the study of the holy Fathers of East and West, and of the ancient liturgies. Catholic exegetes and others dedicated to theological studies should, by zealous collaboration, devote their energies so that under the watchful eye of the sacred magisterium, and making use of all apt subsidiary studies, they may investigate and interpret the sacred books. This would provide that as many as possible of the ministers of the divine word may effectively offer to the people of God the sustaining gift of holy Scripture, which may enlighten the mind, strengthen the will, and enkindle the hearts of men with the love of God.[35] The sacred Council encourages those sons of the Church who are occupied with biblical studies that they may continue with constantly renewed vigour in the task they have successfully undertaken, and may carry out all their studies according to the mind of the Church.[36]

24. Sacred theology is based upon the written word of God, linked with sacred Tradition, as on a perpetual foundation, being thereby firmly strengthened and constantly renewed as it examines in the light of faith every truth contained in the mystery of Christ. Holy Scripture contains the word of God, and, since it is divinely inspired, truly is the word of God; therefore the study of holy Writ should be, as it were, the soul of theology.[37] Likewise the ministry of the word, which includes

---

[35] Cf. Pius XII, Encycl. *Divino afflante Spiritu*: EB 551, 553, 567. Pontifical Biblical Commission, Instruction on proper teaching of sacred Scripture in Seminaries and Religious Colleges, 13 May 1950: AAS 42 (1950), pp. 495-505.
[36] Cf. Pius XII, ibid.: EB 569.
[37] Cf. Leo XIII, Encycl. *Providentissimus Deus*: EB 114; Benedict XV, Encycl. *Spiritus Paraclitus:* EB 483.

pastoral preaching, catechetical teaching and all types of Christian instruction, and in which liturgical homilies should have an important
position, is advantageously sustained and spiritually fortified by the
words of holy Scripture.

25. Hence it is necessary that all clerics, more especially priests and
those who, as deacons and catechists, are lawfully engaged in the ministry of God's word, should remain in close contact with the Scriptures
by means of reading and accurate study of the text, in order not to become like 'one who vainly preaches the word of God externally, while
he does not listen to it inwardly'.[38] A preacher ought to make known
to the faithful under his care the vast riches of God's word, more especially in the sacred liturgy. Similarly the sacred Council earnestly and
expressly calls upon all the faithful especially Religious, to acquire by
frequent reading of holy Scripture 'the excellent knowledge of Jesus
Christ' (*Phil* 3:8). 'Ignorance of the Scriptures', writes St Jerome, 'is
indeed ignorance of Christ'.[39] They should, then, willingly make an
approach to the sacred text, whether by means of the holy liturgy, so
rich in the divine utterances, or by means of spiritual reading or of
instructions suited to the purpose or by other aids, which with the approval and assistance of the Church's pastors, are in our time laudably
to be found everywhere. It must be remembered that prayer should
accompany the reading of holy Scripture, in order that there may be a
dialogue between God and man, for 'we speak to him when we pray,
and he speaks to us when we read the divine utterances'.[40]

It is the duty of bishops, 'with whom is the apostolic doctrine',[41] to
instruct the faithful committed to them in the correct use of the Bible,

---

[38] St Augustine, *Serm.* 179, 1: PL 38, 966.

[39] St Jerome, *Commentary on Isaiah*, Prol.: PL 24, 17. Benedict XV, Encycl. *Spiritus Paraclitus:* EB 475–480; Pius XII, Encycl. *Divino afflante Spiritu:* EB 544.

[40] St Ambrose, *On the duties of ministers* 1, 20, 88: PL 16, 50.

[41] St Irenaeus, *Adv. Haer.* IV, 32, 1: PG 7. 1071; (Same as 49, 2) Harvey 2, p. 255.

especially the books of the New Testament, and, in the first place, the Gospels, by means of versions of the sacred text, which should be furnished with requisite and really sufficient explanatory notes, so that the Church's sons may be securely and usefully made acquainted with the Scriptures, and may be filled with their spirit.

Furthermore, editions of holy Scripture provided with suitable notes should also be prepared for the use of non-Christians in a manner adapted to their needs. The pastors of souls, or Christians generally should take care to circulate these with enthusiasm and discretion.

26. In this manner, by the reading and study of the sacred books, may the word of God 'spread rapidly and be glorified' (2 *Thess* 3:1) and may the treasure of revelation entrusted to the Church more and more fill men's hearts. Just as persevering devotion to the eucharistic mystery augments the Church's life, so it is permissible to hope that a new impulse will be given to the spiritual life as a result of increased veneration for that word of God 'which endures for ever' (*Is* 40:8; 1 *Pet* 1:23-25).

Each and all of the matters pronounced in this Constitution have been approved by the Fathers of the sacred Council. And We, by the apostolic authority given Us by Christ, together with the Venerable Fathers, approve, appoint and decree its contents in the Holy Spirit, and order that what has been decided in the Council be promulgated to the glory of God.

✠ **PAUL**, *Bishop of the Catholic Church*
St Peter's, Rome, 18 November 1965
The signatures of the Fathers follow.

PASTORAL CONSTITUTION ON THE CHURCH IN THE MODERN WORLD

Gaudium et Spes

INTRODUCTION
by Cardinal Angelo Scola

A Constitution for Dialogue[1]

The majority of historians and theologians agree in affirming that *Gaudium et Spes* represents an exceptionally significant expression of the Church's changed attitude to the contemporary world from the time of the Second Vatican Council.

The category of dialogue as explored by the Magisterium of Paul VI in the encyclical *Ecclesiam Suam* provided the keystone for the development of this different way of looking at reality. *Gaudium et Spes* refers to it, though less according to the letter (cf. GS 40, 43, 56, 85, 92) and rather more according to the spirit. However, ecclesial events and theological reflection since the Council have made it very obvious that many aspects of the subject of dialogue still await clarification.

The Fathers and Conciliar experts were perfectly aware of this and explicitly stressed how it was in the nature of a pastoral Constitution to remain open to later developments, as we can see from the judgement of one of the best accredited witnesses to the process of composition of *Gaudium et Spes*. I am thinking of Tucci's statement: 'The Council did not therefore intend this document to bring an end to research, but rather to anticipate research and stimulate it, to establish a point of departure and to set out the prerequisites for a fruitful dialogue. There is no doubt that the Church had what a shrewd observer called 'the courage to be imperfect', the courage to be content with imperfect things, i.e. to launch out trustfully into the future with humble faith both in God and in man his image'.[2]

Vatican II gave the Church a Constitution defined as pastoral, and in this Constitution the programmatic intention clearly expressed in

---

[1] The themes discussed here find an organic development in: A. SCOLA, *'Gaudium et Spes': dialogo e discernimento nella testimonianza della verità'* in R. FISICHELLA (a cura di), *Il Concilio Vaticano II. Recezione e attualità alla luce del Giubileo* (San Paolo: Cinisello Balsamo, 2000), 82-114.

[2] R. TUCCI, 'Introduzione storico-dottrinale alla Costituzione Pastorale Gaudium et spes' in AA.VV., *La Constituzione Pastorale sulla Chiesa nel mondo contemporaneo*, Elle Di Ci, Turin, 1968, p. 134.

the Preface and the Introductory Statement—which lay particular stress on the pastoral task, as it is called—is connected to the urgent problems of the Second Part where the traits of a pastoral nature are present for the most part in *actu exercitu* (i.e. in practice).

The category of dialogue thus emerged at the end of the Council as emblematic of the new phase that had opened in the life of the Church. Among other things this explains very simply why the post-Conciliar era developed (especially in its initial period) under the sign of *Gaudium et Spes*.

Gaudium et Spes seems to me to have two fundamental principles, and they relate both to its content and to its method.

The first of these principles for interpreting and practising the teaching of *Gaudium et Spes* is constituted by an *anthropology* with Christocentric intentions. This anthropology sought an appropriate foundation for the dignity of the human person as the effective basis for an approach to what were considered the most urgent problems—contained in the Second Part—aside from their natural evolution.

The question of the *pastoral* nature of the Constitution on the Church in the contemporary world emerges as the second crucial principle. The pastoral dimension which the Council—attentive to the so-called signs of the times—sees as the way to present Jesus Christ to the human family, is perceived by the Conciliar Fathers as giving expression to the essence of the salvific mission of the Church: 'God ... wants everyone to be saved and reach full knowledge of the truth' (1 *Tim* 2, 4).

These two elements—a vision of man as related to Jesus Christ (Christocentric anthropology) and an emphasis on the salvific-sacramental mission of the Church (her pastoral mission)—are the basis of the attitude of dialogue and discernment which the Church maintains towards the world in order to bear testimony to the truth: 'Since the Church's mission is to spread the light of the Gospel through the world and unite all men of whatever nation, race or culture in one Spirit, she is the sign of that brotherhood which makes possible and encourages a sincere dialogue' (GS 92).

Introduction—Cardinal Angelo Scola

a) A Christocentric anthropology

What motivated the Fathers of Vatican II to introduce this kind of anthropological discourse into the redaction of *Gaudium et Spes* was the fact that it formed the whole basis of the attitude of dialogue so forcefully advocated by John XXIII in his opening address to the council and organically deepened by Paul VI in the encyclical *Ecclesiam suam*.

What kind of anthropology are we speaking of here?

The clearly Christocentric dimension of the anthropology underlying the Constitution is quite undeniable. It suffices to cite the *loci classici* in this regard: GS 10, 22, 32, 38-39, 40-41, 45. In particular, GS 10 makes explicit the nexus between Christocentric anthropology and dialogue: 'In the light of Christ, the image of the invisible God, the first-born of all creation the Council means to address itself to everybody, to shed light on the mystery of man and cooperate in finding solutions to the problems of our time.'

At the same time it has to be recognized that this intention was carried out only fragmentarily. Taking account of the passing of time and the changed socio-cultural situation, and paying due attention to subsequent analytical and organic studies relative to revelation, Christology and the anthropology of the Council, we can say that while the anthropology of the Pastoral Constitution is clearly Christocentric in intention, it remains fragmentary and overly indebted to the neo-scholastic manuals in actual expression. That said, it does nonetheless contain plenty of sections offering the features of an objective Christocentric anthropology in embryo.

If this judgement that there is a lack of harmony between the intention of the Fathers and the effective result in *Gaudium et Spes* is valid, we can better understand perhaps why the standard accounts conclude that the initially enthusiastic reception of its anthropology gave way after ten years to a certain disappointment, indeed even to a certain neglect. In fact, once the initial phase of the positive reverberation of the Christocentric dimension had passed and attention came to be focussed on attempts at the application and deeper hermeneutic of the text of the *Constitution*, there was a growing awareness of the objectively tentative character of the choice of the Conciliar Fathers and therefore of the imperative need for an organic reconsideration of the subject.

b) The pastoral dimension

As we have already noted, in *Gaudium et Spes* the pastoral preoccupation is expressed in terms of the theme of dialogue, and it found a particular resonance in the themes of *aggiornamento* and of the *signs of the times*. From the beginning the pastoral imperative was a mark of the conciliar proclamation in Pope John XXIII himself. In a nutshell: Pope Roncalli and after him Paul VI and the Conciliar Fathers intended to emphasize the salvific nature of the Church precisely by pointing to her pastoral task. The Church offers testimony to the truth that is Jesus Christ through the fact of conceiving herself essentially as *propter homines* (i.e. for, or on behalf of, men), and as a function of this salvific movement she discerns error while having compassion for the person who errs.

The debate on the pastoral dimension was one of the trickiest issues in the development of the conciliar assembly. Staying with *Gaudium et Spes*, a significant proof of this (in addition to the adjective *pastoral* inserted in the title itself and already referred to) is the famous *Nota I* on the need to look at the Constitution as 'a single whole' in which there is no conflict between pastoral intention and doctrinal intention. It has to be admitted that this tricky issue not only was not resolved during the Council, but in many ways remains still to be resolved. The problems classified as being of a pastoral nature, problems which had already emerged in the Council sessions, were rather summarily dealt with from the time of the first commentaries on the *Constitution*. These problems can perhaps be reduced to three heads.

First of all, the question of a language adequate to express the dialogical (pastoral, in fact) dimension of the Council. Secondly the problem of the pastoral nature of *doctrine*—with particular reference to magisterial pronouncements. Finally, the delicate question of the relationship between Jesus Christ as absolute Truth and respect for the insuperable freedom of each person. Here we have the three dimensions of the pastoral dimension as focussed on by the Fathers with the aim of identifying the correct dialogical attitude of the Church towards the world.

These three factors provide potent evidence of the connection between the pastoral work of the Church and her witness to truth in conjunction with her discernment about the world: unavoidable issues for a Christianity that aims at an integral adoption of the deepest concerns of the heart of man. *Gaudium et Spes* shows itself quite aware of this not simply in its handling of the urgent problems dealt with in the Second Part but even more so in the way it faces up organically to the theme of atheism, one of the distinctive questions of modernity. We must remember that the Council had to grapple with this crucial problematic of truth-discernment on many occasions—e.g. when tackling religious freedom, ecumenical dialogue and interreligious dialogue.

This attempt to give some kind of introduction to the reading of *Gaudium et Spes* brings us to the following conclusion.

The dialogical motivation of the Conciliar Fathers, found in the themes of Christocentric anthropology and the pastoral dimension its most significant expressions, but its formulation in the text of the Constitution remains inadequate.

Making herself present among men through her various members and institutions, the Church shows herself to be the efficacious sacrament of the Christ-event, speaking to the liberty of man and of the human family. Speaking not so much of herself, but reflecting the face of Christ in her own, she proves herself to be the *Ecclesia de Trinitate,* giving her life concretely in the martyrdom of charity—starting with the poorest. Dialogue is thus properly to be identified with the real communication of the identity of the Christian that puts itself forward in the first person as (sacramental) sign of Jesus Christ, heart of the world, through the Church, *forma mundi*. Jesus Christ, living personal truth, exalts the liberty of each individual, of each people, of each culture, of each religion. He is 'the true light that enlightens all men' (*John* 1, 9). Obedience, inexorably required by truth, never violates liberty because, as was demonstrated by the monks of Tibhirine (the Atlas Martyrs), to communicate the truth implies to disposing oneself when all is said and done to martyrdom, whose power the Father can grant even to the weak and to the helpless. Like the discernment involved in every authentic dialogue, the *noes* of the Church in the moral domain are in reality the positive expression of this attitude of the total offering of self. They reveal the primacy of witness over *critique* or rather they expose a *critique* that is not witness as ultimately unconvincing.

There is no exaggeration in affirming that with *Gaudium et Spes* the Second Vatican Council set in motion a *novum* in the life of the Church. This new thing has begun to bear fruit especially since 1985, even if that fruit still has not been fully revealed. But the reception of *Gaudium et Spes* and of the Council—inevitably connected to its application, which in turn depends on a correct hermeneutics—is still in progress.

In fact the beginning of the new millennium finds Christians engaged in the unfinished process of the reception of the Second Vatican Council. This daily objective task allows us to shun utopian flights into the future in favour of dealing with reality as it is.

+Angelo Cardinal Scola
Translated by Cyprian Blamires

PASTORAL CONSTITUTION ON
THE CHURCH IN THE MODERN WORLD[1]
PROMULGATED BY HIS HOLINESS POPE PAUL VI
ON DECEMBER 7, 1965

PREAMBLE

1. The joy and hope, the sorrow and anxiety of the men of our time, especially of the poor and of those who are in any way suffering; these Christ's disciples make their own, and there is nothing human that does not find an echo in their hearts. For the Christian community is made up of men; they are brought together in Christ, guided by the Holy Spirit along their pilgrim way to the Father's kingdom, and they have received a message of salvation as something to be offered to everybody. Hence the Christian community feels itself closely linked with the human race and its history.

2. For this reason the Second Vatican Council, having already examined more deeply the mystery of the Church, now speaks unhesitatingly not only to the Church's sons and to those who call on the name of Christ, but to all men, anxious to explain to all how it understands the presence and function of the Church in the world of today.

The world the Council has in mind then is the world of men, the entire human family, its whole environment; the world which is the theatre of human history, marked with man's industry, his triumphs and disasters. It is the world which the faithful believe to be made

---

[1] *About the title:* The Pastoral Constitution on the Church in the World of Today consists of two parts which nevertheless make up a single whole.

The Constitution is called 'pastoral' because, resting on doctrinal principles, it sets out to explain the relation of the Church to the world and the men of today. There is no lack of pastoral intention in the first part nor of doctrinal intention in the second.

In the first part the Church develops her doctrine of man, of the world in which he is involved and of her own relation to both. In the second she considers more closely various aspects of contemporary life and human society, and especially questions and problems which in our time seem more pressing. Hence it is that this latter part, though resting on doctrinal principles, has certain provisional as well as permanent elements.

The Constitution is to be interpreted, then, according to the general rules of theological interpretation, bearing in mind, especially in the second part, the changeable circumstances naturally surrounding the matters there treated.

and sustained by the Creator's love. It was enslaved indeed to sin, but Christ crucified and risen from the dead has freed it, so that according to God's design it may be transformed and achieve its fulfilment.

3. In our time men are moved to admiration at their own inventions and power, yet often wonder anxiously about the way the world is developing, about the place and function of man in the universe, about the direction of individual and collective effort, about the final purpose of things and of men. The Council witnesses to and expounds the faith of the whole People of God. It cannot show how close it feels to the human family to which it belongs, how it loves and respects it, more eloquently than by entering on a discussion with that family of these various problems—bringing the light of the Gospel to bear on them, lending mankind the support of that strength the Church draws from her Founder under the guidance of the Holy Spirit. Men must be saved, human society restored. Our discourse then will hinge completely on man whole and entire—body and soul, heart and conscience, mind and will.

The Council proclaims man's high vocation, insists on a certain seed of divinity he carries within him; for this reason it offers the human race the Church's sincere co-operation in establishing that universal brotherhood which answers to such a vocation. The Church is moved by no earthly ambition; she wants one thing only: led by the Holy Spirit to carry on the work of Christ, who came into this world to witness to the truth—to save, not to judge, to serve, not to be served.[2]

---

[2]Cf. *Jn* 3:17; 18:37; *Mt* 20:28; *Mk* 10:45.

INTRODUCTION

MAN'S CONDITION IN THE WORLD OF TODAY

4. To carry out this task the Church must continually examine the signs of the times and interpret them in the light of the Gospel. Thus she will be able to answer the questions men are always asking about the meaning of this life and of the next and about the relation of one to the other, in a way adapted to each generation. So the world in which we live, its expectations, its aspirations, its often dramatic character must be known and understood. Some of the principal features of the contemporary world can be outlined as follows.

Humanity is passing through a new phase of its history, in which profound and rapid changes are gradually affecting the whole world. Prompted by man's intelligence and creative industry, these changes recoil on man, on his judgements and desires, individual and collective, on his manner of thinking and acting towards things and towards his fellows. We can in fact speak of a social and cultural transformation, which reacts also on religious life.

As happens in any crisis of growth the transformation brings with it considerable difficulties. Thus though man extends his power so widely he is not always able to harness it to his service. Trying to penetrate more deeply the inner recesses of his own mind he often seems still more uncertain of himself. Slowly unfolding the laws governing social life, he remains doubtful what direction to give it.

The world has never enjoyed such wealth, resources and economic powers, and yet a very large part of the earth's inhabitants are plagued by hunger and want and countless people are ignorant and illiterate. Men have never had so acute a feeling for liberty as they have today— just when whole new types of social and psychological slavery are appearing. While the world is vividly aware of its unity, of the dependence of men on each other, of the need of solidarity, it is torn apart by contending forces. Bitter rivalries, political, social, economic, racial and ideological, still persist; so does the danger that war might destroy everything utterly. The communication of ideas increases, but the words in which important ideas are expressed have very different meanings in different ideologies. Finally, the search for a better temporal order is unflagging, but spiritual growth does not keep pace.

In such complex conditions many of our contemporaries are hindered from recognizing enduring values and reconciling them with new discoveries. Buffeted between hope and anxiety, questioning themselves about the present course of events, they carry a burden of disquiet. These questions call for, even compel, answers.

5. Today's disturbance of minds and changed conditions of living are connected with wider upheavals—with the increasing weight of mathematics and the natural sciences in education and of the techniques derived from them in practical training.

This 'scientific mind' fixes the pattern of culture and ways of thinking quite otherwise than in previous times. Technical progress has transformed the face of the earth and now sets out to subdue outer space. The human intellect in a fashion is also extending its sway over time: over the past by historical knowledge, over the future by prediction and planning.

Advances in biology, psychology and social science help man not only to know himself better but even to bring techniques to bear in directly modifying social life. At the same time the human race thinks more and more of forecasting and controlling its own population growth.

The course of history is accelerating so rapidly that the individual cannot follow it. Human destiny is being unified and is no longer a matter of several different histories. Humanity is passing from a static to a dynamic and evolutionary conception of things. Thus does a vast new complex of problems come to birth, which call for new analyses and syntheses.

6. This means that traditional local communities such as patriarchal families, clans, tribes, rural communities, a variety of groups and social associations are changing more radically every day.

An industrial type of society is gradually spreading, bringing affluence to some nations and radically altering age-old social ideas and conditions. The glamour of city life and the hankering after it grows, whether cities and their populations are enlarged or urban ways of life are extended to country folk.

New and more efficient mass communications spread news and habits of thinking and feeling very rapidly and widely, causing many closely linked repercussions.

Nor is it a small matter how many people there are who are led to emigrate, and thus change their whole manner of life.

Thus the demands men make on each other are steadily multiplied, and the very process of 'socialization' induces further demands, but without promoting a comparable maturing of personality and personal relations ('personalization').

This kind of development is more clearly evident in countries which already enjoy adequate standards of economic and technical progress, but it also stirs less advanced peoples, still straining after progress, who want the benefits of industrialization and urbanization for their own lands. These, especially if tied to older traditions, at the same time feel the urge to a greater and more mature personal liberty.

7. A change of outlook and social structures frequently prompts people to question inherited values; this is especially true of the young—they become impatient, restlessness turns them into rebels; conscious of their own importance, they are in a hurry to have a part in social life. Parents and teachers hence find it steadily more difficult to perform their tasks.

The institutions, laws, habits of thought and feeling left us by our ancestors do not always seem well adapted to present-day conditions. Hence fashions and standards of behaviour are seriously upset.

Finally, these new conditions affect religious life itself. On the one hand, sharper critical faculties purify it of a magical conception of the world and of surviving superstitions, and call for a more personal and active commitment to faith, so that many achieve a more lively sense of God. On the other hand greater numbers practically give up religion. In contrast to earlier times, to deny God or religion or to ignore them is no longer something unusual or likely to attract attention; it is often alleged to be demanded by scientific progress or by humanism. These things are in many places no longer confined to the speculations of philosophers but very widely affect literature, the arts, the sciences, the interpretation of history and even the law, so that many minds are disturbed.

8. Such rapid and often uncontrolled change, as well as the keener awareness of contrasts in the world, sets up or aggravates tension and strain.

Often there is a strain in the personality between the modern 'practical' understanding and the inability to synthesize data within the framework of a theory. Strain occurs between the concern for practical efficiency and the demands of conscience, between social demands and those of personal thinking or contemplation; and there is strain between specialization and a comprehensive vision.

Discords arise in families, whether from the strain of numbers and from economic and social problems, or from differences between successive generations, or from social tension between men and women.

There are race discords, class discords, discords between affluent nations and weak or poor nations; between international bodies born of the general wish for peace and the ambition to spread ideologies or the collective greed of nations and other groups.

Hence mutual distrust and enmity, conflict and crisis of which man is at once the cause and the victim.

9. Meanwhile the conviction grows that man not only can and should strengthen his control over created things: it is also his business to establish a more serviceable political, social and economic order, an order more helpful to individuals and groups in vindicating and maintaining their dignity.

Many sharply demand those things which they clearly realize they are deprived of by injustice and unequal distribution. Developing nations, those, for example, recently become autonomous, want an economic as well as a political share in the good things of contemporary civilization. They want to be free to play their full part, yet every day they fall further behind and depend more on the richer and more rapidly-progressing nations. Peoples suffering famine beg from the richer countries. Women claim equality, legal and practical, with men, where they do not have it already. Town and country workers do not want to work merely to survive—they want to exploit their talents and play a part in the ordering of their own economic, social, political and cultural life. For the first time in history everybody is convinced that the benefits of culture can and should be extended to everybody.

Beneath all these demands there lies a deeper and wider aspiration: individuals and groups thirst for a fuller, freer life more worthy of man—a life in which they may bend to their service everything that the world of today can abundantly supply. Nations too become steadily more committed to the achievement of some universal community.

In the light of all this our world appears as at once powerful and weak, capable of achieving the best or the worst; the way lies open to freedom or slavery, to advancement or slipping back, to brotherhood or hatred. Further, man is realizing that it is up to him to control properly the forces he has conjured up and which can either oppress him or serve his ends. Therefore he questions himself.

10. The strains under which the world labours today are connected with these more fundamental tensions. In man himself several elements are opposed. While as a creature he feels himself limited in several ways, at the same time he is aware of unlimited aspirations and of a call to a higher life. He is attracted by many things—he must always reject some and select others. Weak and sinful, he often does what he would prefer not to do and fails to do what he would like.[3]

---

[3]Cf. *Rom* 7:14 ff.

201

He is divided against himself: from this it is that so many discords arise in society at large. Obviously many who in practice live as materialists are distracted from this internal drama, or at least are hindered by extreme want from thinking about it. Many find refuge in various general theories about life. There are those who look forward to the full liberation of mankind by mere human effort, and are convinced that man's coming reign over the whole earth will satisfy all the desires of his heart. There are those who, themselves despairing of finding any meaning in life, praise the courage of men who deny life any general significance and dedicate themselves arbitrarily to self-fulfilment. None the less, in the face of present day developments more and more people ask, or feel deeply the need of asking, absolutely fundamental questions: What is man? What is the meaning of pain, of evil, of death—things which persist in spite of so much progress? What are all our hard-won conquests worth? What can a man bring to society, what can he expect from it? What will come after life on earth?

The Church believes that Christ, who died and rose from the dead for all of us,[4] gives man through his Spirit light and strength enough to live up to his high vocation; nor is there any other name under heaven given among men by which we must be saved.[5] She believes that the key, the centre and purpose of all human history is to be found in her Lord and Master. The Church claims that beneath all change there are many things unchanging which have their ultimate foundation in Christ who is the same yesterday and today and forever.[6] In the light of Christ, the image of the invisible God, the first-born of all creation[7] the Council means to address itself to everybody, to shed light on the mystery of man and cooperate in finding solutions to the problems of our time.

---

[4]Cf. 2 *Cor* 5:15.
[5]Cf. *Acts* 4:12.
[6]Cf. *Heb* 13:8.
[7]Cf. *Col* 1:15.

PART I

THE CHURCH AND MAN'S VOCATION

11. Believing that they are led by the Spirit of the Lord who fills the whole earth, the People of God sets out to discover among the events, needs and aspirations they share with contemporary man what are the genuine signs of the presence and purpose of God. For faith sheds new light on everything and reveals the divine intention about man's entire vocation, thus guiding the mind towards fully human solutions of problems.

First the Council means to assess in this light those values which are today most highly esteemed and to trace them back to their divine source. These values, coming as they do from the nature bestowed on man by God, are thoroughly good; but through the corruption of the human heart they are often distorted and need purifying.

What does the Church think of man? What seems commendable in building contemporary society? What is the ultimate meaning of human effort in the world as a whole? An answer is expected to these questions. From this it will appear that the People of God and the whole human family of which it forms part are of assistance to each other—that the Church's religious mission is by the same token a human one.

CHAPTER I

THE DIGNITY OF THE HUMAN PERSON

12. Believers and non-believers are practically agreed that man is the centre on which all things on earth focus—the apex of nature.

But what is man? He has voiced and still voices many different and even contrary opinions about himself, either exalting himself as the absolute standard or belittling himself to the point of despair. So he is puzzled and anxious. In sympathy with these difficulties, the Church can put forward an answer based on Revelation, describing the true condition of man, explaining his infirmities, at the same time acknowledging his dignity and vocation.

The Scriptures teach that man is created 'in the image of God', capable of knowing and loving his Creator, established by him as Lord of creation[8] to rule over and use created things for God's glory.[9] 'What is man that you are mindful of him, and the son of man that you care for him? Yet you have made him little less than the angels, and you crown him with glory and honour. You have given him dominion over the works of your hands; you have put all things under his feet' (*Ps* 8:5-7).

But God did not create man to be alone: from the beginning 'male and female he created them' (*Gen* 1:27)—the first form of personal communion. Man in his most intimate nature is a social being, and can neither live nor develop his gifts except in relationships with others.

God, then, as we read again in Scripture 'saw everything that he had made, and behold it was very good' (*Gen* 1:31).

13. Made just by God, man nevertheless from the outset of his history was persuaded by the Evil One to abuse his freedom, set himself up in opposition to God and seek his fulfilment elsewhere. When men knew God they did not glorify him as God: their foolish minds were

---

[8] Cf. *Gen* 1:26; *Wis* 2:23.
[9] Cf. *Ecclus* 17:3-10.

clouded and they served the creature rather than the Creator.[10] What Revelation teaches, experience confirms: man looking into his heart finds himself prone to evil and sunk in many evils which cannot come from his good Creator. Often he refuses to acknowledge God as his first beginning and disrupts the harmony which should govern his relations with God, with himself, with other men and with all created things.

So is man divided against himself; so does human life, personal or collective, seem a struggle, and a dramatic one, between good and evil, between light and darkness. Man finds himself unable by his own efforts to repulse the attacks of evil—everyone feels himself in chains. But the Lord himself came to free and comfort man, inwardly renewing him, casting out the prince of this world (cf. Jn 12:31) who had held him enslaved to sin.[11] But sin diminishes man, holding him back from attaining his fulfilment.

In the light of this Revelation we really understand why man is conscious at the same time of a sublime destiny and of a profound wretchedness.

14. Man is a unity of body and soul; by virtue of his bodily condition he is compounded of elements of this material world—elements which indeed reach their highest in him and raise their voice in free praise of their Creator.[12] It is wrong therefore to despise our bodies. On the contrary we are bound to honour them, and esteem them as good since they are created by God and will rise at the last day. But since he is wounded by sin man finds his body resisting control. Human dignity demands that he should glorify God in his body[13] and not allow it to serve those of his heart's desires which are wrong.

Man is not deceived when he recognizes himself to be superior to bodily things—to be no mere speck in nature or anonymous element

---

[10]Cf. *Rom* 1:21-25.
[11]Cf. *Jn* 8:34.
[12]Cf. *Dan* 3:57-90.
[13]Cf. 1 *Cor* 6:13-20.

in the body politic. There are interior resources in him which can transcend the world of experience. He is deeply aware of this when he looks into his heart,[14] where God, who searches hearts, awaits him and where he discerns his own destiny through the eyes of God. When he recognizes his own soul as spiritual and immortal he is not the victim of some vain fancy coming from his physical or social condition, but is penetrating to the heart of the matter.

15. Participating in the light of the divine mind, man rightly judges that his understanding transcends the world of experience. Tireless ingenuity over centuries has brought him remarkable advances in the empirical sciences, in the liberal arts and in technology. Especially in our own time he has been successful in subduing the material world to his purposes. But he has always looked for and found a deeper truth. Intelligence is not confined to phenomena, it can reach a properly intelligible reality with real certainty, even though by reason of sin the grasp is partly weakened and obscured.

Man's intellectual nature is perfected and must be further perfected by wisdom, which draws him gently to the love and pursuit of the true and the good, leads him through visible things to invisible.

More than ever before we need such wisdom to humanize our new discoveries. The future of the world is in danger unless wiser men are to be found. Many of the materially poorer nations who are richer in wisdom may be of great profit to the rest.

It is by faith, by the gift of the Holy Spirit, that man contemplates and savours the mystery of the divine purpose.[15]

16. Deep down man descries the law of conscience. He has not given this law to himself, but he is under obligation to obey it; and wherever the need is, its voice sounds in his heart, always calling on him to love good and shun evil: Do this, avoid that! Man has a law written in his

---

[14]Cf. 1 *Kg* 16:7; *Jer* 17:10.
[15]Cf. *Ecclus* 17:7-8.

heart by God, a law which it is his honour to obey and according to which he will be judged.[16] Conscience is man's most secret core and sanctuary—there he is alone with God and hears his voice most intimately.[17] Conscience marvellously makes known that law which is fulfilled in the love of God and of our fellow-men.[18] Conscience unites Christians with other men in the search for truth, for solutions of individual and social problems of morality which shall be based on truth. The more conscience prevails, the more men exert themselves to live by moral standards which are objective, not blind and arbitrary. Yet not seldom it happens that conscience can be wrong through invincible ignorance. In this case conscience does not lose its stature. But we cannot say the same when men have too little care in looking for the true and the good, or when habits of sin gradually almost blind conscience.

17. Man cannot embrace what is good other than freely, and this liberty our contemporaries greatly value and aim at enthusiastically. Clearly they are right; yet often they foster it in a wrong way, as though it were a licence to do anything pleasurable, even evil. But true liberty is an outstanding sign of the image of God in man. God wished to leave man 'in the power of his own inclination'[19] so that he might spontaneously seek his Creator and by cleaving to him perfect himself so as to be ready for heaven. Man's dignity then demands that he should act in accordance with a free and conscious choice, personally, inwardly persuaded, and not by either blind impulse from within or coercion from without. Man attains such dignity when he frees himself of the bondage of passion and pursues his purpose, freely choosing what is good and achieving it by appropriate means and his own persistent effort. Because of the legacy of sin, free human action will not be thus

---

[16]Cf. *Rom* 2:14-16.
[17]Cf. Pius XII, Broadcast on the right formation of a Christian conscience in the young, 23 Mar. 1952: AAS 44 (1952), p. 271.
[18]Cf. *Mt* 22:37-40; *Gal* 5:14.
[19]Cf. *Ecclus* 15:14.

wholly and actively centred on God except by the help of his grace. Everyone will have to give an account before the judgement-seat of God of his own manner of life, good or evil.[20]

18. The enigma of the human condition becomes greatest when we contemplate death. Man suffers not only from pain or the slow breaking down of his body, but also from the terror of perpetual extinction. It is a sound instinct that makes him recoil and revolt at the thought of this total destruction, of being snuffed out. He is more than matter, and the seed of eternity he bears within him rebels against death. All technical undertakings, however valuable, are powerless to allay man's anxiety; prolonging his span of life here cannot satisfy the desire for a future life inescapably rooted in him.

While all imagination fails us in the face of death, the Church appeals to Revelation in telling man he is created by God, for blessedness, beyond the wretchedness of this life. The Christian faith teaches that bodily death, from which man would have been delivered had he not sinned,[21] will yet be conquered because the almighty and merciful Saviour will give back to man the salvation he lost through his own fault. God called man and still calls him to an eternal imperishable communion of his whole nature with the divine life. This is the victory Christ gained in rising from the dead, since by dying himself, he freed man from death.[22] To any thinking man, then, to offer faith supported by solid reasons is to offer an answer to his anxieties about his future destiny. At the same time it is to offer him the means of communion in Christ with his loved ones already dead, since faith gives hope that they have attained true life with God.

---

[20]Cf. 2 *Cor* 5:10.
[21]Cf. *Wis* 1:13; 2:23–24; *Rom* 5:21; 6:23; *Jas* 1:15.
[22]Cf. 1 *Cor* 15:56–57.

The Dignity of the Human Person

19. The highest reason for human dignity is man's vocation to communion with God. From the outset man is invited to a close familiarity with God. He only exists because God's love created and continually sustains him; nor does he live fully and truly unless he freely acknowledges that love and commits himself to his Creator. Many of our contemporaries either have no conception of this intimate and vital communion with God, or they explicitly reject it. Atheism in fact is a very serious feature of our time and must be carefully examined.

The word stands for many very different things. Some expressly deny there is a God; others think that man can say absolutely nothing about God; others again examine the question in such a way that it appears meaningless. Many extend the positive sciences beyond their proper sphere and offer a merely scientific answer to the question, or go to the other extreme and refuse to admit any absolute truth. Some make so much of man that all vitality is taken out of faith in God—they seem more concerned to insist on man than to deny God. For some the God they reject is a fantasy of their own making, which has nothing to do with the God of the Gospels. Others never even raise questions about God, since they never seem to feel any religious disquiet, or see why they should bother about religion. Again, atheism not rarely results either from violent protest against evil, or from giving an absolute character to some human value, so that it takes the place of God. Contemporary civilization itself can often make the approach to God more difficult, not directly or of its nature but simply because it is too much involved with the things of this world.

Obviously those who deliberately shut out God from their hearts and, in defiance of their conscience, try to evade religious questions are not blameless. None the less, believers themselves often carry a share of responsibility for this. Atheism, fully considered, is not something spontaneous or fundamental, but the result of various causes among which we must list critical reaction against religion, which in some places means chiefly against the Christian religion. Believers then can play no small part in the genesis of atheism; when religious education is neglected, doctrine misleadingly expounded or short comings evident in the religious, moral and social life of believers, then we must admit that the true face of God and of religion is veiled rather than revealed.

20. Modern atheism often takes a systematic form; one reason for this is that the concern for man's autonomy is pushed to such lengths that it raises difficulties about any dependence on God. Atheists of this kind take liberty to mean that man finds his ultimate purpose within himself, is the sole fashioner and arbiter of his own history. This they reckon incompatible with acknowledging the Lord, the author and end of all things—or at least they think it makes such an acknowledgement superfluous. The sense of power man gets from contemporary technical progress can lend colour to this view.

We must not overlook that form of present-day atheism which chiefly expects man's liberation to follow from his social and economic freedom, and maintains that religion is an obstacle to this, because by deceptively raising man's hopes of a future life it holds him back from bettering his condition here.* When the advocates of this doctrine achieve political power they strongly oppose religion and spread atheism by using, especially in educating the young, those means of exercising pressure which political power affords.

21. The Church, loyal to God and to men, cannot refrain from sorrowfully but decisively reproving, as she has before reproved,[23] these doctrines and policies which contradict reason and common experience, and drag man down from his native excellence.

---

*I have avoided literally translating 'a civitatis terrestris aedificatione' since the phrase might mean little or nothing to those unacquainted with St Augustine. TRANS.

[23]Cf. PIUS XI, Encycl. Divini Redemptoris, 19 Mar. 1937: AAS 29 (1937), pp. 65-106; PIUS XI, Encycl. Ad Apostolorum Principis, 29 June 1958: AAS 50 (1958), pp. 601-614; JOHN XXIII, Encycl. Mater et Magistra, 15 May 1961: AAS 53 (1961), pp. 451-453; PAUL VI, Encycl. Ecclesiam suam, 6 Aug. 1964: AAS 56 (1964), pp. 651-653.

The Dignity of the Human Person

Nevertheless she tries to discover in the atheist mind the hidden cause of the denial of God. She is aware of the seriousness of the questions which atheism raises, and out of charity towards all men she believes that those questions should be deeply and seriously examined.

The Church holds that it is in no way contrary to man's dignity to acknowledge God, since that dignity is founded in God and finds its perfection there. God the Creator established men in the society of other men, intelligent and free, but chiefly he is called as a son to communion with God and to participation in God's happiness. She holds further that other worldly hopes in no way slacken the momentum of earthly business, but rather add the support of fresh motives in carrying it out. On the other hand, when a divine foundation and hope of eternal life are lacking, man's dignity, as is often evident nowadays, is seriously harmed, the riddles of life, death, pain and suffering remain without solution and men are not seldom thrown into despair.

Meanwhile every man goes on, obscurely recognizing himself as an unanswered question. It is a question no man can avoid asking himself at some moments in his life, least of all when great things happen to him. It is a question to which only God gives a full and certain answer, calling man to think more deeply and enquire more humbly.

The remedy for atheism must come from properly presented teaching and from the whole life of the Church and her members. It is up to the Church to make God the Father and his incarnate Son present, we might say visible, by increasingly renewing and purifying herself, under the guidance of the Holy Spirit.[24] This will come about in the first place by the witness of a living and adult faith educated to recognize clearly, and overcome, difficulties. Many martyrs have given and do give remarkable testimony of this faith. This faith should show itself fertile, penetrating the entire life of believers—their everyday life as well—rousing them to justice and love especially towards the poor.

---

[24]Cf. Vatican Council II, Dogmatic Constitution on the Church, c. 1, n. 8: AAS 57 (1965), p. 12 [CTS Translation Do 349].
[25]Cf. *Phil* 1:27.

211

The presence of God is most manifest in the fraternal charity of the faithful, 'with one mind striving together for the faith of the Gospel'[25] and appearing as a sign of unity.

The Church, though she completely rejects atheism, sincerely maintains that all men, believers and unbelievers, should work together to build properly this world in which they live together. This certainly cannot be done without sincere and prudent dialogue. She must complain therefore of some governments unfairly discriminating between believers and non-believers, and thereby failing to acknowledge fundamental human rights. For believers she asks that active freedom which will allow them to set up the temple of God in this world. In a humane spirit she invites atheists to consider the Gospel of Christ without prejudice.

Before all else the Church knows that her message is in harmony with the most secret desires of the human heart, since it insists on the dignity of man's vocation and gives back hope to those who have begun to despair of their higher destiny. Far from belittling man, her message generously offers him light, life and liberty, and apart from it nothing can satisfy the heart of man. 'You have made us for yourself, Lord, and our hearts are restless till they rest in thee'.[26]

22. The mystery of man becomes clear only in the mystery of the incarnate Word. Adam, the first man, was a type of the future,[27] that is of Christ our Lord. Christ the new Adam, in revealing the mystery of the Father and his love, makes man fully clear to himself, makes clear his high vocation. No wonder then that in him the above truths find their source and their culmination.

He who is 'the image of the invisible God' (*Col* 1:15)[28] is the perfect man who restored to the sons of Adam the divine likeness which

---

[26]St Augustine, Confessions I, 1.:PL 32, 661.

[27]Cf. *Rom* 5:14; cf. Tertullian, *De carnis resurrectione*, 6: 'Whatever was the form and expression which was then given to the clay (by the Creator) Christ was in his thoughts as one day to become man': PL 2, 282; CSEL 47, p. 33, 1. 12-13.

[28]Cf. 2 *Cor* 4:4.

the first sin distorted. Since he took to himself human nature, not extinguishing it,[29] by the same token that nature is in us raised to a sublime dignity. For the Son of God by his incarnation did in a fashion unite himself with every man. He worked with human hands, thought with a human mind, acted with a human will,[30] loved with a human heart. Born of the virgin Mary he became truly one of us, like us in everything except sin.[31]

Freely shedding his blood as an innocent lamb, he merited life for us, and in him God reconciled us to himself and to each other.[32] He delivered us from the slavery of the devil and of sin so that each of us can say with the Apostle: the Son of God 'loved me and gave himself up for me' (*Gal* 2:20). By suffering for us he not only left us an example that we should follow in his steps,[33] but renewed the road, so that as we follow it life and death are sanctified and take on a new meaning.

The Christian, conformed to the image of the Son who is the first-born among many brethren,[34] receives 'the first-fruits of the Spirit' (*Rom* 8:23), by which he becomes capable of fulfilling the new law of love.[35] Through the Spirit, which is 'the guarantee of our inheritance' (*Eph* 1:14), the whole man is inwardly restored, even to 'the redemption of our bodies' (*Rom* 8:23). 'If the Spirit of him who raised Jesus from the dead dwells in you, he who raised Jesus Christ from the dead will give life to your mortal bodies also through his Spirit who

---

[29]Cf. COUNCIL OF CONSTANTINOPLE II, can. 7: 'without either the Word being transformed into the nature of the humanity or the humanity changing over into the nature of the Word': DENZ. 219 (428) [for each remains what it is by nature even after the hypostatic union. TRANS.]. Cf. also COUNCIL OF CONSTANTINOPLE III: 'His most holy and innocent body, animated by his soul, was not to be taken away by being "divinized" (theôtheisa ouk anarèthè), but stayed true to its own determinate nature': DENZ. 291 (556). Cf. COUNCIL OF CHALCEDON: '(Christ) must be acknowledged in two natures without any commingling or change or division or separation': DENZ. 148 (302).

[30]Cf. COUNCIL OF CONSTANTINOPLE III, 'in the same way his human will was not taken away either by being "divinized"': DENZ. 291 (556).

[31]Cf. *Heb* 4:15.

[32]Cf. 2 *Cor* 5:18-19; *Col* 1:20-22.

[33]Cf. 1 *Pet* 2:21; *Mt* 16:24; *Lk* 14:27.

[34]Cf. *Rom* 8:29; *Col* 1:18.

[35]Cf. *Rom* 8:1-11.

dwells in you' (*Rom* 8:11).[36] Certainly the need and duty of battling against evil through many trials presses on the Christian, and the need of undergoing death; but he partakes in the paschal mystery, becomes like Christ in his death and will encounter the resurrection fortified with hope.[37]

Nor does this hold only for those who believe in Christ: it holds for all men of good will in whose hearts grace works in an invisible fashion.[38] Christ died for everybody;[39] everybody's ultimate vocation is the same, divine vocation; then we must hold that the Holy Spirit offers everybody the possibility of sharing in some way known to God in this paschal mystery.

Such is the mystery of man as the Christian Revelation expounds it to believers. Through Christ and in Christ, then, light is shed on the puzzles of pain and death which, considered apart from the Gospel, overwhelm us. Christ rose, by his death destroying death, giving us abundant life,[40] so that as sons united in the Son we can cry out in the Spirit 'Abba, Father'.[41]

---

[36]Cf. 2 *Cor* 4:14.
[37]Cf. *Phil* 3:10; *Rom* 8:17.
[38]Cf. VATICAN COUNCIL II, Dogmatic Constitution on the Church, c. II, n. 16: AAS 57 (1965), p. 20.
[39]Cf. *Rom* 8:32.
[40]Cf. Byzantine Paschal Liturgy.
[41]Cf. *Rom* 8:15 and *Gal* 4:6; cf. also *Jn* 1:12 and 1 *Jn* 3:1-2.

CHAPTER II

THE COMMUNITY OF MAN

23. One of the principal features of the contemporary world is the multiplication of ways in which men depend on each other. This is something to which technical progress greatly contributes; but at a deeper level fraternal dialogue among men is realized in a community of persons, which demands reverence for each other's full spiritual dignity. The Christian Revelation helps greatly to promote this personal communion, and at the same time leads us to a deeper understanding of the laws of social life which the Creator has written in the moral and spiritual nature of man.

Since, however, recent official Church teaching has fully expounded social doctrine,[42] the Council merely calls to mind some of the more important truths and explains their basis in the light of Revelation. It then goes on to emphasize certain consequences which are especially important for our time.

24. God, who is a father to everybody, wants all men to be one family and behave to each other as brothers. We are all created in God's image: 'He made from one every nation of men to live on all the face of the earth' (*Acts* 17:26) and called us all to the same end, that is himself.

This is why the greatest and the first commandment is the love of God and of our neighbour. Scripture teaches us that the two cannot be separated: '…(These) and any other commandment are summed up in this sentence: You shall love your neighbour as yourself … Therefore love is the fulfilling of the law' (*Rom* 13:9-10; cf. 1 *Jn* 4:20). This is clearly of the first importance to men every day more dependent on each other and to a world every day more unified.

Indeed the Lord Jesus, when he prays to the Father 'that they all

---

[42]Cf. JOHN XXIII, Encycl. *Mater et Magistra*, 15 May 1961: AAS 53 (1961), pp. 401-464; *Encycl. Pacem in terris*, 11 Apr. 1963: AAS 55 (1963), pp. 257-304. PAUL VI, Encycl. *Ecclesiam suam*, 6 Aug. 1964: AAS 56 (1964), pp. 609-659.

may be one ... even as we are one' (*Jn* 17:21-22), opening up prospects inaccessible to human reason, hints at some likeness between the union of the divine Persons and the union of the children of God in truth and charity. This likeness shows that man, the only creature on earth that God wanted for its own sake, cannot fully find himself except in sincere self-giving.[43]

25. The social character of man shows that the advancement of human personality and of society go hand in hand. The beginning, subject and end of all social institutions is and should be the human person who by his nature so completely needs social life.[44] It is because social life is not something adventitious to man that his gifts blossom and he measures up to his vocation in company with others, in mutual service, in fraternal intercourse.

Of the social ties which are necessary to man's development some, like the family and the political community, are more closely linked with his intimate nature; others are matters rather of free initiative. In our time, for various reasons, connections and interdependence multiply continually, and lead to a variety of associations and institutions public and private. This fact, which is called 'socialization', though it is obviously not without dangers, has also many advantages in confirming and enhancing personal qualities and safeguarding personal rights.[45]

If human persons profit a good deal from this social life in finding even their religious fulfilment, it cannot be denied that often men are diverted from doing good and driven to evil-doing by the social environment in which they are immersed from infancy. Disturbances frequent in the social order are certainly traceable in part to tensions in the economic, political and social structures. But at bottom they are the result of the selfishness and pride of man-vices which pervert

---

[43]Cf. *Lk* 17:33.
[44]Cf. St Thomas, 1 Ethics Lect. 1.
[45]Cf. John XXIII, Encycl. *Mater et Magistra*: AAS 53 (1961), p. 418. Cf. also Pius XI, Encycl. *Quadragesimo anno*, 15 May 1931 : AAS 23 (1931), pp. 222 ff.

even the social environment. Where good order is affected by the consequences of sin, man, who is born with a certain inclination to evil, finds new incitements to sin which he cannot overcome except with strenuous efforts helped by grace.

26. As interdependence grows steadily closer and extends to the whole world, the common good (i.e., the sum of those social conditions which allow individuals and groups to achieve their proper purposes more fully and quickly) assumes a universal scale and entails rights and duties belonging to the human race as a whole. Any group must take account of the needs and legitimate aspirations of other groups, indeed of the common good of the human family.[46]

Yet at the same time we are growing more aware of the exalted dignity of the human person, since he excels all other things in importance and his rights and duties are universal and inviolable. He should therefore have ready access to everything necessary for living a truly human life: food, clothing, housing, freedom to choose a state of life and found a family, education, work, reputation, respect, adequate information, freedom to live according to a right conscience, protection of his privacy and a just religious liberty.

The social order then should constantly tend to the good of persons; the management of things should be subordinate to personal values and not vice-versa, as our Lord implied when he said that the sabbath was made for man and not man for the sabbath.[47] This order of things must be gradually evolved, founded on truth, built on justice, vitalized by love; a humane balance in the matter of liberty must gradually be found.[48] This will all need fresh thinking and ample social changes.

The Spirit of God who with marvellous providence directs the course of history and renews the face of the earth broods over this

---

[46] Cf. JOHN XXIII, Encycl. *Mater et Magistra*: AAS 53 (1961), p. 417.
[47] Cf. *Mk* 2:27.
[48] Cf. JOHN XXIII, Encycl. *Pacem in terris*: AAS 55 (1963), p. 266.

evolution. The ferment of the Gospel rouses in man's heart a demand for dignity that cannot be stifled.

27. Coming down to more practical and urgent conclusions, the Council insists on respect for man. Everyone should respect his fellow man without exception as 'another self', and have due regard for his life and for what he needs to live it worthily.[49] We must not imitate the rich man who had no care for the poor man Lazarus.[50]

Nowadays we have a special obligation to make a neighbour of any man, and actively serve him where need is, whether he be old and neglected, or a foreign worker unjustly despised, or an exile, or an illegitimate child suffering for a sin which is not his, or a hungry man who appeals to our conscience by reminding us of our Lord's words: 'as you did it to one of the least of these my brethren, you did it to me' (*Mt* 25:40).

Whatever is inimical to life, such as homicide, race murder, abortion, euthanasia and voluntary suicide; whatever violates personal integrity, as mutilation, bodily or mental torture, attempts to coerce minds; whatever offends human dignity, as subhuman living conditions, arbitrary imprisonment, deportation, slavery, prostitution, trafficking women and young people, shameful working conditions in which workers are mere tools of profit and not free and responsible persons; these things and others like them are infamous, and while they are harmful to civilization they dishonour the Creator and they defile those who are actively responsible more than those who are the victims.

28. We owe respect and charity to those who think differently from us in social, political and also religious matters. The more humanity and charity leads us to a deeper understanding of their ways of thinking the easier it will be to enter upon a dialogue with them.

Obviously this charity and friendliness must not make us indifferent to truth and goodness. Charity itself drives the disciples of Christ

[49]Cf. *Jas* 2:15-1 6.
[50]Cf. *Lk* 16:19-31.

to tell salutary truths to all men. But we must distinguish between error, which must always be rejected, and the person in error, who always retains his personal dignity even though he has false or inaccurate religious ideas.[51] God alone is the judge and searcher of hearts and forbids us to pass judgement on the inner guilt of anybody.[52]

Christ's teaching demands that we should forgive injuries,[53] which extends our obligation to love even to our enemies: such is the commandment of the new law: 'You have heard that it was said, you shall love your neighbour and hate your enemy. But I say to you: Love your enemies, and pray for those who persecute you' (*Mt* 5:43-44).

29. All men have a rational soul and are created in God's image; they share the same nature and origin; redeemed by Christ, they have the same divine vocation and destiny; so it should be more and more recognized that they are essentially equal.

Men are plainly not equal in physical, intellectual and moral powers. But we should overcome and remove every kind of discrimination which affects fundamental rights, whether it be social and cultural discrimination, or based on sex, race, colour, class, language or religion. All such discrimination is opposed to God's purposes. It is really deplorable that the fundamental rights are still not everywhere securely guaranteed—as when women are not allowed freely to choose a husband or adopt some other state of life, or are denied educational or cultural equality with men.

Moreover, although there are just differences between men, equal personal dignity demands that we should move towards a more human and equal standard of living. Excessive social and economic inequalities between the members or peoples of one human family are scandalous, and contrary to social justice, equity, human dignity and international peace.

Human institutions, private or public, must serve man's ends and minister to his dignity. They should be bulwarks against any kind of

---

[51]Cf. JOHN XXIII, Encycl. *Pacem in terris*: AAS 55 (1963), p. 299 and 300.
[52]Cf. *Lk* 6:37-38; *Mt* 7:1-2; *Rom* 2:1-11; 14:10-12.
[53]Cf. *Mt* 5:43-47.

political or social slavery and guardians of basic rights under any kind of government. Indeed such institutions should be gradually brought into harmony with spiritual purposes, which are the highest of all, though this may take a long time.

30. Profound and rapid change makes it more imperative that no one should be so heedless of the course of events or so sunk in idleness as to be satisfied with a merely individualistic ethic. Justice and charity increasingly demand that each of us should, within the limits of our capacities and of others' needs, concern ourselves with the common good. We should promote and help public and private institutions likely to better living conditions. There are those who voice broad and generous opinions but in practice live as though they had no care for the needs of society. In fact many in various parts despise social laws and regulations. Some are not ashamed to avoid just taxes and other social dues by various tricks and devices. Others take little account, e.g., of regulations for safeguarding health or of highway codes, forgetting that by such carelessness they endanger their own and other people's lives.

It should be sacred to everybody to put social requirements high among present-day duties, and to observe them. The more the world is united the more men's commitments go beyond particular groups and gradually become world-wide. This cannot come about unless individuals and groups cultivate the moral and social virtues and spread them abroad, so that with the necessary help of divine grace we shall have new men and fashioners of a new humanity.

31. The huge resources available today should be used to broaden men's minds so that they will more precisely carry out the demands of conscience towards each other and towards the groups of which they are members. First of all the education of the young of all classes should be permanently such as to raise up men and women not only accomplished but large-minded—the sort that are urgently needed in our time.

Man will hardly attain this sense of responsibility unless the conditions of his life allow him to be aware of his dignity and to fulfil his vocation by giving himself unsparingly in the service of God, and of his fellows. Human liberty is commonly weakened when man falls into extreme want, just as it deteriorates when he falls to easy living in comfortable seclusion. It is fortified when he accepts the inescapable demands of social life, faces up to the many-sided requirements of human fellowship and bends his energies to serving the community.

Everybody should be roused to resolution to play his part in common enterprises. Admirable is the practice of those nations in which the greater number of citizens take part, with true liberty, in political life. But regard should be paid to the real condition of each nation and to the need to maintain public authority at a reasonable level of vigour. If citizens are to be willing to take part in the life of social institutions, they need to find in them adequate incentives which will attract them to the service of others. We are justified in thinking that the future of mankind is in the hands of those who can hand on to future generations grounds for living and hoping.

32. Just as God created man to live socially and not in isolation, so also it 'pleased him not to sanctify them singly and unrelatedly but to make of them a people who should acknowledge him in truth and serve him in holiness'.[54] Hence from the outset of the history of salvation he chose men not only as individuals but as members of some community. Disclosing this plan, God called these chosen ones 'his people' (*Ex* 3:7-12), and moreover made a covenant with them on Mount Sinai.[55]

This community pattern was perfected and brought to its completion by the work of Christ. The incarnate Word himself chose to share in human fellowship. He was at the marriage of Cana, visited the home of Zachaeus, ate with publicans and sinners. He revealed his Father's love and man's sublime vocation by reference to the commonest

---

[54]Cf. Dogmatic Constitution on the Church, c. II, n. 9: AAS 57 (1965), pp. 12-13.
[55]Cf. *Ex* 24:1-8.

features of ordinary social life and the use of familiar language and imagery. He sanctified human ties, especially family ties, which are the basis of social thinking, and freely submitted to the law of the land. No less willingly he lived the life of a workman of his period and place.

In his preaching he clearly ordered the sons of God to behave to each other as brothers. In his prayer he asked that all his disciples should be 'one'. Even unto death he offered himself for all, the redeemer of all. 'Greater love has no man than this, that a man lay down his life for his friends' (*Jn* 15:13). He charged the apostles to preach the Gospel message to all nations, so that the human race might become God's family in which love would be the fulfilment of the law.

The first-born of many brethren, following his death and resurrection he sets up among all who receive him in faith and charity a new fraternal communion, in his own body, which is the Church, in which all, members of one another, serve one another according to the gifts they have received.

This solidarity must continue to grow until the day on which it will find its completion—the day on which men saved by grace will give perfect glory to God as his family and the family of Christ their brother.

CHAPTER III

THE ACTIVITY OF MAN IN THE WORLD AT LARGE

33. Man has always tried to enlarge the scope of his life by his work and skill. But today, chiefly by means of science and technology, he has extended and is extending his mastery over almost all nature. The human family is gradually recognizing and establishing itself as a worldwide community, mainly by virtue of the increased facilities for many-sided commerce between nations. So it is that man now gets by his own industry many benefits for which at one time he looked mainly to heavenly powers.

In the face of this immense effort which pervades the whole human race, many questions arise. What is the meaning and value of this industry? How are all these things to be used? To what purpose are the exertions of the individual and of society? The Church guards the deposit of God's word from which religious and moral principles are derived. Without having ready answers to every question, she wishes to join the light of Revelation with general experimental knowledge to illuminate the way on which mankind has lately set out.

34. Believers are clear that human enterprise, individual and collective, the enormous effort by which men in the course of centuries have improved their living conditions, in itself answers to God's design. Man, created in God's image, was commanded to subdue the earth and everything in it, to rule the world in justice and holiness,[56] to refer all things to God as his acknowledged Creator, so that through man's mastery the name of God should be honoured over the whole earth.[57]

This has a profound bearing on everyday tasks. Men and women who provide sustenance for themselves and their families in such a way that at the same time they employ their energies for the benefit of

---

[56]Cf. *Gen* 1:26-27; 9:2-3; *Wis* 9:2-3.
[57]Cf. *Ps* 8:7 and 10.

society are justified in thinking that by their own labour they advance the work of the Creator and benefit their fellow-men, and that their personal industry contributes to the carrying out of the divine plan in history.[58]

Christians then, far from supposing that the achievements of man's skill and power are opposed to the power of God, as though the rational creature were a rival of his Creator, are convinced rather that mankind's triumphs are signs of God's greatness and the fruit of his sublime plan. But the greater men's power the wider their responsibility, whether as single persons or in community. So the Christian message does not distract men from building up the world nor induce them to neglect the welfare of their fellows, but rather obliges them more strictly to these tasks.[59]

35. Human enterprise, which proceeds from man, is also directed to man. When man works he not only effects changes in things and society, he perfects himself. He learns much, he develops his talents, he advances outside and above himself. Gain of this sort, properly appreciated, is more worthwhile than any profit that may accrue. Man is more valuable for what he is than for what he has.[60] Equally, everything he does to further justice, brotherhood and a more human social order is more valuable than technical progress. This last can provide the material for human progress but can never by itself bring it about.

This then is the norm of human enterprise, that it should by the divine plan and purpose harmonize with the real good of the human race, and allow man individually and in society to fulfil his vocation wholly.

---

[58]Cf. 301 JOHN XXIII, Encycl. *Pacem in terris*: AAS 55 (1963), p. 297.
[59]Cf. Message to all men by Council Fathers at the beginning of Vatican Council II, Oct. 1962: AAS 54 (1962), p. 823.
[60]Cf. PAUL VI, Allocution to Diplomatic Corps, 7 Jan. 1965: AAS 57 (1965), p. 232.

36. Many of our contemporaries seem to be afraid that the autonomy of man or society or science will be prejudiced if human enterprise and religion are more closely associated.

If by this autonomy we understand that created things and society itself have their own laws and values which man must gradually learn, use and control, it is perfectly right to insist on it. It is not only the concern of our contemporaries—it is in harmony with the Creator's will. It is a feature of creation that all things have their own stability, truth, goodness; their inner law and coherence which man should respect, recognizing the methods proper to each of the sciences and arts. Research in any branch of learning, conducted scientifically and in a moral way, will never clash with faith, because secular things and the things of faith take their origin from the same God.[61] In fact anybody who tries humbly and perseveringly to penetrate the secrets of nature is, however unknowingly, led by the hand of God who sustains all things and makes them what they are. It is right then to regret that habit of mind which has sometimes existed among Christians who failed to appreciate the proper autonomy of science. By thus provoking contention and controversy they led many people to suppose that faith and science were in opposition.[62]

But if 'autonomy of temporal things' means that created things do not depend on God and that man can use them without regard for the Creator, no one who acknowledges God can fail to see that this is false. What is created becomes nothing without the Creator. All believers of whatever religion have always heard God's voice and presence in the language of created things. Indeed, to forget God is to cast the creature into shadow.

37. Holy Scripture is at one with the lessons of history in teaching the human family that human progress is a great good carrying with

---

[61]Cf. VATICAN COUNCIL I, Dogmatic Constitution on the Catholic Faith, c. III: Denz. 1785-1786 (3004-3005).
[62]Cf. Mgr PIO PASCHINI, *Vita e opere di Galileo Galilei*, 2 vol. Vatican edition, 1964.

it a great temptation. If the hierarchy of values is upset and good confounded with evil, individuals and groups become self-seeking and disregard others. So it comes about that there is no room in the world for true brotherhood, and man's increased powers threaten to destroy humanity itself.

A hard struggle against the powers of darkness runs all through history—we have the word of our Lord[63] that it began with the world and will go on to the last day. Immersed in this struggle, man needs to strain always to hold fast to what is good, nor without hard work and the help of God's grace can he achieve unity within himself.

While trusting in the divine plan of the Creator and recognizing that human progress can contribute to man's true happiness, Christ's Church cannot but echo the Apostle's warning: 'Do not be conformed to this world' (Rom 12:2), meaning to that spirit of vanity and malice which distorts human enterprise from the service of God and man into an instrument of sin.

If anyone asks what is the way out of this dismal state of things, Christians answer that all human enterprises, though they are everyday threatened by pride and egoism, are to be purified and brought to perfection by Christ's cross and resurrection. Redeemed by Christ and made a new creature in the Holy Spirit, man can and should love the things created by God. He got them from God—he regards and respects them as flowing from God's hands. Grateful to his Benefactor, using and enjoying created things in detachment and freedom of spirit, he enters into true possession of the world 'as having nothing and yet possessing everything'.[64] For 'all are yours, and you are Christ's, and Christ is God's' (1 Cor 3:22-23).

38. The Word of God, by whom all things were made, was himself made flesh and dwelt here on earth.[65] The perfect man, he entered history, taking it up, summing it up in himself.[66] He reveals to us that

---

[63]Cf. *Mt* 24:13; 13:24-30; 13:36-43.
[64]Cf. 2 *Cor* 6:10.
[65]Cf. *Jn* 1:3 and 14.
[66]Cf. *Eph* 1:10.

The Activity of Man in the World at Large

'God is love' (1 *Jn* 4:8); he teaches us that the fundamental law of human fulfilment and hence of the transformation of the world is the new commandment of love. He assures those who believe in divine charity that the way of love is open to all men, and that the effort to establish universal brotherhood is not a vain effort. At the same time he warns us that this charity is not to be cultivated only in great matters but primarily in everyday circumstances. Suffering death for every one of us sinners,[67] he sets us an example—to bear that cross which the flesh and the world puts on the shoulders of all who dedicate themselves to peace and justice. Christ was established as Lord of all by his resurrection—the Lord to whom all authority in heaven and on earth has been given.[68] He still works in the hearts of men by the power of the Holy Spirit, and he does not merely rouse our desire of the world to come; at the same time he stimulates, purifies, reinforces those generous aspirations by which the human family bends its energies to make its own life more humane and to subdue the earth to this purpose. The gifts of the Spirit are various. He calls some to bear witness clearly to the desire for heaven and to keep that desire alive among men. Others he calls to devote themselves to serving humanity here—a ministry which provides material for the kingdom of heaven. To all he brings liberation, that setting aside self-interest and putting all earth's powers to human purposes, they may reach out towards a future in which humanity itself will become an offering acceptable to God.[69]

A pledge of this hope, sustenance for this journey, our Lord left us in that sacrament of faith in which natural elements cultivated by men are turned into his glorious Body and Blood, the supper of fraternal communion, the foretaste of the heavenly banquet.

39. We know nothing of when the earth and the human race will come to an end,[70] nor of how the universe will be transformed. The

[67]Cf. *Jn* 3:16; *Rom* 5:8-10.
[68]Cf. *Acts* 2:36; *Mt* 28:18.
[69]Cf. *Rom* 15:16.
[70]Cf. *Acts* 1:7.

form of this world, distorted by sin,[71] is passing away, but we are taught that God is preparing a new dwelling-place, a new earth in which justice abides,[72] whose blessedness will satisfy and quench all man's thirst for peace.[73] Death will be conquered and the sons of God will be raised up again in Christ and what was sown perishable will be raised imperishable.[74] Charity will remain,[75] and in virtue of it, all that God created for man will be delivered from subjection to futility.[76]

We are admittedly warned that it profits man nothing if he gains the whole world and loses or forfeits himself.[77] None the less, expectation of a new world should not water down but rather stimulate our eagerness to better this one, for here there is growing that body, the new human family which in some degree foreshadows the world to come. By all means distinguish temporal progress from the advancement of the kingdom of God; but insofar as it can contribute to a better ordering of human society, temporal progress is very much in the interest of the kingdom of God.[78]

Human dignity, fraternal comradeship, freedom, these good things are all fruits of our nature and of our industry. After we have propagated them throughout the world we shall rediscover them, cleansed of every stain, shining and transfigured; when Christ restores the eternal and universal kingdom to his Father—'a kingdom of truth and life, a kingdom of holiness and grace, a kingdom of justice, love and peace.'[79] Here on earth this kingdom is already present though in a manner veiled; with the Lord's coming it will be consummated.

---

[71]Cf. 1 *Cor* 7:31; St Irenaeus, *Adv. Haer,* v. 36: PG 8, 1221.
[72]Cf. 2 *Cor* 5:2; 2 *Pet* 3:13.
[73]Cf. 1 *Cor* 2:9; *Rev* 21:4-5.
[74]Cf. 1 *Cor* 15:42 and 53.
[75]Cf. 1 *Cor* 13:8; 3:14.
[76]Cf. *Rom* 8:19-21.
[77]Cf. *Lk* 9:25.
[78]Cf. Pius XI, Encycl. *Quadragesimo anno:* AAS 23 (1931), p. 207.
[79]Preface for the Feast of Christ the King.

CHAPTER IV

THE CHURCH'S FUNCTION IN THE CONTEMPORARY WORLD

40. Everything we have said of human dignity, of the human community, of the profound significance of human enterprise, constitutes the basis of the relation between the Church and the world and of the dialogue between them.[80] In this chapter we take for granted what the Council has already said of the mystery of the Church, and consider the Church as it exists in this world, as it lives and acts with the world.

Taking rise from the eternal Father's love,[81] founded in time by Christ the Redeemer, gathered together in the Holy Spirit,[82] the Church has an eschatological purpose, a purpose concerned with salvation, a purpose which cannot be achieved fully except in the next world. But she is present here and now, made up of men, of citizens of the earthly city; men whose mission it is to give shape in human history to the family of the sons of God which will go on growing until our Lord's second coming. What brings this family together is the concern for heavenly benefits; by these it is enriched; but Christ 'founded and organized it as a society in this world',[83] furnished it with 'appropriate bonds of visible and social union'.[84] Thus the Church, at once 'a visible assembly and a spiritual community',[85] marches with the whole of humanity, shares the fortunes of the world here below, exists as the leaven, we might say the soul, of human society,[86] to renew it in Christ and transform it into God's family.

---

[80]Cf. PAUL VI, Encycl. *Ecclesiam suam*, III: AAS 56 (1964), pp. 637-659.
[81]Cf. *Tit* 3:4: '*philanthropia*'.
[82]Cf. *Eph* 1:3; 5-6; 13-14; 23.
[83]Dogmatic Constitution on the Church, c. I, n. 8: AAS 57 (1965), p. 12.
[84]*Ibid.*, c. 11,0.9: AAS 57 (1965), p. 14; cf. also n. 8: AAS *loc. cit.*, p. 11.
[85]*Ibid.*, c. I, n.8: AAS 57 (1965), p. 11.
[86]Cf. *ibid.*, c. IV, n. 38: AAS 57 (1965), p. 43, with note 120.

This intermingling of the earthly and heavenly cities can only be perceived by faith—indeed it remains the mysterious factor in human history, since that history itself remains troubled by sin until the full revelation of the glory of the sons of God. In pursuing her own end, salvation, the Church not only communicates divine life to man but in a fashion diffuses the reflected light of that life through the entire world. She does this most of all by restoring and enhancing human dignity, reinforcing the social structure and giving deeper meaning and importance to man's everyday tasks. So the Church believes that she can contribute a good deal through her members, whether singly or as a community, to enhance the human qualities of men and their history.

The Church is moreover glad to value highly what other Christian churches and ecclesiastical communities have done and are doing to co-operate in the same task. She is also firmly convinced that in preparing the ground for the Gospel she can be much helped in various ways by the world—by the abilities and industry whether of individuals or of society. We here set out some general principles for promoting this co-operation and mutual help in spheres which the Church and the world have to some extent in common.

41. Contemporary man is in the process of developing his personality more fully and finding out and asserting his rights. The Church is charged to show forth the mystery of God, man's last end. Simultaneously she shows man the meaning of his existence, the intimate truth about himself. The Church knows that only the God she serves can satisfy the deepest desires of the human heart, which is never content with earthly nourishment. She knows further that man, constantly stirred by the Spirit of God, will never be altogether indifferent to religious problems; the experience of past ages and the multiple testimony of our times confirms this. Man will always want even though only vaguely, to know the meaning of his life, of his activity, of his death. The very presence of the Church reminds him of these problems.

Only God, who created man in his own image and redeemed him from sin, provides the full answer to these questions through revelation in Christ his Son made man. Whoever follows Christ, the perfect man, himself becomes more of a man.

By this belief the Church sets man's dignity above the fluctuations of opinion which, for example, exaggerates either in depreciating or in extolling the human body. No human law can provide such secure ground for man's dignity and liberty as the Gospel entrusted to Christ's Church. This Gospel announces and proclaims the liberty of the sons of God, rejects all slavery, for this is ultimately the consequence of sin,[87] holds sacred the dignity of conscience and its free decision, admonishes us all to double our talents in the service of God and welfare of man, and commends each of us to the charity of all.[88] This agrees with the basic law of the Christian scheme of things. Though the same God is Saviour and Creator, Lord at once of human history and of the history of salvation, yet it is this very divine order which, far from taking away the rightful autonomy of the creature and particularly of man, rather restores and guarantees his dignity.

The Church then by virtue of the Gospel entrusted to her proclaims man's rights and acknowledges and esteems the modern movement to promote these rights everywhere. It is a movement however which should be in the spirit of the Gospel and protected from any species of false autonomy. There is a tendency to think that our personal rights are only safe if we are free even of divine law. That way human dignity, far from being saved, perishes.

42. The union of the human family is notably strengthened and completed by the unity of the family of the sons of God established in Christ.[89]

---

[87]Cf. *Rom* 8:14-17.
[88]Cf. *Mt* 22:39.
[89]Dogmatic Constitution on the Church, c. II, n. 9: AAS 57 (1965), pp. 12-14.

The mission which Christ entrusted to the Church is not indeed political, economic or social, but religious.[90] But from this religious mission light and strength derive which can help to establish and consolidate the community of men according to the divine law. Again, where circumstances call for it, the Church can and should set on foot projects for the service of all, especially the poor, for example works of mercy and the like.

The Church recognizes what is good in present-day social dynamism (impulses) especially the development towards unity, the process of sound 'socialization' and association in the civil and economic fields. The promotion of unity is in line with the Church's intimate mission, since she exists 'in Christ as a sacrament or instrumental sign of intimate union with God and of the unity of the whole human race'.[91] She shows the world that true external social union flows from the union of minds and hearts, from that faith and charity on which, in the Holy Spirit, her unity is unshakeably based. The force which the Church can inject into present-day society consists simply of that faith and charity brought to bear on life. It does not consist of wielding some external power by merely human means.

Again, because of her mission and nature the Church is not tied to any particular form of human culture or any political system. She can act as the closest link between human communities and nations so long as they trust her and really recognize her true liberty in fulfilling her mission. The Church admonishes Catholics as well as all other men that in this family spirit of God's children they should put an end to all international and racial dissension and consolidate rightful forms of human association.

The Council regards with great respect all the true, good and right elements in the vast variety of institutions which men have founded

---

[90]Cf. Pius XII, Address to Historians and Artists, 9 Mar. 1956: AAS 48 (1956), p. 212: 'Her Founder Jesus Christ gave her no cultural mandate, nor fixed any cultural pattern for her. The end Christ has assigned her is strictly religious ... the Church must lead men to God, that they may bind themselves to him without reserve ... the Church can never lose sight of this strictly religious, supernatural goal; directly or indirectly it must provide the meaning of all her activities, down to the last canon of her Code'.

[91]Dogmatic Constitution on the Church, c. I, n. 1: AAS 57 (1965), p. 5.

and continue to found. It declares that the Church wants to help and promote all such institutions so far as this depends on her and is compatible with her mission. She desires nothing more strongly than to serve the general welfare and develop freely under any regime which will acknowledge fundamental personal and family rights and the requirements of the common good.

43. The Council appeals to Christians, citizens of both cities,* to spare no pains to carry out their earthly duties faithfully and in the spirit of the Gospel. They are wide of the mark who think that because here we have no lasting city but we seek the city that is to come,[92] they can neglect their duty here on earth; they forget that the faith increases their obligation to fulfil those duties in accordance with their vocation.[93] On the other hand, equally wrong are they who think they can immerse themselves completely in this world's business, as though this were something quite unconnected with religion, and religion merely a matter of worship and some moral duties. This breach between faith and daily life among so many must be considered one of the more serious errors of our time. It is a scandal the Old Testament prophets were already vigorously denouncing,[94] and still more did Christ in the New Testament threaten it with severe penalties.[95] Let there be no false opposition between professional and social activity and the life of religion. The Christian who neglects his temporal duties neglects his duties to his neighbour, neglects God and risks his eternal salvation. Instead Christians should be glad of the chance to exercise their earthly talents after the example of Christ who worked as a carpenter. They must fuse all human effort, domestic, professional, scientific and technical in a vital synthesis with religious values, which co-ordinate everything in the highest way to God's glory.

---

*The earthly and the heavenly. TRANS.
[92]Cf. *Heb* 13:14.
[93]Cf. 2 *Thess* 3:6-13; *Eph* 4:28.
[94]Cf. *Is* 58:1-12.
[95]Cf. *Mt* 23:3-23; *Mk* 7:10-13.

Secular offices and tasks belong properly to laymen, though not exclusively. When singly or in association they act as citizens of the world, they will not only respect the laws proper to each field of work or study but exert themselves to acquire real skill in those fields. They will willingly co-operate with others working in the same field. While recognizing the demands of faith and drawing strength from it, they should boldly plan new enterprises and carry them through. Their rightly formed conscience should set the imprint of the divine law on secular life. The laity should expect light and spiritual energy from priests, but not imagine that their pastors are so expert that they can promptly turn out practical solutions for every question that crops up, however serious. This is not what priests are there for. The laity should rather attend to their own business with Christian wisdom and close attention to the Church's teaching.[96]

Often the Christian view of things will itself in certain circumstances incline them to some definite solution, while other believers, no less sincerely and justifiably, assess the same situation differently. If divergent answers are too readily linked with the Gospel, not necessarily by the authors of the answers, we should remember that no one has a right in these cases to claim the authority of the Church for his own views. Those who differ should try to find enlightenment in sincere discussion conducted charitably and with the common good in the forefront of their minds.

Laymen, who have an active part to play in the whole life of the Church, are not only bound to imbue the world with a Christian spirit; they are also called to be witnesses of Christ in all human affairs.

Bishops who have the task of ruling the Church of God, and their priests too, should preach Christ's message so as to shed the light of the Gospel on all human affairs. Pastors should remember that their everyday conduct and ministry[97] is what shows the face of the Church to the world—from it men judge the force and truth of the Christian

---

[96]Cf. John XXIII, Encycl. *Mater et Magistra*, IV: AAS 53 (1961), pp. 456-457: cf. 1: AAS *loc. cit.*, pp. 407, 410-411.

[97]Cf. Dogmatic Constitution on the Church, C. III, n. 28: AAS 57 (1965), p. 35.

message. Together with Religious and their faithful they should show by their lives and utterance that the Church, merely by its presence here with all it has to offer, is an inexhaustible source of those virtues which the world most needs today. They should study hard to equip themselves for their share in a dialogue with the world and with men of every shade of opinion. Especially they should take to heart the words of the Council: 'The human race is uniting more and more nowadays on a civic, economic and social basis. It is all the more necessary, therefore, that priests combine their responsibility and their resources, under guidance of the bishops and the Supreme Pontiff, to eliminate every form of separation, so that the whole human race may be brought into the unity of God's family'.[98]

Though the Church, fortified by the Holy Spirit, has remained the faithful spouse of her Master, and never ceased to be a sign of salvation to the world, she is well aware that some of her members,[99] clerical or lay, have in the course of centuries turned out unfaithful to the Spirit of God. In our time too she does not overlook the gulf between the message she brings and the human weakness of those to whom the Gospel is entrusted. However history may judge these shortcomings, we should be aware of them and strenuously resist them so that they may not hinder the spread of the Gospel. The Church knows too how much she should continually mature in the light of experience, in her relations with the world. Led by the Spirit, the Church as a mother 'is incessantly exhorting her children to purification and renewal, so that the mark of Christ may shine more clearly in the face of the Church'.[100]

44. Just as it is in the world's interest to recognize the Church as a social reality and a leaven in history, so the Church does not ignore how much she has received from the history and development of humanity.

---

[98] *Ibid.*, n.28: AAS *loc. cit.*, pp. 35-36.
[99] Cf. St Ambrose, *On Virginity*, c. VIII, n. 48: PL 16, 278.
[100] Cf. Dogmatic Constitution on the Church, c. II, n. 15: AAS 57 (1965), p. 20.

The Church benefits as much as any from the experience of past ages, the march of science, the treasures hidden in the various cultural traditions. These are things by which man's nature is more fully manifest and new ways to truth are opened. From the outset of her history she learned to express Christ's message in the ideas and languages of different peoples, and tried to illustrate it from the wisdom of philosophers. She aimed to adapt the Gospel both to common understanding and to the demands of the learned. This flexible preaching of the revealed word should still be a law of all evangelization. It means that every nation is able to express Christ's message in its own way; it promotes lively exchanges between the Church and different cultures.[101] To enlarge these exchanges, especially in our time when things change so quickly and ways of thinking vary so much, the Church particularly needs the help of specialists living in the world, whether believers or non-believers. It is the task of the whole People of God, especially pastors and theologians, to listen critically, with the help of the Holy Spirit, to contemporary utterances, to interpret them, and to evaluate them in the light of the divine word. This will help us to penetrate revealed Truth more deeply, understand it better, expound it more effectively.

Since the Church has a visible social structure which is indeed the sign of her unity in Christ, she can and does profit by social development. It is not that there is anything lacking in the constitution given her by Christ, but she can understand this more deeply, give it better expression, accommodate it more happily to our time. She gratefully appreciates that she herself as a community as well as each of her members receives very varied assistance from men of every degree and condition. Whoever furthers the interest of the human community in the sphere of family life, culture, economic and social life, national and international politics, by God's design also helps greatly the Church's community to the extent that this depends on external factors. Indeed,

---

[101] Cf. Dogmatic Constitution on the Church, c. II, n. 13: AAS 57 (1965), p. 17.

the Church admits that she has greatly profited and still profits from the antagonism of those who oppose or who persecute her.[102]

45. The Church, while she helps the world and receives much from it, has one purpose: that God's kingdom may come and the salvation of mankind be accomplished. Every benefit which the People of God can during its earthly pilgrimage bring to the human family arises from the fact that the Church is 'the universal sacrament of salvation',[103] at once manifesting and putting into operation the mystery of God's love for men.

The Word of God, by whom all things were made, was himself made flesh so that as the perfect man he might save all men and sum them all up in himself. Our Lord is the end of human history, the point on which the aspirations of history and civilization converge; the centre of humanity, the joy of all hearts, the fulfilment of all longings.[104] The Father raised him from the dead, and exalted him. Set him at his right hand, appointed him judge of the living and the dead. We, enlivened and brought together in his Spirit, pursue our pilgrimage towards the consummation of human history, which harmonizes entirely with the design of his love: 'to establish all things in Christ which are in heaven or in earth' (*Eph* 1:10).

The Lord himself says: 'Behold I am coming soon, bringing my recompense, to repay everyone for what he has done. I am the Alpha and the Omega, the first and the last, the beginning and the end' (*Rev* 22:12-13).

---

[102]Cf. St Justin, Martyr, *Dialogue with Trypho*, c. 110: PG 6, 729 (ed. Otto), 1897, pp. 391-393: '... the more such things are inflicted on us, the more people are made faithful and good through the name of Jesus'. Cf. Tertullian, *Apologeticus*, c. 50, 13: *Corpus Christ.*, ser. lat. I, p. 171: 'Whenever you cut us, we multiply: the blood of Christians is a seed'. Cf. Dogmatic Constitution on the Church, c. II, n.9: AAS 57 (1965), p. 14.
[103]Cf. Dogmatic Constitution on the Church, c.VII, n. 48: AAS 57 (1965), p. 53.
[104]Cf. Paul VI, Address, 3 Feb. 1965.

PART II

SOME MORE URGENT PROBLEMS

46. The Council has now explained what man's dignity is, what function he is called on to fulfil individually or socially in the world as a whole. Now it directs the attention of all, in the light of the Gospel and of human experience, to certain of the more urgent contemporary problems which worry the human race.

Among many which today cause general anxiety these may especially be noticed: marriage and the family; culture; social-economic life; political life; the solidarity of the family of nations and peace. On each of these we hope that the guiding principles and the light emanating from Christ may guide Christians and enlighten all men in searching out solutions of so many involved questions.

Chapter I

THE DIGNITY OF MARRIAGE AND THE FAMILY

47. Personal well-being, the well-being of human and of Christian society is closely bound up with the happy condition of the marital and family community. Christians, along with all those who place a high value on this community, feel genuine satisfaction at the various ways in which men today are helped to foster this as a community of love and cultivate it in their lives, and to fulfil their exalted duty as married partners and parents. Those who enjoy these benefits should do their best to bring them about.

But the dignity of this institution does not shine out equally everywhere, since it is obscured by polygamy, the plague of divorce, so-called free love and other disfigurements. Married love itself moreover is profaned by egoism, hedonism and unlawful usages aimed against generation. Again, present-day economic, social-psychological and civil conditions upset the institution of the family. Finally, in certain parts of the world we see disquieting problems arising from population increases. By all these things consciences are troubled. On the other hand the strength and power of the institution of marriage and the family are shown in that the profound changes of contemporary society, as well as giving rise to difficulties, often have the effect of emphasizing the true character of marriage.

The Council then, by putting in a stronger light certain leading features of the Church's doctrine, aims to enlighten and give support to Christians who are trying to promote and keep intact the natural dignity and sublime value of the married state.

48. The intimate community character of married life and love, established by the Creator and deriving its structure from his laws, is based on the conjugal pact, an irrevocable personal consent. From this human act by which the parties give and receive each other there arises an institution which by divine ordinance is stable, even in the eyes of society. This bond, which is sacred for the good of the married parties,

the children and society itself, does not depend on men's choice. God who made marriage endowed it with its various values and purposes.[105] All these are of the highest importance for the continuance of the human race, for the personal profit and eternal welfare of the members of families, for the dignity, stability, peace and prosperity of the family itself and of human society as a whole. By their natural character the institution of marriage and married love are ordained for the procreation and bringing up of children; they reach their peak or crown in these activities. Man and woman, who by the conjugal pact are 'no longer two but one' (*Mt* 19:6), help and minister to each other in an intimate linking of their persons and activities; they experience the real meaning of their union and achieve it more every day. This intimate union, two persons giving themselves to each other, demands their full fidelity and argues for their indissoluble unity; so does the good of their children.[106]

Christ our Lord abundantly blessed this manifold love which springs from the source of divine charity and forms a union on the model of his own union with his Church. For just as God once encountered his people in a covenant of love and trust,[107] so now as the Saviour of the world and the Spouse of the Church[108] he encounters faithful spouses in the sacrament of Christian marriage. Moreover he remains with them; just as he loved the Church and gave himself up for it,[109] so do married partners, by a mutual surrender, love each other with a lasting fidelity. Full conjugal love is taken up into divine love, guided and enriched by the redemptive virtue of Christ and the Church's saving action. Thus married people are effectively led to God and helped and strengthened in the sublime function of a father or a

---

[105]Cf. St Augustine, *De bono conjugii*, PL 40, 375-376 and 394; St Thomas, *Summa Theol.*, Supplem. Question 49, art. 3 ad 1: *Decretum pro Armenis* 3: Denz 702 (1327); Pius XI, Encycl. *Casti Connubii*: AAS 22 (1930), pp. 547-548: Denz. 2227-2238 (3703-3714).
[106]Cf. Pius XI, Encycl. *Casti Connubii*: AAS 22 (1930), pp. 546-547: Denz. 2231 (3706).
[107]Cf. *Osee* 2; *Jer* 3:6-13; *Ezech* 16 and 23; *Is* 54.
[108]Cf. *Mt* 9:15; *Mk* 2:19-20; *Lk* 5:34-35; *Jn* 3:29; cf. also 2 *Cor* 11:2; *Eph* 5:27; *Rev* 19:7-8; 21:2 and 9.
[109]Cf. *Eph* 5:25.

mother.[110] Christian married people are fortified in the dignity of their state, consecrated to its duties, by a special sacrament.[111] Carrying out their conjugal and family functions by virtue of this, penetrated by the spirit of Christ who fills their lives with faith, hope and charity, they make steady progress towards their own perfection and mutual sanctification and give glory to God in unison.

Children and indeed all those living in a family circle will, by parents' example and by family prayer, more easily find the way of salvation and holiness. Parents clothed with the dignity and office of fathers and mothers will diligently carry out the task of education which is first and foremost theirs, especially that of religious upbringing.

Children as living members of a family contribute in their own way to the sanctification of their parents. They will respond with gratitude and affection, devotion and trust to the benefits they receive from their parents and, as children should, they will remember their parents' needs in time of trouble or in the loneliness of old age. Widowhood, faced with courage in continuity with the married vocation, will be honoured by all.[112] Families will generously share their spiritual riches with other families. The Christian family, arising as it does from marriage which is the image and participation of the covenant of love between Christ and his Church,[113] will make clear to all the living presence of the Saviour in the world and the full nature of the Church. It will do this by means of married love, generous fecundity, unity and trust, and by the affectionate co-operation of its members.

49. Many times the word of God tells engaged and married couples to nourish and foster their association with the love appropriate to it.[114]

---

[110]Cf. VATICAN COUNCIL II, Dogmatic Constitution on the Church: AAS 57 (1965), pp. 15-16; 40-41; 47.
[111]PIUS XI, Encycl. *Casti Connubii*: AAS 22 (1930), p. 583.
[112]Cf. 1 *Tim* 5:3.
[113]Cf. *Eph* 5:32.
[114]Cf. *Gen* 2:22-24; *Prov* 5:18-20; 31:10-31; *Tob* 8:4-8; *Cant* 1:2-3; 2:16; 4:16-5:1; 7:8-11; 1 *Cor* 7:3-6; *Eph* 5:25-33.

Many in our time too set high value on true love between husband and wife, which is shown variously according to the legitimate customs of different times and peoples. But that love is above all a human thing, something one person gives to another moved by rational volition; it embraces the good of the person loved as a whole; hence it is able to enrich with a characteristic dignity its own manifestations of body and mind—to give them the nobility which belongs to them as the elements, the special tokens of married comradeship. Our Lord himself graciously made whole, perfected, elevated this love with a special endowment of grace and charity. Such a love associating the human with the divine, leads married people to give themselves to each other freely, with tenderness of affection and action; it pervades their lives[115] and grows by its own generous exercise. It is something far beyond mere erotic attraction which, selfishly indulged, quickly and miserably vanishes.

This love is uniquely expressed and perfected in married intercourse. The sexual activity by which married people are intimately and chastely united is honourable and worthy and, if done in a truly human fashion, it signifies and fosters the self-giving by which the couple gladly and gratefully enrich each other. Such love, ratified by mutual fidelity and above all sanctioned by Christ's sacrament, is unshakeably faithful in body and mind, through good times and bad, and so remains a stranger to adultery and divorce. The unity of marriage which our Lord confirmed is strikingly apparent from the equal personal dignity of man and woman, which in its turn is evidenced by their full mutual love. But it takes exceptional virtue to live up to this Christian vocation constantly. Married people then, fortified in a holy life by grace, will cultivate and pray for constancy in love, largeness of mind and a spirit of sacrifice.

Full married love will be more highly valued, and a healthy public

---

[115]Cf. Pius XI, Encycl. *Casti Connubii:* AAS 22 (1930), p. 547 and 548: Denz. 2232 (3707).

opinion about it formed, if married Christians excel in witnessing to it by their loyalty and harmony and by their devotion in bringing up their children; if they play their part in that psychological, social and cultural revival in favour of marriage which we need today. Young people need suitable and timely instruction in the dignity of marriage, in its responsibilities, in its practical side. They must learn to reverence chastity so that having practised it during their engagement they may, at a suitable age, pass on to marriage.

50. Marriage and married love are by their character ordained to the procreation and bringing up of children. Children are the outstanding gift of marriage, and contribute in the highest degree to the parents' welfare. God himself, who said 'it is not good for man to be alone' (*Gen* 2:18) and who 'from the beginning made them male and female' (*Mt* 19:4), wished to give man a special share in his own work of creation—so he blessed the man and the woman saying, 'increase and multiply' (*Gen* 1:28). Hence the proper cultivation of married love and the whole character of family life arising from it have the tendency, without thrusting into the background the other purposes of marriage, of disposing married people to co-operate courageously with the love of the Creator and Saviour, who through them continually enlarges and enriches his own family.

In the task of transmitting and rearing human life, a task which must be regarded as their proper mission, married people know that they are co-operating with, we might say interpreting, God's creative love. In view of this they should fulfil their duty with human and Christian responsibility. They should form a correct judgement by common reflection and effort, bearing in mind both their own good and that of the children born or expected. They will consider carefully the conditions of the time and their own living conditions, material and spiritual, and they should take account of the good of the family community, of society as a whole and of the Church. This judgement married people must ultimately make for themselves in the sight of

God. Yet they must be aware that they cannot proceed arbitrarily. They must be guided by conscience and conscience must be conformed to the divine law; they must submit to the Church's teaching authority which interprets that law authoritatively by the light of the Gospel. The divine law reveals the full meaning of married love, protects it, impels it towards a truly human perfection. So married Christians, trusting in divine Providence and having a spirit of sacrifice,[116] glorify the Creator and grow in Christian perfection when they fulfil the function of procreation with generous, human and Christian responsibility. Among those who thus satisfy the charge given them by God, special mention should be made of those who prudently and courageously agree to have, and of course properly to bring up, large families.[117]

But in fact marriage is not instituted merely for procreation. The indissoluble character of the personal pact and the good of the children themselves demand that mutual love should be properly shown between a married couple, that it should progress and mature. Even therefore if children, often so much desired, are lacking, marriage persists as a lifelong comradeship, and keeps its value and indissolubility.

51. The Council realizes that certain present-day conditions are often obstacles to a harmonious disposition of married life: that circumstances can arise in which the family, for a time at least, cannot be added to, so that it is not easy to maintain mutual love and life faithfully. Where the intimacy of married life if broken off, marital fidelity can be hazarded and due fertility prejudiced, for the upbringing of children and the resolution of mind to increase the family are endangered.

Some put forward wrong solutions of these problems, not shrinking even from taking life; the Church on the contrary reminds us that

---

[116]Cf. 1 *Cor* 7:5.
[117]Cf. Pius XII, *Address Tra le visite*, 20 Jan. 1958: AAS 50 (1958), p. 91.

there can be no contradiction between two divine laws—that which governs the transmitting of life and that which governs the fostering of married love.

God, the Lord of life, committed to man the high responsibility of maintaining life—a responsibility to be carried out in a way worthy of men. So life must from its very conception be guarded with the greatest care. Abortion and infanticide are abominable crimes. Man's sexual make-up and the human procreative faculty are remarkably superior to those found in lower grades of life, hence married sexual activity ordered in accordance with full human dignity is matter for great reverence. Moral behaviour then, when it is a question of reconciling married love with the responsible transmitting of life, does not depend only on a sincere intention and the evaluating of motives, but must be judged by objective standards. These are drawn from the nature of the human person and of its acts, and have regard for the whole meaning of mutual self-giving and human procreation in the context of true love. This cannot be unless the virtue of married chastity is sincerely cultivated. For children of the Church, taking their stand on these principles, it is not lawful to regulate procreation by embarking on ways which the Church's teaching authority, in expounding the divine law, condemns.[118] Certain questions which need other and more careful investigation have been submitted by command of the Pope to a Commission for the study of population, family and birth questions, so that the Supreme Pontiff may give judgement when the Commission has finished its work. In view of this the Council does not intend immediately to propose concrete solutions.

Let it be clear to everybody that man's life and the business of

---

[118]Cf. Pius XI, Encycl. *Casti Connubii:* AAS 22 (1930), pp. 559-561: Denz. 2239-2241 (3716-3718); Pius XII, Address to Italian Midwives, 29 Oct. 1951: AAS 43 (1951), pp. 835-854; Paul VI, Address to Cardinals, 23 June 1964: AAS 56 (1964), pp. 581-589. Certain questions which need other and more careful investigation have been submitted by command of the Pope to a Commission for the study of population, family and birth questions, so that the Supreme Pontiff may give judgement when the commission has finished its work. In view of this the Council does not intend immediately to propose concrete solutions.

transmitting it are not matters confined to this world or to be understood and measured solely by its standards. They always bear on man's eternal destiny.

52. The family is a kind of school of more abundant humanity. But if it is to achieve the fullness of its life and mission it needs affectionate communion of minds, so that the partners share their thoughts and aims and as parents co-operate zealously in bringing up their children. The active presence of their father is of great help in children's training, but their mother's care in the home, which the young especially need, must also be safeguarded, without losing sight of the legitimate social advance of woman. Children should be so instructed that when they grow up they will be capable of responsibly following a calling, even a sacred one, and of choosing a state of life. If they choose marriage, then they should be fit to found their own family in favourable moral, social and economic circumstances. It is for parents and guardians to offer prudent advice to the young about founding a family, and the young should readily listen; but parents should not force them into marriage or into the choice of a partner.

So the family in which different generations live together, helping each other to acquire greater wisdom and to harmonize personal rights with other social needs, is the basis of society. Therefore all who influence society and its various groupings should actively contribute to furthering the cause of marriage and the family. The civil power should as a sacred duty acknowledge, protect and nourish their true character, safeguard public morality, and look after domestic prosperity. The right of parents to have children and bring them up in the family circle should be protected. Those who unhappily are deprived of family life should be looked after and assisted by legislation and by other measures.

Faithful Christians, redeeming the present time,[119] distinguishing the eternal from the changeable, should diligently further the good of

---

[119] Cf. *Eph* 5:16; *Col* 4:5.

marriage and the family by the witness of their own lives and by co-operation with men of good will. Anticipating difficulties, they should provide for the needs and convenience of families in a way suitable to the present day. Great helps to this will be the Christian sense of the faithful, a general correct moral conscience and the wisdom and skill of experts in the sacred sciences.

Those learned in other sciences, especially biology, medicine, the social sciences and psychology, can also greatly serve the cause of marriage and the family and peace of conscience, if by comparative studies they try to elucidate better the conditions favourable to a lawful regulation of procreation.

The priest's part is to foster the vocation of married people by a variety of pastoral methods: preaching, liturgical worship and other spiritual aids to their married and family life; also to support them humanely and patiently in their difficulties and fortify them in charity, so that really radiantly good families may be formed.

Such enterprises as family associations should try hard to support by advice and practical help the young persons and married people, especially the recently married, and train them for family, social and apostolic life.

Finally, married people themselves are made in the image of God and have true personal status. Let them be joined in equal affection, harmony of mind, and mutual sanctity.[120] Following Christ, the source of life,[121] in the joys and sacrifices of their calling, may they by their loyal love become witnesses of that mystery of love which our Lord revealed to the world by his death and resurrection.[122]

---

[120]Cf. *Gregorian Sacramentary*: PL 78, 262.
[121]Cf. *Rom* 5:15 and 18;6:5-11; *Gal* 2:20.
[122]Cf. *Eph* 5:25-27.

Chapter II

THE PROPER PROMOTION OF CULTURAL PROGRESS

53. It is characteristic of man that he cannot achieve true and full humanity except through culture, that is by cultivating natural resources and spiritual values. Wherever human life is involved, then, nature and culture are closely connected.

The word 'culture' in a general sense stands for everything by which man develops and refines his various gifts of mind and body. We speak of culture whenever he devotes himself to subduing the world to his control by knowledge and labour; when he humanizes social life on the family scale and on the civic by the progress of manners and institutions; lastly, when in the course of time he expresses in his own achievements, great spiritual experiences and aspirations, communicating and preserving them so that they may profit many, even the whole human race.

This means that human culture necessarily has a historical and social aspect—that the word 'culture' often takes on a sociological and ethnological meaning. In this sense we can speak of a plurality of cultures. From different ways of using things, of setting to work, of self-expression, of practising religion and fashioning morals, of establishing laws and legal institutions, of furthering the arts and sciences and cultivating beauty; from all these emerge different sets of living conditions and different patterns for organizing the resources of this life. So every human community has its own patrimony of traditional institutions. So every man of whatever people and period forms part of a definite and historic movement from which he draws resources to promote human and civil culture.

248

Section 1: THE CONDITIONS OF CULTURE IN THE CONTEMPORARY WORLD

54. Socially and culturally modern man's conditions of life have profoundly changed, so much so that we can speak of a new age of human history.[123] As a result new ways are open of perfecting culture and spreading it widely. Enormous advances in the natural and social sciences, in the humanities, in technology, in means of communication have all contributed to this. Hence present-day culture has certain distinctive marks. The exact sciences fully develop the critical sense. Recent psychological studies explain human activity more deeply. Historical studies lead to things being viewed in the light of change and evolution. Manners and customs tend steadily towards uniformity. Industrialization, urbanization, and other causes are creating a mass culture which in turn creates new ways of thinking, acting and using leisure. Increased exchanges between various peoples and social groups opens up more widely the resources of various cultures to all and sundry, so that gradually a more universal type of culture is formed. This promotes and expresses the unity of mankind, in proportion as it respects the particular features of each culture.

55. There is a growing number of men and women of every class and nation who realize that they are the architects of this community of culture. Everywhere there is growing steadily a sense of autonomy and responsibility extremely important for the spiritual and moral maturity of men. This responsibility becomes clearer if we bear in mind that the world is becoming united and the charge is laid on us of building a better world in truth and justice. In this way we see that a new humanism is being born in which man is defined by his responsibilities to his fellow man and to history.

---

[123]Cf. The Introduction to this Constitution, n. 4 and ff.

249

56. It is not surprising that in these conditions man, who feels himself responsible for cultural progress, has higher hopes but at the same time views anxiously the many anomalies he still has to resolve.

How shall he prevent increased cultural exchanges, which should be bringing about a really fruitful dialogue between various groups and nations, from upsetting the life of communities, overturning ancient wisdom and threatening the native qualities of different peoples?

How can the impulse and expansion of the new culture be encouraged without destroying real fidelity to the inheritance of tradition? This problem is especially acute when scientific and technical culture has to be reconciled with the various streams of 'classical' tradition.

How can rapidly growing specialization be reconciled with the need for a synthesis and for preserving men's capacity for contemplation and wonder, which leads to wisdom?

How to ensure that all men share the world's cultural wealth when the attainments of experts are becoming ever more abstruse and complex?

How finally are we to recognize the legitimate autonomy of culture without falling into a merely secular or even anti-religious humanism?

Though it is involved in these anomalies, culture has to develop today in such a way that it brings about an orderly development of the human personality and helps men to fulfil these tasks to which the united human family, but Christians especially, are called.

Section 2: CERTAIN PRINCIPLES FOR RIGHTLY PROMOTING CULTURE

57. Faithful Christians making their way to heaven should look for and set their minds on the things that are above.[124] But this increases rather than diminishes the importance of their task of co-operating

---

[124]Cf. *Col* 3:1-2.

with all men in building a more human world. Indeed the mystery of the Christian faith offers them notable incentives and helps, to take greater pains in the task, and especially to understand fully its meaning. Thus will human culture assume a high place in man's vocation as a whole.

For when man by his handiwork and technical skill cultivates the earth to make it yield fruit and become a fit place for living in and when he consciously takes part in the various forms of social life, he carries out the design of God, manifested from the beginning, that he should subdue the earth[125] and perfect the work of creation and he perfects himself; at the same time he observes the great commandment of Christ that he should spend himself in the service of his fellows.

Further, when he applies himself to philosophy, history, mathematics, the natural sciences, or practices the arts, he can contribute in the highest degree to raising the human family to more sublime appreciation of the true, the good and the beautiful, to a more comprehensive value judgement; he can help it to draw light from that marvellous Wisdom which from the beginning was beside God like a master workman, rejoicing before him always, rejoicing in his inhabited world, and delighting in the sons of men.[126]

By this very means man's mind, less tied to the slavery of material things, can be more readily raised to the worship and contemplation of the Creator. In fact he is thereby disposed under the impulse of grace to acknowledge the Word of God who before being made flesh to save and gather all to himself was already 'in the world' as 'the true light that enlightens every man' (*Jn* 1: 9-10).[127]

Certainly contemporary scientific and technical progress, whose method cannot penetrate the inmost meaning of things, can lead to a kind of mere phenomenalism and agnosticism if that method is taken

---

[125]Cf. *Gen* 1:28.
[126]Cf. *Prov* 8:30-31.
[127]Cf. St IRENAEUS, *Adv. Haer.* III, 11, 8 (ed. SAGNARD, p. 200; cf. also 16, 6: pp. 290-292; 21:10-22, pp. 370-372; and 22:3: p. 378; etc.).

as the only yardstick for investigating truth. There is moreover a danger that man may trust so much in present-day inventions as to think he is self-sufficient and no longer look beyond this world.

But these regrettable results do not follow necessarily from contemporary culture and they should not tempt us to overlook its positive values. These are: rigorous fidelity to truth in scientific enquiry; the need of co-operation which technical enterprises impose; the sense of international solidarity; increasingly lively awareness of the responsibility of experts to help and protect men; the will to improve conditions of life especially for those who suffer from being deprived of responsibility or from poverty of culture. These positive values can afford some preparation for receiving the Gospel message: a preparation which he who came to save the world can animate with divine charity.

58. We find many ties between the message of salvation and human culture. God, progressively revealing himself to his people down to the time of the full manifestation of himself in his incarnate Son, adapted his way of speaking to the culture of each period.

The Church too has lived in various circumstances in the course of her history, and has used the resources of different cultures in preaching to all nations, to spread and expound Christ's message, to examine and understand it more deeply, to express it more effectively in liturgical celebration and in the many-sided life of the community of the faithful.

At the same time, the Church's mission is to all peoples of whatever time and place. She has no fixed and exclusive ties with any race or nation, any code of manners, any customs old or new. Faithful to her own tradition and at the same time conscious of her universal mission she can enter into communion with various forms of culture to her own profit and to theirs.

The Gospel of Christ continually renews the life and culture of fallen man, opposing and eliminating the errors and evils which come from the always menacing enticements of sin. She increasingly purifies and elevates the behaviour of peoples. With heavenly riches she fertilizes, strengthens, complements and restores in Christ the gifts and ornaments of mind of any people and age.[128] Thus in fulfilling her own office[129] the Church contributes to and stimulates civilized and humane life, and by her activity, including her liturgy, she educates men to interior liberty.

59. For the reasons just set out, the Church reminds everybody that culture should be related to the whole perfecting of personality, to the good life of the community and of human society as a whole. Hence everyone must cultivate his mind in such a way as to rouse the capacity for wonder, for inward scrutiny, for contemplation, for forming personal judgement, for developing religious, moral and social sense.

Culture springs from the rational and social nature of man; continually therefore it needs proper liberty to develop itself and scope to operate autonomously. Quite rightly then it commands respect and is in a certain sense inviolable, saving the rights of persons and the community and within the limits of the common good.

The Council, recalling what was taught by the First Vatican Council, declares that 'there are two distinct orders of knowledge', that of faith and that of reason, and that the Church plainly does not forbid that 'human learning and arts ... should use their own principles and methods in their own fields.' In other words, 'recognizing this just liberty', she affirms the rightful autonomy of human culture and especially of the sciences.[130]

All this entails that, within the bounds of morality and the common welfare, man should be free to pursue research, to express and publish his opinions, to practise any art, and that finally he should be accurately informed about public affairs.[131]

---

[128]Cf. *Eph* 1:10.

[129]Cf. Pius XI's words to Fr M.D. Roland-Gossebin: 'We should never lose sight of the fact that the Church's objective is to evangelize and not to civilize. If she civilizes, it is in order to evangelize' (*Semaines Sociales de France*, Versailles, 1936, pp. 461-462).

[130]Vatican Council I, Dogmatic Constitution on the Catholic Faith, c. IV:Denz. 1795, 1799 (3015, 3019). Cf. Pius XI, Encycl. *Quadragesimo anno*: AAS 23 (1931), p. 190.

[131]Cf. John XXIII, Encycl. *Pacem in terris*: AAS 55 (1963), p. 260.

It belongs to public authority not to decide the patterns of culture but to provide conditions and help to further cultural life among all, even minorities within the nation.[132] Above all it must be insisted that culture must not be turned from its proper purposes to serve political or economic power.

Section 3: CERTAIN MORE URGENT DUTIES OF CHRISTIANS IN THE MATTER OF CULTURE

60. Nowadays very many have the chance to free themselves from the misery of ignorance; so it is a duty entirely in harmony with the age, for Christians, especially, to work out those basic judgements in economics and in politics, in the national and international fields, which will recognize and put into practice everywhere the right of all men to a civilized way of life, whatever their race, sex, nation, religion or social status. Enough cultural opportunities should be available to everybody, especially of the kind which make up what is called fundamental culture; otherwise too many will be hindered from making any really human contribution to the common good because they are illiterate or barred from responsible activity.

No effort should be spared to enable those with the necessary talents to proceed to higher studies—in such a way too that they will as far as possible follow careers suitable to their talents and skill.[133] Thus any man and any class of men will be able to attain a full development of their social life adapted to their gifts and traditions.

There should be equal concern to make everybody conscious of his right to culture and of his duty to acquire it and to help others. Sometimes living and working conditions are obstacles to men's efforts in this field and even kill any desire for self-improvement. This holds especially for workers on the land and in industry, and they should be given working conditions which help, not hinder humane

---

[132]Cf. JOHN XXIII, Encycl. *Pacem in terris*: AAS 55 (1963), p. 283; cf. PIUS XII, Broadcast on Christmas Eve, 24 Dec. 1941: AAS 34 (1942), p. 16-17.
[133]Cf. JOHN XXIII, Encycl. *Pacem in terris*: AAS 55 (1963), p. 260.

culture. Women are now working in almost every field. It is desirable that they should play their part fully in accordance with their natural gifts and there should be general interest in recognizing and promoting their proper and necessary share in cultural life.

61. It is more difficult today than in past times to achieve a synthesis of the various branches of knowledge and the arts. An increased mass and variety of elements go to make up a culture: it becomes less possible for individuals to absorb and organize them, so that the image of the 'universal man' is steadily vanishing. All the same each of us still has the duty of keeping in view the human personality as a whole—the person in whom above all we find those values of intelligence, will, conscience, and brotherhood which are founded in God the Creator and wonderfully integrated and elevated in Christ.

The mother and nurse, so to speak, in this education is the family, in which the children, lovingly cherished, more easily learn the right order of things together, and their minds are cultivated almost naturally, by absorption, as they grow up.

There are opportunities for the same education in present-day society from the increased spread of books and from new instruments of cultural and social communication which can favour a universal culture. The widespread shortening of working hours brings greater opportunities for many. There are proper holidays for relaxation and health, with spare-time activities and studies and foreign travel which refine men's minds and help them to get to know each other more thoroughly. Playing or watching games too helps to preserve mental balance even for the community and to establish friendly relations between men of all conditions, nations and races. Christians should co-operate to ensure that collective activities of a cultural kind such as are characteristic of our age should have a human and Christian spirit.

But all these advantages will not educate man to an integral culture if we neglect to consider deeply the meaning of culture and science for the human personality.

62. Though the Church has contributed much to the progress of culture, experience shows that to combine culture with Christian training sometimes, though not necessarily, involves difficulties.

These difficulties are not necessarily harmful to the life of faith in fact they can stimulate our minds to a more accurate and deeper understanding of the faith. Recent studies and discoveries in science, philosophy and history raise new questions which have their repercussions on life and call for fresh investigations by theologians too. Theologians moreover are called upon to examine, according to their own methods and requirements, more suitable ways of putting their teaching to their contemporaries. For the deposit, or truths, of Faith is one thing, the way it is stated is another—though the sense and purpose remains the same.[134] The discoveries of the secular sciences, especially psychology and sociology, should be adequately recognized and employed in pastoral care—not merely theological principles; in that way the faithful will be led to a purer, more mature life of faith.

Arts and literature too are important in their own way for the Church's life. They probe into man's character and problems, into the story of his efforts to know and improve himself and his world. They try to discover his place in history and in the universe, shed light on his happiness and misery, his needs and his potentialities, to outline a better future for him. Thus they have the power to uplift human life, which they express in so many forms in different times and places.

We should see to it that those who practise these arts feel that the Church acknowledges their efforts, that they enjoy reasonable freedom, that their relations with the Christian community become easier. New art styles, which are adapted to contemporary life and express the genius of various nations and regions, should be recognized by the Church. When they raise the mind to God and are appropriate

---

[134]Cf. JOHN XXIII, Speech opening the Council, 11 Oct. 1962: AAS 54 (1962), p. 792.

in their manner of expression to the liturgy, they should be welcomed in the sanctuary.[135]

Thus God will be better known and the preaching of the Gospel will be clearer to men—seem almost engrafted into their way of life.

The faithful should live very close to their contemporaries and apply themselves to understanding fully the latter's ways of thinking and feeling as these are expressed culturally. New scientific and scholarly information, knowledge of the latest inventions, should be combined with the teaching of Christian doctrine and conduct. Religious growth and integrity of mind should advance hand in hand with learning and technical accomplishment; in that way we shall be able to test and interpret everything by fully Christian standards.

Those occupied with theology in seminaries and universities should seek to co-operate intellectually and practically with experts in other sciences. Theological enquiry should aim at deep knowledge of revealed truth without losing touch with its own time; men expert in other fields can then assist a fuller knowledge of the faith. These combined studies will be of the greatest advantage in the training of the Church's ministers, enabling them to explain the Church's teaching about God, man and the world more suitably to our contemporaries and ensure it a more ready hearing.[136] Further, it would be a good thing if more laymen acquired a reasonable knowledge of the sacred sciences; if a good many of them even carried these studies a great deal further at a serious level. But if clerics or laymen are to do their task properly they must be allowed a just freedom of research and thought and be allowed to express themselves humbly yet courageously in those matters in which they are expert.[137]

---

[135]Vatican Council II, Constitution on the Sacred Liturgy, n. 123: AAS 56 (1964), p. 131; Paul VI, Discourse to Roman artists, 7 May 1964: AAS 56 (1964), pp. 439-442.
[136]Cf. Vatican Council II, Decree on Training for the Priesthood [CTS Translation, Do 358], and Declaration on Christian Education [CTS Translation, Do 362].
[137]Cf. Dogmatic Constitution on the Church, c. IV, n. 37: AAS 57 (1965), pp. 42-43.

Chapter III

SOCIAL AND ECONOMIC LIFE

63. Even in social and economic life the dignity of the human person and the integrity of his vocation, along with the good of society as a whole, are to be recognized and furthered. Man is the author, the centre and the end of all social and economic life.

The economy of today, like other provinces of social life, is marked by man's growing mastery over nature, closer and more extensive relations and interdependence between citizens, groups and peoples, more frequent intervention by political power. Progress in methods of production and in exchange of goods and services have made the economy capable of providing better for the increased needs of the human family.

But there are grounds for disquiet. There are those, especially in economically advanced regions, who seem to be ruled by economics, their whole personal and social life impregnated with economics— and this not only in the collectivist countries but elsewhere too. At the very moment when economic advance, rationally and humanely directed and co-ordinated, might be reducing social inequalities, it too often exasperates them, or even results in a relapse in the social structure of the weak, and in contempt for the poor. While a vast multitude still lack the necessities of life some, even in backward regions, live extravagantly and wastefully. Luxury and penury exist side by side. While a few enjoy the maximum independence of action, for many there is almost no possibility of acting responsibly and on their own initiative, and these often live and work in conditions unfit for human beings.

Similar defects of economic and social equilibrium can be seen between agriculture, industry and the public services as well as between different parts of the same country. Between the economically more advanced countries and the rest opposition hardens, which can imperil the peace of the world.

Our contemporaries are becoming more vividly aware of these disparities, and are absolutely convinced that the greater technical and economic resources the world enjoys today can and should correct this unhappy state of things. But this calls for social-economic reforms and a change in everybody's thinking and habits. For this purpose the Church in the light of the Gospel has worked out in the course of centuries principles of justice and equity for individual and social as well as for international life—principles based on sound reason—and has put them forward especially in recent times. The Council proposes to reinforce these principles in the context of our day and to add certain orientations, bearing in mind the requirements of economic progress.[138]

Section 1: ECONOMIC PROGRESS

64. Today more than ever we are intent on increasing production in agriculture, industry and the public services, to cope with population increases and the growing wants of the human race. Hence we must encourage technical progress, openness to new ideas, eagerness to create and to expand enterprises, adaptation of methods and strenuous effort by all engaged in production. In a word, everything useful to this advance. But the basic purpose of production is not mere increase of goods, nor gain, nor domination, but the service of man—of man in his entirety, with attention to his material needs and his intellectual, moral and spiritual demands in the proper order; the needs of any man, let us add, any group of men, any race or region. So economic enterprise must be carried out, according indeed to its own methods and laws, within the bounds of the moral order,[139] so that God's plan for men is fulfilled.[140]

---

[138]Cf. Pius XII, Broadcast, 23 Mar. 1952: AAS 44 (1952), p. 273; John XXIII, Address to Italian Catholic Trades Unionists, 1 May 1959: AAS 51 (1959), p. 358.

[139]Cf. Pius XI, Encycl. *Quadragesimo anno*: AAS 23 (1931), p. 190ff.; Pius XII, Broadcast, 23 Mar. 1952: AAS 44 (1952), p. 276 ff.; John XXIII, Encycl. *Mater et Magistra*: AAS 53 (1961), p. 450; Vatican Council II, Decree on the Media of Social Communication, c. 1, n. 6: AAS 56 (1964), p. 147.

[140]Cf. *Mt* 16:26; *Lk* 16:1-31; *Col* 3:17.

65. Economic progress should remain under man's control, not at the mercy of a few men or groups wielding too much economic power, nor of the political community, nor of some of the more powerful nations. On the contrary, at any level as many men as possible and, where international relations are concerned, all nations ought to have an active part in its direction. Equally the private enterprise of individuals or associations should be properly co-ordinated with public works and government schemes.

Development should be left neither to the mechanical working of private enterprise nor to the power of public authority. Hence they are wrong who oppose reforms in the name of a false liberty; equally wrong are they who subordinate fundamental personal or group rights to collective organization.[141]

Citizens should remember that they have the right and duty, which the civil power should recognize, of contributing what they can to the true progress of their own community. In the underdeveloped countries especially, where all resources urgently need to be exploited, they seriously endanger the public welfare who keep their wealth lying barren or—saving the personal right of emigration—deprive the community of the material or spiritual assistance it needs.

66. Justice and equity demand that, without prejudice to personal rights or the character of particular peoples, we strenuously try to remove as quickly as possible the present huge and growing economic inequalities, which involve unfairness to men and to sections of society. In many regions which have difficulty in growing and marketing agricultural produce, workers on the land need help in increasing production and finding markets, in introducing development and new methods, in getting a fair wage. Otherwise, as often happens, they will

---

[141]Cf. Leo XIII, Encycl. *Libertas: Acta Leonis* XIII, v.VIII, p. 220ff.; Pius XI, Encycl. *Quadragesimo anno*: AAS 23 (1931), p. 191 if.; Encycl. *Divini Redemptoris*: AAS 39 (1937), p. 65 if.; Pius XII, Christmas Broadcast 1941: AAS 34 (1942), p. 10ff.; John XXIII, Encycl. *Mater et Magistra*: AAS 53 (1961), pp. 401-464.

remain second-class citizens. But they themselves, especially the young ones, must seriously set about perfecting their professional skill, without which there can be no progress in agriculture.[142]

It is also a fact that mobility of labour, so absolutely necessary in a developing economy, should be regulated so as not to make the lives of men and their families uncertain and insecure. There should be no discrimination in working conditions or pay against foreign workers who co-operate in furthering the economy. All, especially public authorities, should regard them not as mere tools of production but as persons, help them to send for and decently house their families, and encourage them to become part of the social life of the country. Yet as far as possible opportunities of work should be created in the countries they belong to.

In economies which are in a phase of transition, for example those new types of industrial society in which automation is on the increase, it will be necessary to see that enough and suitable work as well as adequate technical and professional training is provided, and sustenance and dignity safeguarded for those who are gravely handicapped by sickness or old age.

Section 2: SOME PRINCIPLES GOVERNING SOCIAL AND ECONOMIC LIFE AS A WHOLE

67. Human labour, employed in the production and exchange of goods and in supplying economic services, is the chief element in economic life—all else is instrumental.

Such work, whether done independently or managed by others, proceeds directly from a person, who puts his seal on the things of nature and submits them to his will. By his work man normally maintains his life and the lives of those dependent on him, is united with his fellow-men and serves them, can exercise charity to the full and associate himself with perfecting the divine creation. Indeed we hold

---

[142]On agricultural problems cf. especially JOHN XXIII, Encycl. *Mater et Magistra*: AAS 53 (1961), p. 341 ff.

that by his labour man is associated with the redemptive work of Christ, who conferred surpassing dignity on labour by working with his own hands at Nazareth. Hence arises an obligation for each to work loyally, and also a right to work. Society on its part must, according to its circumstances, help its members to find adequate opportunities for work. Then wages must be paid which will give adequate scope for living, materially, socially, culturally, spiritually, considering each man's job, his productivity, his working conditions and the general welfare.[143]

Economic enterprise is generally an affair of collaboration—thus it is wicked and inhuman to arrange and organize it to the detriment of anybody involved. Yet it often happens even in our time that those who work are made slaves to their own work. No 'economic laws' can justify this. The whole process of productive labour should be geared to the personal needs and to the way of life of whoever is doing it; in the first place to domestic life, and this especially applies to mothers and families. Age and sex should always be respected. Workers should be given the scope to express their own gifts and personality in their work. When they have applied their time and energy to it in a responsible way, they should enjoy sufficient rest and leisure to live their family, social, cultural and religious life. Indeed they should have opportunities to develop their capabilities and energy, if these are lacking in their trade or profession.

68. In economic enterprises it is persons who work together, that is, free and independent men created in God's image. So long as unity of direction is assured, a suitable share in management should be aimed at for everybody—proprietors, employers, management and workers.[144]

---

[143]Cf. Leo XIII, Encycl. *Rerum Novarum*: ASS 23 (1890-91), p. 649, and p. 662; Pius XI, Encycl. *Quadragesimo anno*: AAS 23 (1931), pp. 200-201; Pius XI, Encycl. *Divini Redemptoris*: AAS 29 (1937), p. 92; Pius XII, Christmas Broadcast, 1942: AAS 35 (1943), p. 20; Pius XII, Address, 13 June 1943: AAS 35 (1943), p. 172; Pius XII, Broadcast to Spanish workers, 11 Mar. 1951: AAS 43 (1951), p. 215; John XXIII, Encycl. *Mater et Magistra*: AAS 53 (1961), p. 419.

[144]Cf. John XXIII, Encycl. *Mater et Magistra*: AAS 53 (1961), pp. 408, 424, 427: The word *'curatione'* [here rendered as 'management', Trans.] is taken from *Quadragesimo anno*: AAS 23 (1931), p. 199. From the standpoint of the development of the question cf. also Pius XII. Address, 3 June 1950: AAS 42 (1950), pp. 485-588; Paul VI, Address, 8 June 1964: AAS 56 (1964), pp. 574- 579.

But since economic and social conditions, and hence the future of workers and their children, often depend not on the firm they work for but on higher-level institutions, workers should have a share in these too, either directly or through their freely-elected delegates.

One fundamental human right that workers have is that of freely setting up unions which can genuinely represent them and contribute to a proper organizing of economic life; they have also the right to participate freely in union business, without fear of victimization. This kind of orderly participation, combined with progressive economic and social training, will increase everybody's awareness of his position and duties, and make each feel associated, according to his capacities and attainments, with the whole work of economic and social progress and with the universal welfare.

When social-economic conflict arises the aim should be to settle it peacefully. But though negotiation should come first, strikes can remain a necessary last resort, in present conditions, for protecting rights and realizing the rightful demands of labour. As soon as possible, however, ways and means should be sought to resume negotiations and bring about reconciliation.

69. God intended the earth and all it contains for the use of all men and peoples, so created goods should flow fairly to all, regulated by justice and accompanied by charity.[145] Whatever forms property may take according to legitimate custom and changing circumstances, this universal destiny of the earth's resources should always be borne in mind. In his use of them, man should regard his legitimate possessions not simply as his own but as common in the sense that they can benefit others as well as himself.[146] But everybody has a right to a share of the earth's goods sufficient for himself and his family. So thought

---

[145]Cf. Pius XII, Encycl. *Sertum laetitiae*: AAS 31 (1939), p. 642; John XXIII, Consistorial Address: AAS 52 (1960), pp. 5-11; Encycl. *Mater et Magistra*: AAS 53 (1961), p. 411.
[146]Cf. St Thomas, *Summa Theol.* II-II, q. 32, art. 5, ad. 2; and q. 66, art. 2; cf. Leo XIII's explanation in *Rerum Novarum*: ASS 23 (1890-91), p. 651; cf. also Pius XII, Address, 1 June 1941: AAS 33 (1941), p. 199; Christmas Broadcast, 1954: AAS 47 (1955), p. 27.

the Fathers and Doctors of the Church, who taught that men were obliged to help the poor, and that, not merely with what they did not need themselves.[147] In fact he who is in extreme need has a right to supply this need from the riches of others.[148] Since so many in the world suffer from hunger, the Council urges men and authorities to remember that saying of the Fathers: 'Feed a man who is dying from hunger—if you have not fed him you have killed him.'[149] Each as far as he can must share and spend his wealth in coming to the assistance especially of these suffering individuals or peoples so that they may thereby be enabled to go on to self-help and self-development.

In under-developed countries the community often has its own customary and traditional ways of ensuring that goods are distributed, so that each member receives what he absolutely needs. Customs should not be regarded as unchangeable if they no longer answer to present-day requirements; but neither should they be rashly discarded if they can still be so adapted as to remain useful. Similarly in economically advanced nations, a network of institutions designed to provide social security can give practical form to the distribution of wealth. Family and social services should be further promoted, especially those taking account of education and the cultivation of the mind. But in setting up all these things we should be careful that people are

---

[147]Cf. St Basil, *Homily on the text of St Luke's Gospel*. 'I will put down my barns' (*Lk* 12:18) n. 2; PG 31, 263; Lactantius, *Divinarum Institutionum*, Bk.V, on justice: PL 6, 565 B.; St Augustine, *On the Gospel of St John*, 50, n. 6: PL 35, 1760; *Enarratio in Psalmos* CXLVII, 12: PL 37, 192; St Gregory the Great, *Homilies on the Gospel*, Hom. 20: PL 76, 1165; and *Regulae Pastoralis liber*, par. III, c. 21: PL 77, 87; St Bonaventure *In III Sent*, d. 33, dub. 1 (ed. *Quaracchi III*, 728) and In *IV Sent.*, d. 15, par. IL, art 2, q. 1 (*ibid*. IV, 371b); *Quaestio de superfluo*, (ins. in the *Biblioteca Communale* at Assisi, 186 if. 112a–113a); St Albert the Great, *In III Sent.*, d. 33, art. 3, sal. 1. (ed. Borgnet XXVIII, 611) and *In IV Sent*, d. 15, art. 16 (*ibid*. XXIX, 494-497). On the reckoning of surplus in our time cf. John XXIII, television Broadcast, 11 Sept. 1962: AAS 54 (1962), p. 682: 'The duty of every man, the compelling duty of the Christian is to estimate surplus by the needs of others, and to take good care that created goods are administered and distributed to the advantage of all.'

[148]In this case the old principle holds 'in extreme necessity all things are common, that is, to be shared.' On the other hand, for the rationale, extension and manner of application of the principle cited here, cf. besides reputable modern authors St Thomas, *Summa Theol*. II-II. q. 66. art. 7. It will be clear that to apply the principle correctly all the morally necessary conditions must be observed.

[149]Cf. Gratian, *Decretum*, C. 21, dist. LXXXVI, (ed. Friedberg I, 302) The assaying is already found in PL 54 591A (Cf. *Antonianum* 27 (1952), pp. 349-366).

not encouraged in a certain social inertia—that they do not become irresponsible about their work and disinclined for service to others.

70. Investments should be aimed at providing opportunities for work and adequate pay now and in the future. Whoever controls investments and regulates economic life—individuals, groups or public authority—are bound to keep these purposes in view. They must also recognize that they have a grave duty of watching that there is provision for a decent standard of living for individuals and the community. They must look to the future and establish a correct balance between the needs of present-day consumers—individuals or groups—and of investment for future generations. The urgent needs of under-developed countries and regions should never be forgotten. Monetary policy must not be damaging to one's own country or to others. Care should be taken that the economically weak do not suffer unfairly from fluctuations in the value of money.

71. Since property and other forms of private ownership of external wealth contribute to the expression of personality and afford opportunities for social and economic service, it is a good thing that some access to them should be encouraged whether for individuals or for communities.

Private property or some control over external goods gives a certain elbow-room for personal and family independence and can be regarded as an extension of human liberty. Since also it provides incentives to responsible work, it is in some sense a condition of civil liberties.[150]

The forms such property and ownership take today are various and becoming more so. But in spite of public funds and the claims and

---

[150]Cf. Leo XIII, Encycl. *Rerum Novarum*: ASS 23 (1890-91), pp. 643-646; Pius X, Encycl. *Quadragesimo anno*: AAS 23 (1931), p. 191; Pius XII, Broadcast, 1 June 1941: AAS 33 (1941), p. 199; Christmas Broadcast, 1942: AAS 35 (1943), p. 17; Broadcast, 1 Sept. 1944: AAS 36 (1944), p. 253; John XXIII, Encycl. *Mater et Magistra*: AAS 53 (1961), pp. 428-429.

services provided by society, property is still an important element in security. This is true not only of material property but of such non-material assets as professional skills.

The right of private property is no obstacle to the right inherent in various forms of public ownership. The transference of wealth to public ownership cannot be made except by competent authority and within the limits of the common good, as well as with fair compensation. Moreover it is the business of public authority to see that no one abuses private ownership against the common interest.[151]

Private ownership itself has naturally a certain social character, founded in the law that goods are destined for all in common.[152] If this social aspect is neglected, property too often becomes the occasion of greed and serious disturbance, and its opponents are given excuse to call the right itself in question.

In many under-developed regions there are large, even vast country estates, poorly cultivated or for reasons of gain left uncultivated, while the majority of people have no land or only the smallest plots—all this, when an increase in productivity is evidently urgent. Sometimes those who are employed by landlords or till land rented from landlords are given a wage, or keep, unworthy of men, not decently housed, or they are exploited by middlemen. Lacking all security, they live so like serfs that they have practically no chance of acting freely and responsibly and are debarred from all cultural development or part in social or political life. A variety of reforms are therefore necessary: wage increases, better working conditions, greater security of employment, incentives to work willingly; indeed, the redistribution of insufficiently cultivated estates among those able to make them productive. In this case the necessary means should be furnished; especially, training should be

---

[151]Cf. PIUS XI, Encycl. *Quadragesimo anno*: ASS 23 (1931), p. 214; JOHN XXIII, Encycl. *Mater et Magistra*: AAS 53 (1961), p. 429.
[152]Cf. PIUS XII, Whitsun Broadcast, 1941: AAS 44 (1941), p. 199; JOHN XXIII Encycl. *Mater et Magistra*: AAS 53 (1961), p. 430.

subsidized and reasonable facilities given for co-operative organization. But whenever the common good requires confiscation, compensation should be fairly estimated according to all the circumstances.

72. Christians who have an active part in present-day social-economic development and contend for justice and charity should be assured that they have much to contribute to prosperity and peace. Singly and socially they should set a shining example in these activities. Equipped with the necessary skill and experience, they should maintain the right scale of values in the world's business, faithful to Christ and his Gospel, so that their whole life, personal and social, may be full of the spirit of the Beatitudes, and particularly of poverty.

Whoever in obedience to Christ seeks first the kingdom of God, draws from this a stronger and purer love to help all his fellow men and perfect the work of justice under the inspiration of charity.[153]

---

[153]For New Testament teaching on the right use of goods cf.: *Lk* 3:11: 10:30 ff.; 11:41; 1 *Pet* 5:3; *Mk* 8:36; 12:39-41; *Jas* 5:1-6; 1 *Tim* 6:8: *Eph* 4:28; 2 *Cor* 8:13 ff.; 1 *Jn* 3:17 ff.

CHAPTER IV

THE LIFE OF THE POLITICAL COMMUNITY

73. In our time profound transformations are to be seen in social structures and institutions, the consequences of cultural economic and social evolution. These transformations greatly influence the life of the political community, especially as to rights and duties in the exercise of civil liberty and in the achievement of the general welfare; in the matter too of regulating the relations of citizens to public authority.

A livelier consciousness of human dignity has aroused in various parts of the world an eagerness to build a juridical-political order in which personal rights affecting public life are better protected. Such are the rights of free assembly, free association, freedom of expression and of religious profession private or public. The safeguarding of personal rights is indispensable if citizens are to take part, singly or in association, in public life and in government.

Cultural, economic and social progress is reinforcing the desire to take a greater part in active politics. Conscience gives many a growing concern for the rights of minorities—not forgetting the corresponding duties of these to the political community. Respect is increasing for men of other opinions or religion; there is wider co-operation to ensure that all and not just the privileged shall really enjoy their personal rights.

Those political systems, in force in some regions, cannot be approved which impair civil and religious liberty, multiply victims of the greed and crimes of politicians and divert the exercise of authority from the general welfare to the advantage of some faction or of the rulers themselves.

Nothing is better for establishing a truly human political life than to foster a deep sense of justice, goodwill and public service and to strengthen fundamental convictions about the true nature of a political community and about the purpose, the right exercise and the limits of public authority.

74. Men, families and the various associations who make up the political community are aware that they cannot of themselves provide the basis for a fully human life, and they realize the need for a wider community in which all shall join forces continually to foster the common good.[154] For this reason they make up political communities of various forms. The political community, then, exists for the common good, has its full justification and meaning in the common good, and draws its original and distinctive right from that source. Now the common good comprises the sum of those social conditions in which men, families and associations can more quickly perfect themselves.[155]

But many men of different kinds can come together in a political community and legitimately disagree on policies. If the community is not to be torn apart by everybody following his own opinion, authority is needed to direct the energies of all to the common purpose, not mechanically or despotically but primarily as a moral force based on liberty and a sense of duty and responsibility.

Political community and public authority are founded in human nature and thence belong to the order determined by God, though it may rest with the citizens to decide freely the type of regime and personnel of government.[156]

It follows that the exercise of political authority, whether in a community as such, or in representative institutions, must always be carried out within the framework of the moral order, in pursuit of the common good dynamically understood and according to a lawfully established juridical system. The citizens are then bound in conscience to obedience.[157] This argues the responsibility, dignity and importance of those who are in authority.

Where the citizens are oppressed by a public authority which exceeds its competence, they should not on that account refuse what is objectively required of them for the common good, but it must be

---

[154]Cf. JOHN XXIII, Encycl. *Mater et Magistra*: AAS 53 (1961), p. 417.
[155]Cf. *ibid*.
[156]Cf. *Rom* 13:1-5.
[157]Cf. *Rom* 13:5.

allowable for them, within the limits of the law of nature and the Gospel, to defend their rights and those of their fellow citizens against this abuse of authority.

The concrete ways in which the political community organizes its structure and government can vary with the native traditions of different peoples and the course of history, but they should always serve to produce a civilized, peaceful man of general goodwill, to the profit of the human family as a whole.

75. It is entirely consonant with human nature to find juridico-political systems which make it possible for all citizens without discrimination to play an increasingly effective part in establishing the legal foundations of the political community, in deciding the scope and purpose of various institutions and in electing governments.[158] All should therefore remember their right and duty of using their free vote for the common good. The Church has praise and esteem for those who devote themselves to public service and assume the burdens of office.

If conscientious co-operation in public life is to have a happy result, there is need of a positive juridical order embodying a suitable division of public functions and institutions, and also protection of rights which shall be effective and immune from pressure. The rights of all persons, families and associations and the exercise of them, should be recognized, maintained and promoted[159] along with the duties which bind all citizens. Among these last should be remembered the duty of rendering material and personal services which are officially imposed for the common welfare. Governments should avoid hindering associations for family or cultural or general social purposes or intermediate corporations and institutions, or depriving them of a legitimate

---

[158] Cf. Pius XII. Christmas Broadcast, 24 Dec. 1942: AAS 35 (1943), pp. 9-24; *ibid.* 24 Dec. 1944: AAS 37 (1945), pp. 11-17; John XXIII, Encycl. *Pacem in terris:* AAS 55 (1963), pp. 263, 271, 277 and 278.
[159] Cf. Pius XII, Broadcast, 1 June 1941; AAS 33 (1941), p. 200; John XXIII, Encycl. *Pacem in terris; loc. cit.,* p. 273 and 274.

field of action; they should rather be glad to promote such things in a regular fashion. Citizens singly or in association should avoid overestimating the power of public authority, demanding too many services and benefits from it and thereby reducing the responsibility of persons, families and social groups.

In the involved circumstances of today public authority is often forced to interfere in social, economic and cultural affairs to improve conditions and to assist more effectively the free pursuit of human welfare by citizens and free associations. Relations between 'socialization'[160] and personal autonomy and progress can be differently understood in various places and at different stages of development. But where the common good temporarily restricts the exercise of rights, freedom should be restored as soon as circumstances allow. It is inhuman that political authority should take totalitarian forms or dictatorial forms injurious to personal and social rights.

Citizens should be magnanimous and loyal but not narrow patriots—they should at the same time keep their minds on the good of the whole human family which binds races, peoples and nations by so many ties.

All Christians should feel it their special vocation in the political community to set an example of conscientious attention to their task and devotion to the general welfare, thus demonstrating in a practical way how authority is combined with liberty, personal initiative with social solidarity and commitment, appropriate unity with healthy variety. They should acknowledge legitimate differences of opinion in temporal matters and respect those, whether individuals or parties, who honestly disagree with them. Political parties should adopt those policies which in their judgement are called for by the common good; they must never put their own advantage before the common good.

If all citizens are to play their part in political life, the great need, especially for the young, is civic and political education, which should

---

[160] Cf. JOHN XXIII, Encycl. *Mater et Magistra*: AAS 53 (1961), p. 416.

be carefully provided for. Those who are suited, or can become suited, for practical politics—an art as difficult as it is noble[161]—should train and devote themselves regardless of private advantage and mere gain. They should take action prudently and with moral integrity against wrong and oppression, against the arbitrary rule of one man or party. They should dedicate themselves to the good of all sincerely and impartially, with charity and political courage.

76. It is important especially in pluralistic societies that there should be a proper regard for the relation between the political community and the Church and a clear distinction between what Christians singly and collectively do in their own name, as citizens guided by a Christian conscience, and what they do in conjunction with their pastors in the name of the Church.

By virtue of her function and field of action the Church is quite distinct from the political community and uncommitted to any political system; she is at once the sign and the guarantee that human personality transcends the field of politics.

The political community and the Church in their respective fields are independent and autonomous; but under different titles they are both helping the same men to fulfil their personal and social vocation. The more they co-operate reasonably, with an eye on the circumstances of time and place, the more effectively they will perform this service to everybody's advantage. Man is not confined to the temporal order: living in human history he keeps his eternal vocation intact. The Church, rooted in the Redeemer's love, helps to make justice and charity flourish more vigorously within nations and between nations. She preaches the gospel truth and brings the light of her teaching to bear on every province of human affairs with the witness of her faithful. Thus she respects and promotes political liberty and responsibility.

---

[161]Pius XI, Address to the University Catholic Federation: Discourses of Pius XI, (ed. Bertetto), Torino, Vol. I, 1960, p. 743.

The Life of the Political Community

The apostles, their successors and those who assist (the bishops), sent to announce Christ the Saviour of the world to men, rely on the power of God, who often shows the strength of the Gospel through the weakness of its witnesses. Whoever devotes himself to the ministry of God's word must use ways and means appropriate to the Gospel, and very different from the ways and means of the world.

Certainly, the things of this world and those which in the human sphere go beyond this world are closely bound up, and the Church uses temporal things so far as her mission requires. But her hope does not lie in the privileges offered by civil authority; indeed she will give up the exercise of lawfully acquired rights where she is satisfied that to continue to use them will call in question the sincerity of her witness, or where new circumstances of life call for new arrangements. But always and everywhere she must be allowed to preach the faith with true freedom, teach her social doctrine, carry out her task among men unhampered and pass moral judgement even on matters concerning politics when fundamental rights or the salvation of souls require it. She will use all the helps, and only the helps, which according to times and circumstances are in keeping with the Gospel and the general welfare.

Keeping faithfully to the Gospel and carrying out her mission in the world, the Church whose business is to nourish and exalt the good, the true, the beautiful, wherever it is found in the human community,[162] supports peace among men to the glory of God.[163]

---

[162]Cf. Vatican Council II, Dogmatic Constitution on the Church, n. 13: AAS 57 (1965), p. 17.
[163]Cf. *Lk* 2:14.

CHAPTER V

FOSTERING PEACE AND PROMOTING THE INTERNATIONAL COMMUNITY

77. During these current years, in which the gravest distress and anxieties persist among men because of war either raging or threatening, the entire human family has reached a supremely critical moment in its progress towards maturity. It is gradually being unified and everywhere better realizing its unity; but it is unable to carry out the task which weighs on it, of building a more humane world, unless all are renewed in mind and converted to the cause of peace. Hence it is that the Gospel message is in harmony with the highest human ideals and aspirations and shines with a new splendour when it calls the peacemakers blessed 'for they shall be called sons of God' (*Mt* 5:9).

The Council therefore means to elucidate the true and most noble idea of peace; after condemning the frightfulness of war, it means to call on Christians fervently to co-operate with all men, with the help of Christ the author of peace, in establishing peace in justice and love and in preparing the necessary instruments for achieving this.

78. Peace is not the mere absence of war. It cannot be reduced to mere balance of power. It does not come of tyrannical domination. It is rightly and properly called 'the work of justice' (*Is* 32:7). It exists as the fruit of the order built into human society by its divine Founder, an order to be given practical expression by men ever thirsting for more perfect justice. Since the common good of mankind in its primary meaning is regulated by the eternal law, but its concrete requirements continually change with the course of time, peace is never achieved once for all, but has to be constantly fashioned. Since moreover the human will is prone to waver and is wounded by sin; to maintain peace calls for the constant mastery of the passions of each of us and the vigilance of lawful authority.

Nor is this enough. There can be no peace on earth unless personal welfare is safeguarded and men spontaneously and confidently exchange the riches of their minds and genius. The construction of peace absolutely demands a firm resolve to respect other men and peoples, and the practical determination to be brothers. Thus peace is also the fruit of love, which advances beyond what justice can supply.

Earthly peace, which comes from love of our fellow-men, is a type and a result of the peace of Christ issuing from God the Father. The incarnate Son himself, the Prince of Peace, reconciled all men to God through his cross, restoring the unity of all in one people and one body. In his own flesh he killed hatred,[164] and after he had risen he poured out the Spirit of charity in the hearts of men.

Hence we earnestly beg of all Christians that, 'speaking the truth in love' (*Eph* 4:15) they unite with truly peaceful men to implore and establish peace.

In the same spirit we cannot but praise those who renounce violence in defending their rights and use means of defence which are available to the weakest, so long as this can be done without harm to the rights and duties of others or of the community.

Insofar as men are sinners the danger of war hangs over them and will hang over them till the coming of Christ; but insofar as, united in charity, they overcome sin, they overcome violence too, until the words are fulfilled 'They shall beat their swords into ploughshares and their spears into pruning-hooks. Nation shall not lift up sword against nation, neither shall they learn war any more' (*Is* 2:4).

Section 1: AVOIDING WAR

79. In spite of the fact that recent wars have inflicted the greatest material and moral damage on our world, every day, in some part of the world, war continues its devastations. In fact while scientific weapons of any kind are employed in war, its savage character threatens to

---

[164]Cf. *Eph* 2:16; *Col* 1:20-22.

reduce the combatants to a barbarism far beyond that of past times. Besides, the complexity of present-day conditions and the intimate relations between nations allow concealed wars to drag on by new, insidious and subversive methods. In many cases the use of terrorism is considered a new way of waging war.

In view of this dejected state of humanity, the Council's intention is before all else to call to mind the permanent force of the natural law of nations and its universal principles. The conscience of human kind itself more and more firmly asserts these principles. Actions therefore which are deliberately opposed to them, as well as the orders prescribing such actions, are criminal, nor can blind obedience excuse those who carry out such orders. First among such actions are those by which an entire people, nation or racial minority is systematically and methodically wiped out; horrible crimes, to be vehemently condemned, but most praiseworthy is the spirit of men who are not afraid to resist openly those who give such orders.

There exist various international agreements about war, to which a large number of nations have subscribed, for the purpose of humanizing military action and its consequences: e.g., agreements about the treatment of prisoners and wounded, and the like.

These agreements are to be observed, in fact governments and experts are bound to do everything possible to improve them, so that they may check the frightfulness of war more effectively. It seems fair moreover that laws should make humane provision for conscientious objectors, so long as they accept another form of service to the human community.

War has decidedly not been eradicated from human affairs. So long as the danger of it persists and we have no competent international authority equipped with adequate force, it will not be possible to deny governments the right of legitimate self-defence, given that they have exhausted every peaceful means of settlement. Rulers and others sharing the responsibility have the duty of looking to the safety of those in their charge, and must handle such grave matters with proper seriousness. But military policy based on rightful defence is one thing, to want to subdue other nations is quite another. Nor does the possession of war potential make every military or political use of it lawful. Nor does everything between the belligerents become lawful once war has unhappily broken out.

Those who are serving their country in the armed forces should regard themselves as servants of the people's security and liberty. While they are fulfilling this duty they are genuinely contributing to the establishment of peace.

80. The increase of scientific weapons has increased the horror and wickedness of war immensely. Action carried out with these weapons can cause vast and indiscriminate destruction which goes far beyond the limits of legitimate defence. Indeed if the armament already possessed by the great nations were fully made use of, each side would almost entirely destroy the other, to say nothing of the devastating results in the world at large and the deadly side-effects.

All this forces us to examine war in an entirely new frame of mind.[165] Our contemporaries should know that they will have to give a very serious account of their waging war. The future will hang very largely on their present decisions.

Bearing this in mind, the Council makes its own, the condemnations of total war already issued by recent Popes[166] and declares:

All warfare which tends indiscriminately to the destruction of entire cities or wide areas with their inhabitants is a crime against God and man, to be firmly and unhesitatingly condemned.

The peril peculiar to war today is this: that it offers to those who possess the latest scientific weapons occasion to commit such crimes and can by a kind of inexorable escalation drive men to the most atrocious decisions. Lest this should ever happen, the assembled bishops of

---

[165]JOHN XXII, Encycl. *Pacem in terris*, 11 Apr. 1963: AAS 55 (1963), p. 291: 'Thus, in this age which boasts of its atomic power, it no longer makes sense to maintain that war is a fit instrument with which to repair the violation of justice' [CTS Translation, S 264: *Peace on Earth*, § 127].

[166]Cf. PIUS XII, Address, 30 Sept. 1954: AAS 46 (1954), p. 589; Christmas Broadcast, 24 Dec. 1954; AAS 47 (1955), pp. 15 ff.: JOHN XXII, Encycl. *Pacem in terris*: AAS 55 (1963), pp. 286-291; PAUL VI, Address to the United Nations General Assembly, 4 Oct. 1965.

the world implore all, especially statesmen and military leaders, never to stop pondering such a responsibility before God and humanity.

81. Scientific weapons are not accumulated only to be used in war. Since the defensive strength of either side is reckoned to depend on its being equipped for lightning reprisals; stockpiling of arms, heavier year by year, helps in a novel way to deter likely enemies. Many think this the most effective of all ways of keeping international peace nowadays.

Whatever may be thought of this method of dissuasion, men should be convinced that the armaments race in which so many nations compete is no safe way to guarantee peace, nor is the 'balance' resulting from it sure and genuine peace. It slowly aggravates the causes of war instead of doing away with them. While vast wealth is spent on new weapons it is impossible to provide adequate remedies for so much destitution throughout the world. International disputes, instead of being thoroughly healed, are spread to other parts of the world. A change of heart must lead us to new ways of removing this scandal and restoring true peace to a world freed from the burden of anxiety.

Hence we must declare afresh: the arms race is a most serious injury to humanity and an intolerable one to the poor. It is greatly to be feared that if it lasts it will bring fatal disaster, the means of which it is already preparing.

The calamities mankind has made possible should be a severe warning to us. Providentially we are allowed a breathing space: we should use it more responsibly to find ways of settling our differences in a fashion more worthy of man. Divine Providence urgently commands us to rid ourselves of the ancient slavery of war. If we refuse to make the attempt, who knows where the evil road we have set out on will lead us?

82. It is clear that we should give all our energies to hastening the day when by common consent of the nations, war may be altogether banned. This obviously calls for the setting up of some universal public

authority recognized by everybody, commanding effective power, to guarantee for everybody security, regard for justice and respect for rights. Before this authority can be set up, the present international bodies should devote themselves zealously to studying better ways of achieving general security. Peace must be born of mutual trust between nations, not imposed on them by armed terror. So all must work to see an end of the arms race and a real beginning of disarmament; to see, moreover, that this disarmament proceeds not unilaterally but *pari passu* and by agreement, and is protected by adequate guarantees.[167]

Meanwhile we should not undervalue the efforts which have been and are being made to remove the danger of war. Rather we should support the goodwill of the many who are weighed down by the cares of high office, yet feel it part of their very grave duty to strive to abolish war, which they hate, though they cannot altogether ignore the complex facts. We should earnestly ask God to give them strength to persevere with and strongly finish this work—the brave work of making peace, which is the highest work of love. Most certainly it demands of them today that they stretch their mind and spirit beyond the boundaries of their own country, lay aside national egoism and the ambition to dominate others, and nourish a deep respect for all humanity, which is already struggling towards greater unity.

The strenuous and ceaselessly prolonged examinations of peace and disarmament problems, and international conferences about them, must be considered the first steps towards a solution, which need to be pressed forward with greater urgency in the future if they are to achieve practical results. Nevertheless men should beware of committing themselves only to the efforts of others without taking trouble about their own minds. Statesmen are not only answerable for the public welfare of their own nation but also promoters of the universal welfare; yet they depend very much on public opinion and sentiment.

---

[167]Cf. JOHN XXIII, Encycl. *Pacem in terris*. where disarmament is dealt with: AAS 55 (1963), p. 287.

It is no use their setting out to establish peace so long as feelings of hostility, contempt and mistrust, racial hatreds or obstinate ideologies divide men and set them against each other. Our greatest need is to re-orientate people's minds, to re-educate public opinion. Educators, especially of the young, and those who shape public opinion should think it a most serious duty to create in the minds of all a new feeling for peace. All of us indeed must change our hearts, looking to the wide world and to those tasks we can perform together to help our race to better itself.

We should not be deceived by false hopes. Unless enmities and hatreds are put aside and firm and sincere agreements for universal peace are concluded, humanity, already in grave danger in spite of its marvellous scientific attainments, may reach that fatal hour in which it will know no peace but that of a terrible death. Nonetheless, the Church of Christ places herself at the heart of contemporary anxieties, and while she issues these warnings she does not cease to hope resolutely. She is determined to put to our age repeatedly, in season and out of season, the apostolic message: 'Behold now is the acceptable time' for a change of heart: 'behold now is the day of salvation'.[168]

Section 2: SETTING UP THE INTERNATIONAL COMMUNITY

83. To establish peace we need above all to root out the causes of dissensions among men, on which war thrives—and especially injustices. Not a few of them come from excessive economic inequalities and from delay in applying needful remedies. Others come from the desire to dominate and from contempt for persons and, if we ask for deeper reasons, from human envy, mistrust, pride and other selfish passions. Since man cannot tolerate so many disorders, they result in the world being plagued with quarrels and violence even when war is not actually raging. And since the same evils are found in international

---

[168]Cf. 2 *Cor* 6:2.

relations, we badly need better co-operation, better co-ordination between international institutions to overcome or forestall these crises, to check unbridled violence. We need also to stimulate the creating of organizations for peace.

84. In these days the citizens of any country are becoming continually more closely dependent on each other. So are the countries of the world. If in these conditions we are to aim properly and effectively at the common welfare, the community of nations must organize itself in a way adequate to present-day tasks, especially in regard to those regions which still suffer intolerable want.

For these purposes the institutions of the international community should adapt themselves to the various needs of men, not only in the social sphere to which belong food, health, education, labour, but also in those special conditions which can arise in some places, e.g., the need of encouraging the advance of the developing nations, of relieving the wants of refugees scattered throughout the world, or also of helping immigrants and their families.

Existing international or regional institutions have certainly deserved well of mankind. They stand out as the first attempts at laying international foundations for the whole human community with the aim of solving the great questions of our time, furthering progress throughout the world and preventing war in any form. In all these fields the Church rejoices at the spirit of brotherhood flourishing between Christians and non-Christians—a spirit dedicated to more intense efforts at relieving widespread destitution.

85. The present unity of the human race demands greater international co-operation in the economic field. For though nearly all peoples have become politically independent they are very far from being free of excessive inequalities or independent in every way they should be, nor are they free of serious internal difficulties.

The growth of a nation is dependent on man-power and finance. The citizens of every country must be prepared by education and professional training to face the various duties of social and economic life. This calls for the help of foreign experts who, while they are giving it, should not behave like overlords but like helpers and collaborators. If the developing nations are to be given material aid, the habits of present-day world trade will have to change profoundly. Other kinds of help should be given by the developed nations in the form of gifts or loans or money investments offered on the one side with generosity and without greed, accepted on the other with all honesty.

To establish a genuine universal economic order we need to get rid of excessive concern for profit, national ambitions, the appetite for political mastery, militaristic scheming, devices for propagating and imposing ideologies. Many economic and social systems are advocated. It is desirable that experts should discern among these systems the common foundations of a sound world trade. This will happen more easily if they drop their prejudices and show themselves ready for honest discussion.

86. For this co-operation the following guiding principles seem opportune:

(a) The developing nations should take care that they expressly and firmly make the full human perfection of their citizens the goal of progress. They should remember that progress originates and grows chiefly from their own work and talents; that they should not lean only on foreign resources but first fully develop their own and cultivate their own genius and tradition. The most influential in the community ought to take the lead in this.

(b) It is the very serious duty of the developed nations to help the under-developed to carry out these tasks. They should adjust themselves, mentally and materially, to establish this universal co-operation. Thus in doing business with the weaker and poorer nations they should continually have the latter's good in mind. For these nations need the profit they make from selling their produce for their own sustenance.

(c) It is the task of the international community to regulate and stimulate development in such a way that the subsidies for this purpose are effectively and fairly assigned. It should also, while observing the principle of subsidiary function, direct world economic policy in the interests of justice.

Suitable institutions should be founded for promoting and regulating international trade, especially with the less developed nations, and compensating for the handicaps caused by excessive inequalities of power between nations. This kind of control, combined with technical, cultural and financial assistance, should help nations which are trying to make progress towards a satisfactory economic growth.

(d) In many cases economic and social structures badly need revising. But we should beware of facile technical solutions, especially when put forward by those who offer men material advantages but are hostile to their spiritual nature and profit. For 'man shall not live by bread alone, but by every word that proceeds from the mouth of God' (*Mt* 4:4). Any part of the human family retains in its best traditions some part of the spiritual inheritance entrusted to mankind by God, even though many know nothing of where it comes from.

87. There is great need of international co-operation today in regard to those who often suffer, besides so many other difficulties, those arising from rapid increase of population. There is urgent need for all, especially the richer countries, to co-operate fully and earnestly in exploring ways of providing the necessities of life and adequate instruction, and distributing them among the world community. Some people could better their own living conditions if they were adequately instructed—if they could replace old methods of farming with new production techniques judiciously adapted to their own situation; if finally they could achieve a better social order and a fairer distribution of wealth.

Within the limits of its competence and within its own frontiers each government has rights and duties regarding its population problems, e.g., regarding social and family legislation, migration from the countryside to cities, information about the state of the country and its needs. Since there is such deep concern about these problems today it is to be hoped that Catholic experts, especially in universities, will study them intelligently and on a larger scale.

But many maintain that the world's population growth, or at least that of some nations, should be drastically diminished by any and every means of government intervention. The Council exhorts everybody to avoid solutions, publicly or privately promoted, or sometimes imposed, which are against the moral law. The inalienable right of man to marriage and offspring entails that decisions about the size of their families rest with the right judgement of parents and can by no means be committed to the judgement of public authorities. But since the judgement of parents depends on a rightly formed conscience it is important that all should be given the chance to cultivate a right and really human responsibility, looking to the divine law in the context of present realities. This in turn demands that social and educational conditions should be widely improved, and especially that religious training or at least complete moral instruction should be given. Men should be suitably informed about scientific advances in methods of regulating procreation which are clearly sound and morally justifiable.

88. Christians should co-operate readily and wholeheartedly in building an international order with true respect for rightful liberties, with men accepting each other as friends and brothers; the more so since the greater part of the world still suffers such extreme poverty that in the persons of the poor Christ himself seems to call loudly on the charity of his disciples. We should not therefore allow the scandal to continue that some nations with a nominally Christian majority enjoy abundance while others are short of the necessities of life and wracked with hunger, disease and every kind of misery. The spirit of poverty and charity is the glory and witness of Christ's Church.

We must praise and help those Christians, the young especially, who volunteer as helpers to other men and nations. Indeed it is for all the People of God at the word and example of their bishops to do all they can to relieve the wants of our time—and to do this, as was the ancient custom in the Church, not only from what is superfluous but from what they would normally use themselves.

Subsidies should be collected and distributed not with rigid uniformity but in orderly fashion on a diocesan, national or worldwide scale, in co-operation with other Christians wherever this seems advisable. The spirit of charity, far from forbidding social and charitable action to be provident and well organized, rather demands that it should. Hence those who intend to devote themselves to the service of the developing countries should be properly trained for the job.

89. When the Church, relying on her divine mission, preaches the Gospel to men and pours out the treasures of grace, she contributes to establishing peace and laying the foundation of human and international brotherhood, which is knowledge of the divine and natural law. On this account the Church should certainly be present in the community of nations to foster and stimulate co-operation among men. And this not only by means of her public institutions but also through the full and sincere collaboration of all Christians, given with the sole motive of service.

It will help here if the faithful themselves, as part of their personal and Christian responsibility, do all they can in their own environment to rouse a desire to co-operate readily with the international community. Pastoral care should be given to training people for this, especially young people, in both the religious and the civil fields of education.

90. An undoubtedly excellent form of international work on the part of Christians is that which they do in existing institutions for international relations, and will do in others still to be founded. Of great service also to the community of nations can be the various Catholic

international associations, which should be strengthened, their trained personnel and subsidies increased and their organization improved. In our time efficiency and the need for dialogue both demand common enterprise. Such associations help much to develop a universal outlook appropriate to Catholics and make them aware of universal solidarity and responsibility.

It is desirable that Catholics should do everything to co-operate actively and positively with the separated brethren who share with us the profession of evangelical charity, and with all men who thirst for true peace. This is part of the proper fulfilment of their duty in the international community.

The Council, thinking of the vast scale of the troubles which still afflict men, believes that it would be opportune to create some organism of the universal Church to further justice and the love of Christ for the poor; its task would be to stir up the Catholic community to promote the advance of the poor areas of the world and international justice.

CONCLUSION

91. What the Council puts forward from the treasury of the Church's doctrine has the purpose of helping all men, whether they believe in God or do not explicitly recognize him; of helping them to understand better their vocation as a whole, to make the world more worthy of the surpassing dignity of man, to aspire to a wider and deeper brotherhood and under the impulse of love to try generously together to respond to the urgent demands of our age.

Obviously in view of the immense variety of conditions and of patterns of human culture in the world, what is offered is in many parts deliberately only general in character. Indeed, although it sets out doctrine already received in the Church, where it treats matters subject to constant development it will have to be carried further and amplified. Yet we are confident that many of the things which we have proposed in reliance on the word of God and the spirit of the Gospel can be of valid assistance, particularly when the faithful under the guidance of their bishops have adapted them to each people and mentality and given them practical form.

92. Since the Church's mission is to spread the light of the Gospel through the world and unite all men of whatever nation, race or culture in one Spirit, she is the sign of that brotherhood which makes possible and encourages a sincere dialogue.

This requires that first of all we promote mutual esteem, reverence and harmony, allowing for every legitimate difference, so that we can begin a dialogue among the People of God, pastors or faithful, which may become steadily more fruitful. The things that unite the faithful are stronger than those that divide them. Let there be unity in things essential, liberty in things doubtful, charity in all things.

Our thought also embraces those brethren not yet in full communion with us, and their communities, to whom nonetheless we are united in the confession of the Father, the Son and the Holy Spirit, and in the bond of charity. We remember that Christian unity is awaited and desired today even by many unbelievers—for the more it prospers in truth and charity under the powerful impulse of the Holy Spirit, the more it will be presage of unity and peace for the whole world. We must devote ourselves to brotherly co-operation in the service of the human family, which in Christ Jesus is called to be the family of the sons of God. To this splendid goal we must co-ordinate our energies and continually adapt our methods to the needs of the present day.

Reasonable prudence being presupposed, we for our part should not wish to exclude anybody from such a dialogue, prompted only by charity and directed towards truth—neither those who cultivate the splendid human values without acknowledging their Author, nor those who in various ways oppose or persecute the Church. Since God our Father is the beginning and end of all, we are all called to be brothers. Sharing this human and divine vocation, we can and should work together without violence, without deceit, to build a world of true peace.

93. Christians, remembering the Lord's words 'by this all men will know that you are my disciples, if you have love for one another' (*Jn* 13:35) can want nothing more ardently than to serve the men of our time ever more generously and effectively. Faithful to the Gospel and drawing strength from it, united with all who love and work for justice, they have undertaken a huge task in this world. They will have to answer for it to him who will judge us all at the last day. Not all who say 'Lord, Lord' will enter the kingdom of heaven, but those who do the will of the Father[169] and set themselves down to the work. It is the Father's will that we recognize and really love Christ our brother in all men, in word and in work, thereby witnessing to the Truth, and that we share with others the mystery of the heavenly Father's love. In this way men all over the earth will be roused to a lively hope—the gift of the Holy Spirit—so that at last they may be taken in peace and high blessedness to that fatherland which shines with the glory of the Lord.

---

[169]Cf. *Mt* 7:21.

Conclusion

'Now to him who by the power at work within us is able to do far more abundantly than all that we ask or think, to him be glory in the Church and in Christ Jesus to all generations, for ever and ever. Amen' (*Eph* 3:20-21).

Each and all of the matters pronounced in this pastoral Constitution have been approved by the Fathers of the sacred Council. And We, by the apostolic authority given Us by Christ, together with the Venerable Fathers, approve, appoint and decree its contents in the Holy Spirit, and order that what has been decided in the Council be promulgated to the glory of God.

✠ **PAUL**, *Bishop of the Catholic Church*
St Peter's, Rome, 7 December, 1965.
The signatures of the Fathers follow.